Food Insecurity and Revolution in the Middle East and North Africa

Food Insecurity and Revolution in the Middle East and North Africa

Agrarian Questions in Egypt and Tunisia

Habib Ayeb and Ray Bush

ANTHEM PRESS

Anthem Press
An imprint of Wimbledon Publishing Company
www.anthempress.com

This edition first published in UK and USA 2019
by ANTHEM PRESS
75–76 Blackfriars Road, London SE1 8HA, UK
or PO Box 9779, London SW19 7ZG, UK
and
244 Madison Ave #116, New York, NY 10016, USA

British Library Cataloguing-in-Publication Data
A catalogue record for this book is available from the British Library.

ISBN-13: 978-1-78527-087-1 (Hbk)
ISBN-10: 1-78527-087-7 (Hbk)
ISBN-13: 978-1-78527-090-1 (Pbk)
ISBN-10: 1-78527-090-7 (Pbk)

This title is also available as an e-book.

This book is dedicated to the memory of Hassanine Kishk (1946–2019).

CONTENTS

ILLUSTRATIONS

Figures

Tables

Maps

ABBREVIATIONS

ASA P	Agricultural Structural Adjustment Programme, Tunisia
BNA	Banque Nationale Agricole
CPG	Compagnie des phosphates de Gafsa
EUR	Euro
FAO	Food and Agricultural Organisation of the United Nations
FS	Food sovereignty
GDP	Gross domestic product
GMO	Genetically modified organism
GoE	Government of Egypt
GoT	Government of Tunisia
IFI	International Financial Institution
IMF	International Monetary Fund
LE	Egyptian pound
LVC	La Via Campesina
MENA	Middle East and North Africa
MNC	Multinational company
NATO	North Atlantic Treaty Organisation
NGO	Nongovernment Organisation
NDP	National Democratic Party (Egypt)
OPTs	Occupied Palestinian Territories
SONEDE	Société Nationale d'Exploitation et de Distribution des Eaux
STEG	Société Tunisienne de l'Electricité et du Gaz
UCPA	Cooperative Units for Agricultural Productions
UGTT	General Union for Tunisian Workers
UNDP	United Nations Development Programme
USAID	United States Agency for International Development
UAE	United Arab Emirates
WFP	World Food Programme
1 feddan	1.038 acres or 0.42 hectares

PREFACE AND ACKNOWLEDGEMENTS

This book marks many years of collaboration and engagement with family farming and agrarian questions in Africa, the Middle East and in particular Egypt and Tunisia. We have benefitted greatly from conversations and discussions with colleagues and farmers in both countries. We are particularly grateful to François Ireton who has supported this work throughout and helped with data collection and organising statistical material to help analyse economic and social underdevelopment in Egypt and Tunisia. Nada Trigui and Sara Pozzi helped with translation from French into English. We have benefitted from membership of *Thimar*, a research collective on agriculture, environment and labour in the Arab World, based in Beirut and coordinated by Martha Mundy and Karim Eid-Sabbagh.

Thanks for comments on parts of the manuscript to Ali Kadri whose critical eye served us well. We are very thankful to Max Ajl who greatly enriched this work through many conversations and made invaluable comments on an early draft. His insight and perspectives have helped sharpen many of our arguments. Thanks also to Giuliano Martiniello who commented on an early draft and whose work on peasants and agrarian questions is so important.

Mark Duffield remains an inspiration.

Drafting this work would have been much more difficult without all the support and we feel honoured to have received it. Usual caveats that we may not have always done what we may have been encouraged to do. We also gratefully acknowledge support from the Open Society Foundation Middle East and the North Africa Programme office in Amman and Tunis.

It is with sadness we completed this book, as our dear comrade Hassanine Kishk passed away. The book is dedicated to his memory – an outstanding comrade.

Chapter 1

INTRODUCTION: AGRARIAN TRANSFORMATIONS AND MODERNISATIONS

Introduction

This book explores the political economy of agriculture and farming in Egypt and Tunisia. It highlights the economic and political significance that small-scale family farming has had historically in these countries and with reference to the wider MENA region. We document many of the pressures and constraints that farmers have had to deal with and we examine the myriad and largely negative policy interventions that have undermined, and often displaced, families and communities with little provision and opportunity for alternative non-agricultural livelihoods. We go further, however, than most analyses of the region, by locating investigation of the uneven consequences for farmers and the abjection that many have experienced, by understanding the impact as part of the way Egypt and Tunisia have been adversely incorporated into the world economy.

Egyptian and Tunisian agriculture has been structured by the interactions between global food regimes and local agricultural systems. This book helps to identify the social actors and conflicts that emanate from and shape these relations and contradictions. Our approach contrasts markedly with mainstream commentary on the MENA region. Although food security has been a major issue in the MENA region since World War II, it has been debated without reference to the producers of food, the farmers and *fellahin* (*fellah* singular or *fellahin* plural refers in the Arab world, but mostly in Egypt, to a peasant or agricultural labourer).

We also highlight how food security has been defined in a very limited and narrow sense that has restricted the opportunities for farmers to be part of a project that ensures the poor can access affordable food at all times.

We account for how the local food system is also the product of, and in turn influences, broad patterns and processes of local and national political economy, as well as structures of the global food regime. Egypt, for example, is second only to Indonesia in its dependency upon imported wheat. An appreciation of global pressures that shape the possibilities for grain imports is an important ongoing dynamic in Egyptian and broader MENA politics. Food security issues have shaped Egyptian state policy since President Abdul Nasser in the 1950s. His consummate political skill ensured that Egypt benefited from its geostrategic rent by playing off the United States and Soviet Union as suppliers of grain. In the contemporary period, as we highlight, it is largely commercial interests and influence that shape the arena of food policy in Cairo and Tunis. However, it does not do so in a political vacuum, internationally or locally, where the companies operate. We therefore examine, among other things, the relations of agricultural production and social reproduction among smallholder producers, their conflictual interactions with land owners and struggles for access to land, crop production and marketing.

Persistent and worsening rural poverty contributed, as we will show, to the 2011 Arab uprisings. Yet it was the urban-based slogans of protesters that captivated commentary on the turmoil. In Egypt protestors chanted, 'Bread, Freedom, Social Justice' and in Tunisia, 'Bread, Water, and No Ben Ali'. These slogans highlighted how food poverty impacted the municipal poor that drove dissent. Deaths in food queues in Cairo in 2008 were ignored by the regime yet they were the culmination of decades of structural adjustment reform that had generated increased poverty and political resistance and protests in both countries for workers and farmers. Demonstrations against poverty, economic reform and the need for increased wages and improved living conditions heralded the end of both dictatorships. The 2000s were highlighted by collective actions of workers protesting economic reform and failed promises of dictatorships to improve living and working conditions of the poor (Beinin 2016). The dramatic increase in the global price of food in 2008, which continued to the end of the decade, acted as a catalyst for popular mobilisation.

We make two major interventions with this book. First, we locate the role of rural struggles and agrarian transformation as part of the backdrop of the uprisings in Tunisia and Egypt and in doing so, draw on new original research of farmer responses to regime change. We examine the role and future of small farmer agriculture, providing insight into debate about agricultural modernisation. Second, we advance the discussion about food security and sovereignty. We assemble a critique of the ways in which food security continues to be the hegemonic mainstream policy position. We do this by examining the policies that have shaped agricultural underdevelopment in Tunisia and Egypt and which remain key challenges in political and economic reconstruction after 2011. In doing this, we build on recent radical and activist scholarship and interventions (Kadri 2014; Hanieh 2013; Achcar 2013). We seek to go beyond, on the one hand, orientalist views that imply Arabs, especially 'backward' peasants, could never protest and displace dictatorships because they simply did not understand the importance of democracy. On the other hand, the dominant views of the World Bank and many advocacy and NGO critiques of authoritarianism that it was dictatorship that limited free markets and opportunities for economic growth (Hanieh 2013, 1–6). While political repression limited representation, and brutalisation of citizens became systemic in both Egypt and Tunisia, we need to go beyond the political superstructure of the respective regimes. To do this, we explore why and how economic crisis persisted, why and how the roots of this lay in the underdevelopment of the countryside, and why and how many of the poor became mobilised against repression.

Our analysis is grounded in a historical materialist understanding of the MENA region and the importance of an approach that embraces the longue durée (Braudel 1960). This approach examines long-term historical processes and structures rather than focus only on events, despite how momentous some of them were. The political and economic structures that emerge over many decades and that influence the rural livelihoods and life chances of peasants in Egypt and Tunisia include shifts in the patterns of production and trade, changes in climate and population as well as in wages and prices. We explore the exploitative relations of production in capitalism, which created conditions for struggles and ultimately led to the ousting of President's Hosni Mubarak and Ben Ali. Government policy and practice is successful or unsuccessful not because of the frailties of government, although efficiency may play a part in policy delivery. Policy is always a product of contested economic and political power shaped by capitalism and its historical development.

This book contributes to the development of particular case studies of rural political economy in the MENA in general, and Egypt and Tunisia in particular. There has been an almost total absence in radical scholarship for many years of locating an understanding of rural underdevelopment in the context of case study analysis. We want to highlight from the outset that case study analysis runs alongside and is not reducible to the simple empirics of the case. We contribute to the development of the ways in which food regime theory and dependency theory continue to offer the most appropriate analytical frame to locate the class dynamics that shape food politics in Egypt and Tunisia. Our analysis is informed by the work of the late Samir Amin (1931–2018). He provided a model to explain both the persistence of underdevelopment in the Third World and what an alternative to late capitalism might look like. We highlight the possibilities for strategic alternatives to the food security tropes of the IFIs in Chapter 7. There we explore the debate about food sovereignty and why and how it is such an epistemic shift from the dominant mainstream discourse. We highlight and document what Amin noted as the crucial contrast between the dynamics of capital accumulation in the centre, what is now more neutrally referred to as the Global North, and the periphery or the Global South. We also use the more common language of North and South, but we use it as a referent to centre/periphery. In doing this, we stress what Amin called the 'self centred system' of capital accumulation in the centre or the imperialist triad of the EU, the United States and Japan (Amin, S. 1974a, 9). The self-centred system of accumulation was established with the European expansion of merchant capital in the fifteenth century as a mechanism to transfer value from the periphery (Amin, S. 1974a; 1974b). It does this in the process of unequal exchange where returns to labour in the periphery are less than returns to labour in the centre.

Samir Amin argued that cheap labour in the periphery produces raw materials and agricultural products for export to the centre, where the value of labour embodied in the final product is higher (Amin, S. 1974; Lawrence 2018). The periphery cannot 'catch up' with the centre because development in the centre is shaped by economic activity that satisfies mass consumer needs and demand for production goods. The masses in the centre are tied into this system of production by a social contract, which also fuels imperialist rhetoric, xenophobia and racism (Amin, S. 2011a). In contrast, Amin argued that the peripheral systems are dominated by the production of luxury goods and exports and the absence of an internal mass market. The consequence of this in the periphery is persistent inequality, dependence upon Western technology and fragmentation of political resistance and marginalisation. The resolution of this dependency upon the centre is for the countries in the periphery to break from the international political economy. In doing so, countries in the periphery can create a productive system not dependent upon imported commodities but the production of goods and services locally for domestic need (Amin, S. 1974b). We explore this further in Chapter 7 as we explore the possible transition towards food sovereignty.

The global framing that we adopt helps explain the main dynamic periods that resonate in our understanding of the political economy of rurality in Egypt and Tunisia and how that is shaped by, although not simply reducible to, the international capitalist processes of expansion and contraction. The moments that resonate in our case studies, in Egypt in the nationalist period 1952–67 mirrored in Tunisia's early period of independence during 1960–69 and then the periods after 1967 and 1969 in Egypt and Tunisia as not least the impact of defeat by Israel and the emerging neo-liberal revolutions, impact directly on rural underdevelopment. Economic reform in Egypt began in the countryside in 1987 predating the formal structural adjustment programme of 1991. The global drive of neo-liberalism has direct consequences for the debates about food security, agricultural strategy and the way Egypt and Tunisia are unevenly incorporated into the world food system.

The dynamics of peripheral capitalism in Egypt and Tunisia is best understood by examining the role of social class to fathom why some outcomes emerge and others do not and why, because policy is contested, there may be unintended consequences of government intervention. We highlight the importance of understanding the dynamics that underpin conflict in Egypt and Tunisia and focus on rural class antagonisms and how they are played out.

Class is an analytical category that represents social relationships of exploitation linked to property and modes of appropriation (Kadri 2014, 12). It is an essential category to help explain the ways in which politics and power, in the formulation and delivery of agrarian political economy, have had varied outcomes. Yet class as an analytical tool is mostly neglected in studies of the MENA region and some authors have been explicitly hostile to its use. It is a relational concept that helps explain how capitalists ensure the 'capacity of labour is realised' (Campling et al. 2016, 1747).

Class helps explain the exploitative relationships in Egypt and Tunisia's countryside. It is part of our analytical toolbox that explores the different dimensions of rural labour, the social relations of production that operate in different spheres of the circuit of capital and the conflictual processes that have helped realise the value of capital. Although we may, among other things, also highlight differences in levels of income among rural producers, these indicators of social stratification are inadequate to explain how and why capitalist agrarian transformation has taken place and who the winners and losers have been (Selwyn 2015).

Class will help explain and show the links between the local and the international political and economic factors that shape the outcomes of food policy. It is a key element in understanding the ways in which uneven capitalist development has displaced farmers, casualised work and has affected women disproportionately. Class may not always be the most evident or even dominant element in our understanding of political economy of agrarian transformation, but it is always determinant in outcomes. We will see how value is generated and how it is appropriated by landowning and business elites. And we will highlight in Chapter 3 how a socio-spatial dynamic is evident in facilitating the extraction and then movement of rural surplus to privileged urban centres in Tunisia and Egypt. We highlight how surplus appropriation from different types of agricultural production help shape political outcomes in both our case studies. In Tunisia we trace, among other things, an agricultural transformation promoted by newly emerging industrial elites that undermine the country's ecology and small farmer interests. We review the colonial agricultural model and the consequences of de-collectivisation, the persistent policy attempts seeking technical modernisation of farming, the consolidation of monopolies and land grabbing. In Egypt we see how land tenure reform in the 1990s accelerated social differentiation and rural class conflict between landowners, tenants and the landless and how policies of agricultural modernisation failed to deliver improved rural livelihoods. But first we need a sense of where farmers and peasants, or in Egypt's case *fellahin*, fit in as a social class in the context of agrarian transformation and the changes historically in the character of the world economy.

Agrarian Transformations: Peasants and Family Farming

Peasant family farming received a boosted recognition in 2014 when the United Nations declared a year to celebrate its importance. The Food and Agricultural Organisation (FAO) estimated there were globally 570 million farms of which 500 million were family owned (FAO 2014a). Of those 500 million, perhaps as much as 3 per cent, were located in the MENA region. We need to be a little cautious, however, when dealing with data in MENA as data quality and accuracy is notoriously poor (Kadri 2014). This poverty of data is the result of government attempts across the region to underestimate the extent of rural impoverishment and to overembellish rural production figures. The reluctance of statisticians to enter the MENA countryside and do more than anything other than make basic projections or generate spurious and poorly formulated surveys is well noted (El Nour 2015a). The estimated figure for family farms globally led the FAO director general, who is himself an agricultural economist, to assert that 'the well-being of farm families [were] inextricably woven into the overall well-being of societies'. He also noted how the prevalence of family farming has immense implications for 'food production and sustainability' (Graziano da Silva, in FAO 2014a, 4).

The FAO achievement of seeking to raise the profile and celebrate family farming was important. It went against the grain that routinely advanced the interests of agribusiness and corporate food giants – something that followed quickly in 2015 with the FAO's 'year of the soil'. We might also note that 2014 was the year of support for Palestinian People but there does not appear to have been any link between these two years of 'support'. We see in Chapter 2 how Israel's invasion of Gaza in 2014 and persistent occupation in the OPTs directly impacted 10,000 Palestinian farmers destroying their livelihoods.

Family farming is a broad descriptive term and rather imprecise. We know, for instance, that many large agricultural companies are also family businesses. Family farming focuses mainly on issues of size of land holding and where the relations of production (class relations) and the ease with which farmers can socially reproduce their households (ensure daily renewal) vary considerably.

When we use the term family farming we refer to those who access 5 hectares, and less, of irrigated land or 20 hectares and less, of rainfed land – 50 hectares of more arid or steppe lands on grassland and shrublands. We then specify whether that access is through ownership, tenancy or other patterns of often mixed access.

Family farm enterprises differ greatly in size and access to land, and other resources, including the different levels of dependence upon family labour. There are some family farms that rely only on family labour, some that hire in labour and may sometimes combine with other labour practices. These may include the accessing of land through a number of different labour processes and ownership arrangements like renting in, sharecropping and working for wages in the community or neighbouring villages, migrating to a nearby town or further afield. But who are these family farmers? In understanding this, we need to reflect on the rather controversial term 'peasant'.

Peasants

Peasants are direct producers of the soil who access their own tools for farming and employ mostly family labour. Peasants may commonly not be involved in wage labour, can access land through tenancy and other arrangements and include agro-pastoralists. Farming is shaped historically by a number of different social and political practices. Shifts in the social relations of production emerge shaped by differences in family size and age profile as well as the gender dynamics of production. Family farming is often lumped together with 'agriculture' but that term usually refers to agribusiness and 'commercial' as opposed to 'subsistence' farming practices.

As we see later, the debate about agricultural modernisation needs to capture the role played not only by the macroeconomic and political actors within the world food system, but also how they interact with, and are also shaped by, farming (class) struggles and practices in the Global South. The debate also needs to understand the influences of patterns of modernisation from struggles between landowners and farmers and those who control access to the means of production including not only land but also seeds and fertilisers.

The transformation of agriculture and the relations between farmers has been examined historically through the lens of modernisation. We look at the notion of modernisation in more detail in the ensuing discussion. In summary, the debate and interventions that relate to social classes and how we label and understand the actions of rural food producers has been posed through three agrarian questions. Questions of accumulation, production and politics refer broadly to issues linked to the transition to capitalist agriculture; to agriculture's ability to meet the food (and other?) needs of a newly emerging working class and what political struggle peasants, small-scale producers and the near landless might engage in the shaping and emergence of democracy (Bernstein 2010; 2014a; 2014b).

By the end of the twentieth century, many commentators noted that agrarian questions were less important for the Global North. This was because production of food and its availability in the Global North, but not for all and not always at affordable prices, had been met. Clearly this was not the case in the Global South. The resolution of the agrarian question for capital assumed that while generalised commodity production may not have commoditised all forms of rural existence, capitalism on a world scale has commoditised subsistence (Bernstein 2010, 102; see also, Akram-Lodhi and Kay 2010a).

If that has indeed been the case, does it mean that the concept or category, 'peasant', has become redundant? Should we instead use the broad term 'classes of labour' to characterise small holder farmers who,

> might not be disposed of all means of reproducing themselves, which marks the limits of their viability as petty commodity producers in farming ('peasants') or other branches of activity (Bernstein 2014b, S97).

If peasant as an analytical (class) category had historical meaning, it was now, according to some commentators, redundant as capital had penetrated all 'circuits of "household" production and reproduction' (Bernstein 2014b, S97). This has meant that the old categories of agrarian classes of landed property, labour and agrarian capital have become much more complex (Kautsky 1988; Lenin 1977). They were perhaps overdetermined by agricultural commodity chains and the dominance of agribusiness. But does this spell the end of the analytical usefulness of the category and social realities informed by the term peasant or *fellahin*? Are peasants not still fighting to retain as much of their agricultural surplus as possible that is generated from their labour time? Although most of Africa, including in the North and Near East, may not have experienced the expansion of large capitalist landed property, although it did in the settler colonies of Algeria and Tunisia and large irrigated schemes in Sudan, was it really the case for the Global South more generally, that the capitalist imperative of generalised commodity production dominated? And if it did, how exactly does it undermine the analytical usefulness of the term peasant (Bernstein 2010, 109)?

Moreover, the importance of a national agricultural surplus for a transition to capitalism may now be less feasible compared with the original industrialisers in Europe and the United States. But the lack of feasibility within existing global capitalism does not mean that the generation of rural surplus and access to it is unimportant. Indeed, we will argue that at a time when there is rather limited debate about alternative development strategies in MENA, we need precisely to look at how rural surpluses may be increased in a way that does not alienate (or dispossess) rural producers or simply estrange foreign interests (Amin, S. 2017a). We find the critique of the usefulness of the term peasant and its substitution of the catch all 'classes of labour' to be unconvincing.

The late Sam Moyo and others (2012) have noted, in their many critiques of the way the category peasant has been dismissed and replaced by petty commodity producer, that the analysis is too Eurocentric, it is structured in the classical debates about agrarian transitions in Europe and the United States, and ignores the realities of rural relations of production and reproduction in the Global South (McMichael 2013; Van der Ploeg 2013). In doing this, the recurrent debate in the post- World War II period of the 'disappearing peasantry' is perpetuated without grounded empirical analysis of really existing farms, farmers and farm practices (Hobsbawm 1994). It is certainly the case that farmers and peasants in the Global South are engaged in a number of different occupational roles or 'pluriactivity' (Van Der Ploeg 2013). The 'limbo' between dependence upon the market, for farming and subsistence, yet the inability to generate access to it because of resource limitations or other restrictions is the particular outcome of modernity, and the fragmentation is synonymous with what has been referred to as a 'deagrarianisation' elsewhere (Bryceson 1999). This refers to an increase in the proportion of rural income that accrues from non-farm income and the downward pressure on farm size. It also refers to intensification of the labour process for those who work on both their own land and as wage labourers for others.

These economic pressures may not, however, detract from or alter the objective position of peasants sui generis. Peasant agriculture is first and foremost structured around the household as a unit of analysis and the ways that household interacts with broader social and economic units. Land-holding peasants can be distinguished from non-farm classes and rural workers who may work on commercial farms, plantations or estates. The complexity of definitions is here highlighted by potential, but not always contradictory, interests between small holders and landless or near landless peasants. We will argue that peasants may be 'only *partially integrated into incomplete markets*' (Ellis 1993, 4 emphasis in original) and continue to retain, although not in an unchanged way, conditions of existence similar to pre- or non-capitalist modes of production (Cross and Cliffe 2017).

The persistent and distinctive character of peasant family farming is demonstrated in the ways farmers and their families and different members of rural communities combat (or acquiesce) to a fundamental dilemma. This is the struggle for 'autonomy and progress in a context characterised by multiple patterns of dependency and associated processes of exploitation and marginalisation' (van der Ploeg 2009, xiv). In trying to fathom why despite their omnipresence, the persistence and distinctive significance of small farm households and peasants are continuously downplayed or redefined, we emphasise that 'there is a critical role for peasants in modern societies and that there are millions who have no alternative to such an existence'. The attempts to marginalise the role of family farming emerge because of the way Empire (globalisation) in its many different forms tends to 'destroy the peasantry along with the values that it carries and produces' (ibid.).

Although it has been asserted that the new agrarian question of labour relates to the multifaceted ways in which classes of rural labour are socially reproduced and that the rule of capital may largely shape that, we need to also investigate patterns of labour process that are unrelated to the dominance of market rules and relations. These may be where the level of rural abjection has denied any wage earning opportunity, where labour migration is prevented, where the majority of rural producers are girls or women and therefore a clearer understanding of power dynamics within households is important. In other words, we need to investigate the evidence for the persistence of non-commoditised and non-market-oriented access to land and water, seeds and other inputs to farming (Martiniello 2015a).

We might be helped in establishing the doggedness of non-commoditised dimensions of rural existence by examining internal dynamics of the household, household relations of production and social reproduction for farmers and farming. In doing this, there is no romanticising of peasant conditions of existence. The feverish debate about agrarian transition to capitalism in Bolshevik Russia foregrounded some themes of a specific peasant economy (Chayanov 1966). We do not promote the idea of a peasant economy but we do give weight to the Chayanovian view that small farmers may at times be driven by motivations that might prioritise family needs over imperatives of profitability per se. In the case of revolutionary Russia in the 1920s and 1930s, Chayanov noted that farmers may make decisions finely tuned to the balance between meeting subsistence needs and the harshness of manual (family) labour (Chayanov 1966).

There are immense differences between farming systems in the Global North and the Global South (Amin, S. 2017b, 155). There are the obvious contrasts in rates of productivity and mechanisation and environmental consequences for established farming practices. Rural poverty in Egypt and Tunisia, as we will see, is far greater than the experiences of the poor in urban centres. Peasants continue to have a high dependence upon subsistence food as this is the most common and important mechanism to ensure survival. Precarious rural conditions of existence spill over into disruptions of urban food markets and, as we will also see in Chapter 3, resistance to neo-liberal reform, and the authoritarian imposition of market reforms emerges from the countryside and continues after 2010–11 in the post-uprising years.

The term peasant and its class significance and specificity need a historically grounded analysis of particular social formations. In doing this, we need to be explicit about what constitutes the agrarian question today (Moyo, Jha and Yeros 2012). We need to concretely explore the role of peasants in a 'context of food and agriculture in relation to capitalist dynamics' (Friedmann 2016,671). In the contemporary period, this involves examining why there is an absence of a problematisation of land and conflicts linked to how access and control over rural property is contested. We will see how land has been repeatedly politicised, and access to it and the different types of land are overdetermined by a range of economic, political and social factors. And we will see how the contestation over land further reflects the abjection of its farmers from rural development. We will highlight the need to inform policymakers about what farmers and peasants do and how the surplus that some may generate is expropriated and by whom. But such knowledge alone is insufficient to change the life chances of peasants. We indicate how farmers resist the expropriation of land and resources more generally and how by doing so they begin to sketch an alternative agenda for rural development. Ultimately our work leads to an analysis and critique of imperialism. This is because we document, among other things, land grabs, corporate dispossession of farmers and their communities, the spread of monopoly supply, and distribution of seeds and other farming inputs. The defense of the peasantry against these challenges is a 'possible anti-imperialist project' (Yeros 2012, 344).

Farming and Modernisation

Modernisation and 'the idea of progress' assert that all societies have an industrial future (Shanin 1997). The modernisation theory of development, so dominant in social science in the 1960s, continues, as we will see, in the twenty-first century. It is very evident in the agricultural policy and practice of Egypt and Tunisia (for the background, see, Huntington 1971; Tignor 1966; Hoogvelt 1997;1982; World Bank 1996 [2001]). The model in relation to farming is that reliance upon small-scale agricultural producers will diminish, as industrial production and agribusiness, resulting from economies of scale, dominate with greater levels of productivity.

In this context the future of family farming and, more specifically, of the peasantry is challenged. The contemporary hegemonic policy position is to downplay the continuing significance of small-scale agricultural producers and patterns of rapid (jobless) urbanisation (Davis 2006). But what have been some of the actual consequences for peasants and their varied livelihoods that are in the process of being recast? To get a handle on this, it is important to structure our analysis in the context of a longue durée of historical enquiry and visit the ways in which international food regimes have emerged as an integral part of capitalist development from the nineteenth century.

The transition to capitalism for Karl Marx involved primitive accumulation. This was 'the historical process of divorcing the producer from the means of production' (Marx 1867, 874) in the creation of labour power as a commodity. Because agriculture was the predominant form of production prior to capitalism, the separation of agricultural labour from the land was a prerequisite for capitalist development. This was understood to take only a relatively brief period of time and did so in Europe and the United States in the eighteenth and nineteenth centuries. In the Global South (and still in parts of the North), however, the dispossession of farmers and the associated violence that has accompanied this has continued (Moyo, Yeros and Jha 2012; De Angelis 1999; Bonefeld 2002). It is a process, moreover, that has always involved the intervention of the state to quell resistance to farmer dispossession. In the UK this was done with more force and more systematically than elsewhere in Europe with the enclosure laws denying farmers access to land for growing crops and common grazing. The state was also involved in limited welfare state provision, helping to regulate healthy supplies of factory labour and regulate the transition to capitalism based on free wage labour (Fine and Saad-Filho 2004).

In the colonies the pattern of primitive accumulation has been less successful in separating farmers from their means of production, and some only partially, and in creating stable supplies of free wage labour. Levels of agricultural productivity are not high enough to retain rural labour in the countryside, and economic growth is inadequate to find employment for the dispossessed. The outcome is for rural genocide and northern development policies that are just enough to prevent widespread dissent. Where there has been an increase in the flow of labour to the towns following rural crisis, land dispossession and farming crisis, the newly and sometimes only partially expelled remain jobless. As Samir Amin noted, 'Capitalism, by its nature, cannot resolve the peasant question: the only prospects it can offer are a planet full of slums and billions of "too many" human beings' (2017b, 156).

Modern imperialism fosters persistent (recurrent) processes of accumulation by dispossession (Luxemburg 1968; Bracking and Harrison 2003; Harvey 2003; 2005; Perelman 2000) and displacement (Araghi 2000; 2009a). Our argument will be that this accumulation by dispossession is ongoing, perhaps a permanent feature of capitalism and very evident in contemporary Egypt and Tunisia. This may largely be because of the resistance to it, not only in our case studies but also more generally in the Global South. That resistance both preserves, albeit in an altered way, and also transforms, as we mentioned earlier, local relations of production and social reproduction (Cross and Cliffe 2017; Cohen 1987; Glavanis and Glavanis 1989; Meillassoux 1981). We will argue throughout this book that while we never glorify or idealise the usually immensely harsh and inhospitable rural conditions of existence, we do seek to demonstrate the importance of understanding them more fully than policymakers have ever tried to do. The struggle of critique is to explain the existing rural conditions and to see them as being underpinned by the contradictions of capitalism, violence, coercive state power and resistance to it (Bush and Martiniello 2017). The next step, if it is indeed to be seen in terms of steps rather to run simultaneously and systemically as part of the critique, is to promote an alternative to the development models adopted and imposed in Egypt and Tunisia. This is an alternative that we will not have time to elucidate in this volume, but we will indicate possible aspects of it that place farmers and peasants centre stage. Unlike the views expressed historically by Kautsky (1988 [1899]) that peasant agriculture will disappear, or asserted more recently that capitalist agriculture prevails subordinating farmers to the rules of the market (Bernstein 2014a), we indicate that family farmers and small-scale farming persists, is reproduced in Egypt and Tunisia and is not entirely subordinated to the market: self-provisioning remains a crucial lifeline for small-scale farmers. The persistence of small-scale farmers is a major social and economic feature of modernity and thus there is a distinction between 'capitalist agriculture and agriculture under capitalism' (Amin, S. 2017b, 151–52). This book is a contribution to understanding the character of agriculture under capitalism in Egypt and Tunisia.

In both countries, to varying degrees, we document the emergence of a separate, but connected, agrarian structure of relatively high-value export produce and smallholder farming for mostly self-provisioning but increased dependence upon local markets. In these circumstances, the dominant farming system and the labour that produces the value within it do not produce crops for local consumption but for external markets. The labour process is shaped by the demands of a circuit of capital that is determined by external capitalist actors, although mediated by local farming structures and practices, which might supply labour, provide diminishing access to land for social reproduction and knowledge. The adverse uneven incorporation of peasants and farmers into an externally driven agriculture is shaped by their ability to resist and the market power of corporate agriculture (Akram-Lodhi and Kay 2010b; Martiniello 2016).

The historical process of primitive accumulation in Egypt and Tunisia by which farmers and urban poor were unevenly dispossessed of the means of production is an historical and persistently contemporary process. Rural modernisation is connected to food production and the ecological limits and dynamics that underpin it: land and water. The broad pattern that can be traced and driven by IFI-imposed policies of structural adjustment lending in the 1980s and 1990s is market deregulation for land and other commodities, farming inputs, and distribution. The rollback of state welfare provision, reduced subsidies on food and energy, and removal of import controls have opened economies, including in Egypt and Tunisia, to agro-exporting regimes that undermine the competitiveness and viability of small-scale farmers (Araghi 2009b; 2009a; McMichael 2016). This pattern of agrarian political economy has been broadly experienced throughout the Global South although unevenly. And the vortex of violence that has accompanied the pattern of agrarian transformation has driven rural migration to the towns and cities in the Global South and to Europe and North America.

The processes that have driven the uneven and adverse incorporation of peasants in MENA can be best formulated by using the structure of world food systems and food regime analysis. This analytical frame was introduced in the early 1980s (Friedmann 1982; 1987; 1993; 1994; Friedmann and McMichael 1989) as a method to help explore the role of commercial agriculture in state formation. The food regime is a 'rule-governed structure of production and consumption of food on a world scale' (Friedmann 1993, 30–31). It provides insights into 'larger dynamics of accumulation, power, class and territory' (Friedmann 2016, 672). It is an analytic frame that is rooted in an historical analysis of commercial agriculture and has been inextricably linked to state formation in Europe and the United States. A summary of the main themes linked to the ways in which food regimes have been driven by capitalist development and the impact on the Global South is highlighted in Table 1.1.

We will ask whether the contemporary period is marked by a fourth 'corporate food regime' that may spell the end to the usefulness of food systems analysis (McMichael 2016). We also explore some of the consequences of an analysis that suggests 'capitalism has fully absorbed agriculture' (Friedmann 2016, 672), making farming just another sector of capital accumulation. This latter view is one that implies the focus of agrarian political economy shifts to analysis of surplus labour as an essential feature of capitalist development rather than an analysis of farming and farmers and peasants. It also suggests we need to advance clearer understanding of the social relations of production and reproduction within the farming communities under investigation.

The two most important economic processes that drive uneven and combined capitalist development in the Global South are the commodification of land and labour. Commodification involves the commercialisation or increased dependence on the market for self-provisioning or household

Table 1.1 World Food Systems

First Food Regime (1870s–1914): Farming to Agriculture	Transition (1914–40s)	Second Food Regime (1940–73s): Agricultural Modernisation during Developmentalism	Third Food Regime (1973–end of Developmentalism) Accumulation by Dispossession
Agricultural industrialisation; steel chemicals; electricity and oil; centrality of settler colonialism; British dominance	Free trade to protection: Roosevelt's new deal	US dominance; Cold War; surplus food, PL480; industrialisation of farming. Northern farm supports; overproduction, depressed prices. Idea of 'right to food' and 'food security'	Grain price inflation in the 1970s and 2005–8; increased competition in agricultural trade; new entrants, end of Cold War signals end of strategic role for food aid. Trade liberalisation, increased power of agri-business, idea of household food security
Global South crop specialisation Asia+Africa	Global South war, national struggles	Global South ISI, capital-intensive industrialisation, labour surplus economies; cheap wheat imports, disarticulated agrarian transitions, debt and encouragement to export food	Global South austerity; SAP; end of farmer supports and ISI; Relative becomes absolute depeasantisation, displacement, enclosures; land grabs; food security versus grabs; food security versus sovereignty; farmer resistance; promotion of food and seeds as more than commodities

Source: Permission to reproduce this table from Bush and Martiniello (2017).

activity. This may involve production for the market to generate income to purchase goods and services to sustain social reproduction. It may also involve the purchase of farming inputs like seeds and fertilisers. This increased subordination or reliance upon the market may increase labour market participation of family farmers. This may not, however, necessarily erode the status of peasants as peasants. We have already noted that peasant households may be dependent upon family labour but may also work as wage labourers or indeed, hire-in labour. Peasants, broadly defined as worker peasants or part of a peasantariat, straddle town and country (Bush, Cliffe and Jansen 1986).

Egypt

Commodification of land and labour highlights the ways in which self-provisioning households may become more vulnerable to (unequal) market conditions or dependence upon the market over which they have little control. In Egypt, attempts at controlling the *fellahin* and the land on which they worked were a persistent feature of the country's political economy since before the nineteenth century. Napoleon's invasion of Egypt in 1798 began a process of seeking greater control over the Ottoman ruler, Muhammad Ali, whose alliance with and control over local Mamaluke beys, or rulers, challenged the Sultan of Turkey. The relative military strength of Muhammad Ali was seen as a threat to Europe and a challenge for accrual of economic surplus that might otherwise be directed to France. Accessing and controlling the country's agricultural wealth was fought over between Muhammad Ali and the French, and during 1882–1956, with the British. Surveillance and increased control of Egypt's peasants, however, predates French and British presence. Until the end of the eighteenth century, farmers had considerable control over the development and maintenance of small-scale irrigation and other local infrastructure and village maintenance. But at the start of the 1750s, control over rural Egyptians became increasingly concentrated around elites linked to the country's rulers (Mikhail 2014; Abbas and el-Dessouky 2012). As one commentator has noted, 'The Ottomans had treated Egypt as one big tax farm for about two and a half centuries. At the end of the eighteenth century, various interests wanted slices of this very big pie' (Mikhail 2014, 11). By the mid-1800s, 'the people of Egypt were made inmates of their own villages' as their mobility was restricted and they were forced to supply their produce to government warehouses (Mitchell 1991, 34). An emerging landowning class and the British colonial administration tried to convert the Nile Delta into an agricultural powerhouse. By so doing, village labour was violently coerced into trying to affirm Egypt as a grain powerhouse. Peasant control and decision-making autonomy was lost. Land was increasingly privatised and social unrest increased. Large canal projects came at an immense cost in the form of human suffering. These projects confirmed for farmers the transition from self-control exercised over their local conditions of existence, farming, self-provisioning and the local environment to a reorganisation of their lives and environment managed by an emerging power of new landlords.

The allocation of land-use rights, within a nominal idea that all land was owned (controlled) by the state, was a means of generating clients and revenue for the Khedive ruler.[1] It challenged the idea and practice that

> Landholding did not refer to land as an object, to which single individuals claimed an absolute right. It referred to a system of multiple claims, and not to the land itself but its revenue (Mitchell 2002, 58).

Food production and access to that food for the Ottoman Empire drove the development and repair of complex and expansive irrigation schemes. At first on a small scale, and then expansively after the mid-eighteenth century, village labour, which was once voluntary and paid, became increasingly and violently coerced as Egyptian elites exacted greater rural surplus to keep their autonomy from the Ottoman Empire (Mikhail 2014). One public works scheme that has been seen to shape Egypt for 200 years was the rebuilding of the Mahmudiyya Canal at the turn of the nineteenth century. Mehmet 'Ali sought to link the Nile's Rosetta branch to Alexandria, Egypt's second city on the Mediterranean coast. The canal development involved 315,000–360,000 corvée[2] labourers – more than the total population of Cairo at that time: more than 100,000 perished in terrible conditions of forced labour (Mikhail 2014, 22).

The increasing scale of public works helped meet elite interests to promote and preserve power and to consolidate a pattern of capital accumulation. This involved generating increasing amounts of tax revenue from peasants as well as stocks of food to feed a growing local population. Between 1810 and 1835 Muhammad Ali gifted land to local dignitaries for them to help maintain authority and police the peasantry. By 1858 land tenure laws allowed individual ownership and community user rights facilitating the growth of capitalist agriculture (Cuno 1992).

The British occupation of Egypt during 1882–1956 affirmed the ideology and practice of the universal right to private property and stressed its legitimacy and authority over any competing claim. British occupation also encouraged a rather simplistic but not necessarily wholly inaccurate, bimodal system of agriculture. The growth and increased dominance of large estates worked by sharecroppers and small peasant farming households often with tiny landholdings with leases that had no legal security. The increased indebtedness of small holders and growing landless or near-landless labourers increased the economic wealth of a developing *pasha* class of absentee landlords. Private property as a legal category was a politically engineered strategy to extract rural surplus from the *fellahin*. Private property was 'based on individual acts, orders, seizures, descriptions and inscriptions' (Mitchell 2002, 58). The impact, however, was to promote the uneven alienation of land and labour. It was uneven because on the one hand, land and peasants were 'made into objects to supervise and control' while on the other, there were, as the result of struggles, 'delaying maneuvers, simplifications, and silences' countervailing processes that problematised the blanket or universal spread of privatisation of land and labour.

Central to the processes that drove alienation of land and labour was the western demand for two industrial crops: cotton and sugarcane. During the first world food system from the 1870s to 1914 demand from dominant Northern economies was for crop specialisation in the South. There had been early failed attempts to produce these crops in Egypt with slave labour from Sudan. From the mid-1820s the authorities began to exercise greater control and regiment labour and farming practices in rural Egypt. Regimentation included the 'Programme for Successful Cultivation by the Peasant and the Application of Government Regulations', 1829, that tried to specify what farmers were to produce and where, and who in the governance hierarchy was to ensure its deliverability (Mitchell 1991, 40–41).

Farmers resisted external control and a change to farming practices but they had been increasingly subordinated to the demands on their labour time in public works. They nevertheless clung onto the practice from before the nineteenth century that if they paid part of their food crop to the state they received in return at least a promise of security and justice (Mitchell 2002, 59). The new imperatives of growing crops for export, to meet the interests of Europe rather than local producers, did not sit easily with the *fellahin*. They were uninterested in growing crops that they could not eat. The state's response was to increase farmer surveillance and the farmer response was to move away from the areas of control and in some cases to leave Egypt completely. The increased control over land extended beyond *fella* farming communities to include populations described as arab or more accurately Bedouin. Communities that had a stronger degree of independence from central government were violently dispossessed from the 1840s by Mohammad Ali who created large estates for his household.

The attempts to impose land privatisation were met with local hostility from farmers and their communities. Mohammad Ali secured for himself the status of governor of Egypt for life and hereditary rights to that office, as Khedive for his three male heirs, Abbas (1848–54), Said (1854–63) and Isma'il (1863–79). Although Isma'il reversed some of the controls on peasant land that had generated resistance, allowing, for example, the return of farmers to parts of their historic plots, he nevertheless accelerated an agricultural system that was more outward-facing than organised to meet local food needs. The period 1848–79 was one of increased opening of Egypt's economy to European markets, borrowing for Suez Canal in 1858 from France, and the recurrent externalisation of the economy led to an unsustainable debt by 1868. Yet Khedive Isma'il pressed forward with the development of sugar plantations and mills, the digging of the Ibrahimiyya Canal (1873), a waterway of more than 400 kilometers dug with forced labour intended to boost production of sugar cane and not develop agriculture for local farmer needs. The boost of export agriculture led to rural opposition, conflict and militarisation of some areas in Upper Egypt where cane production was concentrated. It led to increased vulnerabilities in the Egyptian economy notably in terms of international debt. Isma'il had borrowed from creditors against the prospect of a sustained demand for Egyptian cotton. The end of the American civil war and the return to cotton that followed erased Egypt's competitive advantage and one of its main sources of income. It also compounded the country's debt that had grown as a result of infrastructure projects, cattle and food imports.

The nineteenth century witnessed an increased power and authority of large landowners over farmers and farming communities and from historically shared to exclusive rights to the land (Cuno 1993). By 1900, 40 per cent of the cultivated areas were farms with a size of more than 50 feddan (Baer 1962; Owen 1986). As one commentator noted:

> The Egyptian peasant family, formerly a semiautonomous producer with usufructory land rights and substantial control of labor time and production, was increasingly supervised and subject to widespread control of its land and labor (Tucker 1993, 238).

The commodification of land and labour was very uneven in its impact. That was because of the balance of class forces and the ability of the *fellahin* to resist the regulations that were emerging from an increasingly centralised state and the local power holders used to impose tenure reforms. Part of this unevenness in impact was also gendered. Corvée labour imposed enormous hardship on farming families, those forced to work, those left behind and whose labour regime was intensified as male labour was coerced to work on large estates or infrastructural projects. Women experienced hardship in depopulated areas as they were increasingly excluded from land rights, inheritance and custody battles. The social conflict that was generated from state attempts to accelerate the privatisation of land and labour led to erosion of local historical patterns of familial support (Tucker 1993).

Yet it seems the resistance to the most aggressive dimension to commodification also led to the persistence, albeit transformed, of peasant family farming. The state may have recognised the deleterious impact that forced labour recruitment and privatisation of tenure had on the social viability of farming communities. There was no provision to deal with or manage increased under-mining of farming households that resulted from corvée labour. There was no alternative sustainable employment that would be able to help sustain pre capitalist family farming and there were farmer revolts that threatened rural political order. It may also have been the case that farmer resistance to the ways in which land tenure was being privatised and labour hire commoditised led to farming households protecting the perception of their communities being undermined (Tucker 1993, 250).

We will highlight in later chapters how the struggles around the privatisation of land have played out. We will see how the persistence of large-scale agricultural projects shape the geographical and social space for family farming and the marginalisation of Egypt's *fellahin* in trying to sustain independence and autonomy when confronted by neo-liberal reforms, privatisation, market liberalisation and political authoritarianism.

Tunisia

The Tunisian agricultural sector began to seriously deteriorate after 1815. At the root of this deterioration was the appearance of several episodes of drought and an epidemic of plague. Poor harvests caused by irregular rainfall and the vagaries of the climate caused a sharp deterioration in tax revenues and damage to public finances. In response the state imposed new taxes on primary production.

A succession of European states after 1815 imposed their own conditions and control of Tunisian trade. The drop in the export price of Tunisian olive oil and the loss of export markets for durum wheat and artisanal products were very detrimental to the country's cash flow. Meanwhile, European exports penetrated Tunisian markets. Amid bad harvests and state taxes, part of the countryside began to rebel against the new fees and taxes.

Faced with the new economic and social instability and against the specter of European colonial aggrandisement, the bey[3] reacted in a number of ways. The first was to reform the tax system, both to rationalise it and to also increase the state's extractive capacity. The previous tax system was based on direct and indirect taxes. There had been a tithe on cereal and a more complex tax on date and olive silviculture. This was now expanded to include customs duties and farm proceeds, including local taxes, dues from tax-farming, market taxes and rent taxes (Zouari 1998, 122–27).

Finally, the government experienced a revival of its foreign trade, although it was increasingly linked to soap factories in Marseille and promoted the extraversion of the economy (Chater 1984, 469–82). Tax revenues rose sharply but they were so heavy on rural producers that the inhabitants of

Bizerte registered their animals with the Europeans to avoid paying the taxes. In 1840 there was an anti-tax uprising in Gabes. The fiscal policies of the state provided a disincentive for large landowners close to power and especially small holding peasants less and less inclined to cultivate their land. As a result, the area seeded to cereals fell by 85 per cent, from about 700,000 hectares to 120,000 hectares from 1815 to 1855 (Chater 1984, 556–60). To cope with the burden of taxation, farmers borrowed, often at rates of 20 per cent to 30 per cent per year, raising the levels of rural indebtedness (Zouari 1998, 70).

From 1838, the trade balance was largely in deficit (Chater 1984, 569–82) and European powers (France, Italy and Great Britain) used Tunisia's financial weakness to seize legal rights (Zouari 1998, 74–75). In 1861, they imposed the establishment of a 'constitution' to reorganise the Regency and give foreigners the right to exercise any profession in the country, as well as the right to take direct possession of property and the freedom of commerce. But what was perhaps even more crucial was the rights granted to Europeans to own land (Zouari 1998, 67–68; Liauzu 1976) and European traders were eager to control the olive oil trade. In 1860, France, Italy and Britain controlled 92 per cent of Tunisian trade.

In the early 1840s, Tunisia had one million hectares under cultivation compared with just 150,000 hectares in 1862. After a short and difficult renaissance of olive groves in Mornag,[4] under Mohammed Bey (1855–59), the amount of cultivated land fell from 150,000 hectares (in 1862) to less than 60,000 hectares in 1869. In the middle of the agricultural crisis and fall in revenue associated with it, the Beylik quickly contracted three loans – the first dating from 1863. The French influence in the Beylik was already overwhelming in the early 1860s, with French merchants and landowners eager to control Tunisian production and tertiary circuits (Zouari 1998, 171).

The government doubled a rural personal levy *majba* income tax from 36 to 72 piastres (Zouari 1998, 189). This European financial extraction became a catalyst for the 1864 tax rebellion in vast areas of Tunisia. The tribes started the rebellion. But it took on a national character spreading to more populated areas, negatively impacting rural production in the Sahelian olive groves (Zouari 1998, 10–12). Government troops from the Sahel fled to rebel forces based in their territories, the insurgency operation bleeding Sahelian towns and villages, leading to the end of the revolt (Zouari 1998, 230–37). The government imposed a ruinous compensation on the region equal to twice the country's *majba*. The coastal cities of Sousse, Monastir and Mahdia were the hardest hit with escalating debt leading to widespread bankruptcies (Zouari 1998, 250–57).

This last episode of extracting as much surplus as possible from rural Tunisia led to the final collapse of production in the rural sector that included depressed animal sales, jeopardising any possible recovery. It highlighted the surrender of the endogenous tax system. The European International Finance Commission in 1869, with France, Britain and Italy, took control of the financial future of the Regency of Tunis. The declared purpose of the European powers was to protect the interests of their nationals (Zouari 1998, 260–68). From 1870 to 1877, the financial affairs of the regency were transformed partly due to a reform of tax collection. But the fate of Tunisia's sovereignty was sealed. France invaded Tunisia in 1881 and imposed the 'protectorate'. A colonisation de facto.

French colonisation in 1881 constituted a radical turning point in the agricultural policy and dynamic of agrarian questions. The French profoundly modified the rules of access to agricultural land. They introduced a land register (cadastre) in 1885 (Poncet, 1962; Jouili 2008, 116). It had a dramatic impact on social relations of production, including the appropriation of the most productive land for the benefit of French and European settlers. The French dispossessed the local peasantry of their agricultural resources and initiated the intensification of agricultural production. The policy focus was to orientate Tunisian agriculture towards exports and to do so by mechanisation and use of pesticides. The period of French colonisation set an indelible structure to underdevelopment in the agricultural sector that has persisted. This is detailed in Chapter 5.

During the first period of colonisation (1881–1930), colonial agricultural capital structurally transformed conditions and forms of production. Thus, on the basis of colonial capital, a productive agricultural sector was created limited to agricultural production of three major crops: olive oil (centre in the south), grape and wine production (northeast), and cereals, mainly soft wheat (northwest). Very little of the latter had been cultivated before the arrival of the French but was very much demanded by the French market. The dispossession of the peasants for the benefit of the colonial sector deprived them of the resources necessary to maintain their land and ensure their own food security. Deprived of minimum sources of livelihood, thousands of families left their villages in the direction of the capital, giving birth to the first shantytowns of Tunis. Between the 1930s and the 1950s, the Tunisian countryside experienced a worsening of the process of impoverishment and marginalisation of the small- and medium-sized peasantry. This was particularly with the new difficulties of access to resources and means of production and shrinkage of the labour market.

After independence in 1956, the new state chose to continue the pursuit of the colonial agricultural policy. It adopted the intensive, mechanised, modern and export-oriented model that President Bourguiba publicly declared in August 1964. He noted in a public speech that 'the colonial agricultural model was the right model to follow'. One of the first important political decisions in this area was to nationalise settler lands and integrate them into state land. This was instead of returning land to the heirs of the former owners who had been expropriated by the colonial state that favoured settlers. This choice in the 1960s was justified by the necessity of creating a modern agricultural sector and the sanctity of public and private property. It created the first major political rupture between the ruling elite and the peasantry.

The next stages of postcolonial agricultural policies aggravated the gap between elites and family farmers to the point of transforming, more recently, into a powerful engine of the revolutionary processes that brought down the dictatorial regime of Ben Ali in January 2011. The first step was the experience of the cooperatives during the 1960s, which aimed at the collectivisation of private lands of small and medium farmers to create cooperative production units, led by civil servants. This was accompanied by the decollectivisation of tribal (collective) lands in order to privatise them and to facilitate access for investors. Peasant producers were forced to enter cooperatives with their land but as low paid wage earners. This experience led to the second wave of impoverishment that had been induced by colonisation. When the experiment of the cooperatives was finally abandoned in 1969, the farmers who had been members were allowed to take back their land but this led to their indebtedness. Cooperative members had been allowed to only enter the cooperative with their land. They had to sell their equipment and livestock. Leaving the cooperative after 1969, they found themselves with the land as the only means of production. They had no capital, equipment or animals. They had to go into debt to restart their agriculture. There was little improvement in the livelihoods of family farmers.

Finally, as we detail in Chapters 4 and 5, the third period (1970–2018) has highlighted the liberalisation of the agricultural sector. This was marked in the mid-1980s by a structural adjustment plan imposed by the IFIs, which granted political and economic priority to the large private agricultural sector at the expense of family farming. It imposed the paradigm of food security, based on the export of agricultural products, with high added value (olive oil, off-season fruits and vegetables), and the import of food products, particularly food cereals, of which Tunisia still imports more than half of its basic needs. Faced with the intensive and modernised agribusiness sector, favoured and encouraged by the state, the competitiveness of peasant agriculture has been made almost impossible.

We show that the marginalisation of the small peasantry and the definitive break between it and the political elite has produced a form of socio-spatial class solidarity. This explains the popular uprising of solidarity expressed following the desperate act of Mohemad Bouazizi who took his own life in

December 2010 in Sidi Bouzid and it highlights the rural and peasant origins of the revolutionary processes, still in progress, that had begun in the mining regions of southwest Tunisia in 2008. We demonstrate the basic link between agricultural and food problems and revolutionary processes. We make it possible to better decipher and understand the meaning and scale of the slogans carried by protesters between December 2010 and February 2011, from Sidi Bouzid in Tunisia to Tahrir Square in Egypt before reaching many other parts of those respective countries but also in almost all the other countries of the region: 'Bread, social justice and dignity'. More than anything else, this slogan and its variants captured the same importance – it carried the rural and peasant signature of popular uprisings.

Conclusion

This chapter has begun to map out our theoretical and historical framing for the account of why family farmers were so important in the 2010 and 2011 uprisings in Egypt and Tunisia. We have begun to indicate the significance of an historical account of underdevelopment in Egypt and Tunisia with particular reference to the uneven incorporation of both countries into the global food regimes. Chapter 2 extends our theoretical and empirical framing with a discussion of the significance of economic reform, war and environmental stress in the MENA and in our country cases. Chapter 3 will then offer a new interpretation for regime change, which highlights the roles played by small-scale farmers and rural mobilisation. The specific dynamics of our two cases is examined in detail in Chapters 5 and 6 after we have revisited and concentrated on the ways in which food security has shaped policy doctrine within the world food system and in Egypt and Tunisia.

This book offers a detailed critique of how food security is promoted by the IFIs and how it has been internalised by governments in Egypt and Tunisia. We document the impact this has had on rural underdevelopment, on agrarian questions and farmer resistance. We therefore go beyond the usual trope that food insecurity is linked to or driven by natural resource degradation or population growth. We argue instead that we need to capture the differential impact of commodification of land and labour, the uneven incorporation of Egypt and Tunisia into the world food system and how small farmers have at different historical moments been both subordinated to as well as helped shape, global, national and local capitalist political economies. In Chapter 7 we offer an account of how an alternative food sovereignty agenda might emerge as a counter hegemonic food system.

Notes

1   The Khedive was a ruler of Egypt from 1867–1914 and governed as a viceroy of the sultan of Turkey. Muhammed Ali Pasha, however, the Ottoman Albanian commander became the self-declared Khedive of Egypt and Sudan and ruled from 1805 to 1848.

2   Corvée is unpaid labour for a limited period often used for public works.

3   The Bey of Tunis was originally a simple governor representing the Ottoman Empire in Tunis (Tunisia). From the eighteenth century, beys from the Husseinite dynasty acquired a de facto autonomy, that is, a quasi-independence vis-à-vis their overlord: the Ottoman sultan. The beylical regime quickly transformed into a monarchy and the bey was the sovereign. Although the French protectorate from 1881 weakened its effective power, it is after the independence of Tunisia in 1956, that the beys definitively lost their power. The beylical regime was replaced by the advent of the Republic proclaimed on 25 July 1957.

4   Located southeast of the city of Tunis, Mornag is mainly known for its wide and rich agricultural plain dedicated to the vineyard and the olive tree.

Chapter 2

WAR, ECONOMIC REFORM AND ENVIRONMENTAL CRISIS

Introduction

This chapter traces three dimensions of the political economy context for food security issues in the MENA region with particular emphasis on Egypt and Tunisia. It does so by tracing the ways in which conflict, economic and agrarian reform and environmental struggles have provided a politically and socially overdetermined context for understanding food and agricultural underdevelopment. Overdetermination refers to a myriad of contradictions in the conditions of existence of the complex whole of any social formation (Althusser 2005). The three themes raised here are seldom explored in relation to agricultural underdevelopment or the systemic way in which they are integral to the global capitalist system. Yet as we will highlight, the region is structured by wars and conflict, neo-liberal reform and environmental crises. These persistent features of the region have shaped the ways in which agrarian questions can and should be posed. Agrarian transition, the ways in which capital impacts and may transform rurality and shape food sovereignty takes place in the context of multiple and persistent deleterious factors. These result from the 'globalised neo-liberal system', and as we see throughout this book, confronting the development of global apartheid will require the emergence of new strategies for 'Sovereign Popular Project[s]' (Amin, S. 2017a, 7, 13).

War and Conflict

The MENA region has experienced the highest number of international wars and civil conflict in any region in the world. MENA accounts for 40 per cent of total global battle-related deaths since 1946 and 60 per cent of all casualties since 2000. Between 1945 and 2015, 12 of the 59 conflicts in the MENA region lasted more than eight years each, and in half of these, peace lasted less than 10 years (Rother et al. 2016, 7). The cost of conflict and war has been and continues to be catastrophic for national development. Much of the destruction generated by conflict is the result of direct US and NATO military intervention and indirectly by the arms trade and Western funding of local reactionary surrogate forces. The IMF estimate, among other things, that Syria's GDP in 2015 was less than half the pre-conflict 2010 figure (Rother et al. 2016, 9). Yemen lost up to 35 per cent of its GDP in 2015 – and much more since Saudi and UAE accelerated aggression, aided by US intelligence and UK military supplies to Riyadh. Libya's GDP fell by a quarter in 2014 and West Bank and Gaza has been de-developed as a result of Israeli occupation. Conflict may vary in the extent of its impact relating to the severity of war and destabilisation. The direct economic costs, not only precipitous falls in GDP but also spikes in inflation, may be the easiest to note. Yet the indirect impact of displacements, refugee exodus and consequences for neighbours of housing what have become permanent human encampments in Jordan and Lebanon, for example, is calamitous. It is calamitous for the human suffering and transformation of people's access to land and farming that is so transformed by war.

In South Sudan conflict has had an enormous human and economic cost undermining smallholder farming. The loss of 75 per cent of the country's oil revenue in July 2011 contributed to a contraction of South Sudan's economy by 4.4 per cent in 2012. The WFP noted at the time that 'food security remains fragile' and later in 2017 reminded commentators that 'food insecurity is persistent and exacerbated by conflict and economic crisis' (WFP 2014, n.p. and 2017, n.p.). Conflict in Darfur lasting more than 10 years impacted the lives of 3 million people, half of whom have been displaced, removed from farming and herding and in need of food assistance. Displacements have also disrupted farming and agro pastoralism in Blue Nile and South Kordofan (FEWS 2017).

Following the first Gulf War in 1990, Iraq lost two-thirds of its GDP, and the ensuing sanctions campaign took the lives of one and a half million including 500,000 children (Kadri 2014,118). Sanctions and war dramatically undermined Iraq's food security. Before the oil economy, Iraq was a 'bread basket'. After 1990, however, the country imported 70 per cent of its cereals, legumes, oils and sugar (Woertz 2013,135). Disease and malnutrition flourished in Iraq following the international sanctions regime imposed in 1990 after Saddam invaded Kuwait. The misnamed 'oil for food' programme generated disease and malnutrition. In fact, the programme involved neither oil nor food as the UN 'imposed a near total trade and financial embargo […] Iraq was shut off from international financial transactions and its foreign assets were frozen' (Woertz 2013, 134). Iraq's infrastructure was destroyed by Western bombing, and despite attempts by the state to control cereals and oil seeds production, yields fell as cultivation expanded into marginal soil. Land

and crops were destroyed during the invasion and have not rejuvenated as markets and rural communications have been eclipsed by terror and sectarian violence.

Iraq's farming sector plunged into chaos with the 2003 US invasion as terror restricted agricultural production and marketing. The removal of Saddam Hussein and his regime took the lives of at least 268,000 (Iraq Body Count 2017) but one estimate is that deaths related to the invasion were 461,000 in 2013 and higher again by 2017 as there was no end to violence and instability (Hagopian et al. 2013). Reconstruction has focused on the oil sector and combatting the terror that was unleashed by the invasion. There has been very little concern with developing the agricultural sector.

In Syria the devastating civil war reduced the majority of people to hunger and starvation. Syria was previously self-sufficient in food, but violent conflict, reduced by Russian defense of the regime in 2017, still led to an estimated 465,000 deaths (Reuters 2017). Additionally, up to 14 million were in need of humanitarian assistance, 6 million were internally displaced and 4.8 million Syrians were refugees.

Conflict has been central to the history of Yemen, where more than 70 per cent of the 20 million population is food-insecure. The Republic of Yemen, formed in 1990, was the outcome of a union between the People's Republic of Yemen, established in 1967, and the northern Yemen Arab Republic that was established in 1962. The civil war between 1962 and 1971 impacted on farming resources and agricultural 'policy' at a time when the northern economy was opened to the world market for grain. Conflict accelerated after the 2011 uprisings for greater political liberalisation and democratisation. Most of the Western media parrot the figure of 10,000 fatalities, but that is a gross underestimation. It is now clear that between January 2016 and October 2018, there were 56,000 deaths and many more continued into 2019 as a result of the civil war and the Saudi-led military intervention to deny the Houthi movement for political change (Cockburn 2018). Open conflict intensified after the ouster of the West's flunky, President Abd-Rabbu Mansour Hadi. Conflict was aggravated by a Saudi border conflict and Al Qaeda in the Arabian Peninsula militants targeted by US drones. The use of US cluster bombs and drones have devastated rural communities, intensifying conflict and struggle over scarce resources.

In a country where more than 85 per cent live in small villages but only 3 per cent of the land is farmed, a sinister turn to an already violent conflict emerged after October 2015. There is convincing evidence to indicate that Saudi bombing in Yemen has directly targeted civilians and agricultural production, and urban transport and food processing (Mundy 2017; Beckerie 2017). The cynical targeting of civilians indicates Saudi strategy of devaluing

'Yemen's rural human and animal labour' that is trying to deny Yemen as a continuing political regional actor (Mundy 2017, 16; Nichols 2017).

Another illustration of the targeting of civilians and the destruction of farming as a result of war and conflict is the impact of Israel's occupation of Palestine. Occupation has disrupted and dislocated farmers and their families. Violent dispossession of farmers and herders and agro-pastoralists, the appalling loss of civilian life caused by Israel's invasion and bombing of Gaza in July–August 2014, and operation Protective Edge killed more than 2,000 in Gaza. Israel's bombs destroyed 10,000 homes, ruining the livelihoods of 300,000, displacing 500,000, this latter representing almost one-third of Gaza's population. And this was only the latest of a series of attacks on Gaza in particular and in occupied Palestine more generally.

Small farmer agriculture in occupied Palestine is the most undermined in the region including that of other war-torn areas like Syria and Iraq. It is also in many ways, despite the illegal Israeli occupation, a microcosm of themes linked to the constraints on regional agriculture: dispossession, access to water and social and physical (im)mobility. Almost 65 per cent of Palestinians are less than 24 years old. This is similar to the MENA region as a whole, where more than 100 million are between the ages 15 and 29 and where there are 'higher unemployment levels among the young than in any other region of the world' (OECD 2016, 9). Nevertheless, with an overall decline in regional population growth, the young in the region offer a potentially strong and important 'demographic dividend' (Marcus et al. 2013). A predominantly young population generates two kinds of pressure, even in repressive regional regimes. The first is a high expectation for development to meet young people's aspirations, and the second, linked to this, is to understand the reasons for rural youth out-migration, especially in the context of agricultural crises.

Of the just over 4 million Palestinians under occupation, 707,500 are rural, of which 410,000 are classified as poor. The GDP in occupied Palestine in 2016 was just over US$13 billion. Agriculture accounted for about 4 per cent of GDP in 2016 compared with 6 per cent in 2005 and may have employed about 354,000 in 2010 (World Bank 2017). Agriculture accounted for between 20 and 36 per cent of all formal employment for women and 90 per cent of all informal employment in occupied Palestine between 2000 and 2009.

Agricultural development is determined entirely by Israel's violent occupation. The 22-day operation Cast Lead in 2008–2009 impacted 'almost all of Gaza's 10,000 smallholder farms' (FAO 2009). In 2012, losses to the agricultural sector following Israel's Operation Pillar of Cloud were estimated to be UD$20.6 million (PARC 2012, 7).

Destruction of physical farming assets in occupied Palestine is a direct consequence of Israeli occupation. According to the FAO, 2012 witnessed a 'twofold increase in the destruction of agricultural assets, such as olive and fruit trees and cisterns – and with it lost income' (2012, 4). Much of this happened in Area C in the West Bank, an area that was demarcated after Oslo II Accord as in full Israeli control, but it is the area of occupation where there is really the only space for expansion of family or Palestinian state farming. It includes the Jordan Valley and northern Dead Sea, an area of 1.6 million dunums – 28.8 per cent of the West Bank. It is home for 65,000 Palestinians in 29 communities and a further 15,000 Palestinians live in Bedouin communities. But about 10,000 Israeli settlers live in 37 settlements and outposts intensely exploiting the areas rich in natural resources, denying Palestinian herders grazing access and mining waterways (B'Tselem 2011; Reuters 2016).

Violence and conflict in occupied Palestine intensified following the PNA's bid for statehood to the UN in 2013. Israel continues its sanctions regime on Gaza that began in 2006. This was imposed after the election in Gaza of the Islamic resistance movement, Hamas. In 2007, Israel imposed a blockade restricting all but the bare minimum of goods and services to Gaza. Gaza was put on a 'diet' by the Israeli state of the bare minimum 2,279 calories a day and the state would limit the amount of food that entered Gaza accordingly (Cole 2012). There were Israeli restrictions on the Palestinian fishing fleet. Limited to a 6-mile fishing space, it suffered the double liability of constant daily harassment by Israel's navy and lack of fuel. The blockade on Gaza and West Bank has prevented the exchange of products between the two separated locations and limited all hope and prospects for boosting family farming exports overseas. Palestinian markets have also been dumped with Israeli agricultural products and state-subsidised settlers' products – some of which have been inedible and all of which undermine Palestinian farmer competitiveness.

The most destructive Israeli war in occupied Palestine took place in the summer of 2014. It led to more than 2,200 deaths, of which 490 were children. More than 20,000 Palestinian houses were bombed and destroyed, and during the invasion more than 300,000 Palestinians sheltered in UN facilities (UN 2015). Israel's violent disruption to life is the everyday experience of Palestinians and it undermines and aggravates large numbers of fragmented small-scale farms that are labour-intensive and which, although under immense pressure, provide insurance against the occupation forces. But only 5 per cent of all cultivated land is irrigated and it is located mostly in the lower elevated areas of the West Bank. As Israeli settlers steal more and more Palestinian land, less than 1 per cent of upland districts of Nablus and Ramallah is irrigated.

The World Bank continues to stress the importance of private-sector-led growth but recognises that 'Palestinian enterprises have remained hostage to political instability, unresolved conflict, and continued restrictions on movement, access, and trade' (World Bank 2014, n.p.). There remains little hope that Israel will relinquish its occupation of Palestinian territory and it continues to control Palestinian agricultural development and farmer wellbeing.

The catalogue of MENA war and conflict is not an example of violence that is exogenous or the result of local pathology. War and conflict are the channels through which this region is structured and integrated into the world capitalist system. The wars and conflict we have referred to are part of the grab for value and the ways in which the capitalist core maintains an oil-seignorage system of exploitation that inhibits and restricts alternative development strategies. Militarisation and war increase the opportunities for imperial power to be exerted and reduce the negotiating power of the working class and peasantry (Kadri 2018).

Economic Reform and Adjustment

MENA has experienced a 35-year period of economic reform and structural adjustment. Structural adjustment programmes (SAPs) have transformed the region's farmers, dispossessing many from small holdings, raising prices for inputs to unaffordable levels and promoting export-led growth of largely cash crops rather than staple food crops for consumption locally. Private-sector-led growth has empowered large (and some small) entrepreneurs, who have charged increased prices for essential farming inputs, accelerating rural social differentiation, as small holders and the near landless have been displaced. Private sector growth remains the mantra of the international financial institutions (IFI's) especially the World Bank (2008; 2012) and USAID, the leading bilateral donor, which for many years occupied, for example, several floors in Egypt's Ministry of Agriculture and Land Reclamation (USAID 1999). A central plank in the policy of promoting private sector growth was to change land tenure and to convert wherever possible state land (and farms) into private property that was appropriated by either local elites or foreign investors.

The context in which the reforms and the undermining of agriculture and the well-being of farmers has taken place was the failure for regional states to invest oil revenues in agriculture. High oil prices in the 1970s seldom benefitted small farmers although some did manage to migrate, boosting incomes from labouring in the Gulf, Libya or Iraq (Toth 1999). Income to migrant labour helped ameliorate government preoccupation with extractives, but investment in agriculture across the Arab world fell in the 1970s and 1980s. Oil wealth encouraged states to import food and consumer goods rather than produce them locally. This was encouraged by the IFIs. Agricultural productivity per worker fell across the region as did gross investment in agriculture between 1980 and 1992. In Algeria it fell from 37 per cent to 28 per cent, in Egypt from 31 per cent to 23 per cent and in Morocco from 23 per cent to 22 per cent. It also fell by 2 per cent in Sudan and Tunisia (El Ghonemy 1999,12). The celebrated years of oil-led economic growth and the economic opening or *infitah* created years of agricultural neglect contributing to the (false) idea of the resource curse (inter alia Lynn Karl 1997; Ross 1999).

Governments in the MENA region resisted SAPs longer than any other part of the world. The history of social contracts throughout the MENA and the protests and riots against reform in Egypt, Algeria, Sudan and Tunisia added to the state's reluctance to implement IFI-led reform agenda. Yet governments did not hold out forever, and the march towards privatisation and state withdrawal was extensive. Morocco privatised state-, collective- and religious-endowed land. Land that had previously been farmed collectively was split up with minimum five hectare plots favouring the wealthy who were able to purchase land that accelerated concentration of land ownership among political elites (Hanieh 2013, 79). Tunisia also privatised collectively managed tribal land, and state farms were sold off. Algeria sold its state farms that were declared 'inefficient' and privatisation was declared to benefit family farmers.

Egypt highlights the pressures for privatisation of land, changes in land tenure and removal of state allocation of agricultural resources including credit. Market-led reforms and economic liberalisation were the centerpiece of USAID's US$775 million Agricultural Production and Credit Project (1986–96). After 1996, USAID's Agricultural Policy and Reform Programme increased influence with the government of Egypt (GoE), linking with five ministries emphasising export-led growth, the US farm model and reduction in subsidies. The policy outcomes were praised as increasing agricultural productivity and incomes and deregulating cropping patterns to boost agricultural exports.

Critics have noted that this was an agricultural policy without farmers; investment and GoE support was directed to new investors rather than to family farmers in the old lands of the delta and there was a gap between declared policy and actual outcomes. First, productivity data was unreliable, and improvements in agricultural productivity may have been the result of previous underreporting (Mitchell 1998). The rate of growth in agriculture after 1990 was in fact less than for the pre-reform period of 1980–87 and the strategy to boost revenue from export-led growth failed to resolve the understanding that while Egypt's agricultural imports had a low elasticity of demand – wheat, sugar and edible oils – most of the country's exports had high elasticity. More than two decades of economic reform failed to deliver export-led growth (Bush 2002; 2009).

The harsh impact of economic reform on small farmers was most felt with implementation of changes in land tenancy. Law 96 of 1992 revoked Gamal Abdel Nasser's legislation that had given small farmer rights to lease land in perpetuity.[1] Fully implemented in 1997, more than a million tenants were displaced, and rents were increased by more than 400 per cent. Many of the dispossessed were female-headed households and landlords refused to renew contracts with people thought unable to pay.

Law 96 had not been part of the economic reform package implemented in 1991, but USAID congratulated the GoE on policies that were consistent with privatisation. The law, however, led to considerable levels of rural violence, disruption to productivity, as tenants were reluctant to invest in land over which there was so much insecurity about future cultivation (LCHR 2002). The changes in tenancy together with economic liberalisation contributed to an increase in land concentration. In Egypt between 1990 and 2000 the number of farms of less than one feddan increased from 36.7 per cent of total holdings to 48.5 per cent. Ninety-three per cent of Egyptian farmers work less than 5 feddan while just 3 per cent of landowners control almost 35 per cent of agricultural land with an average holding of more than 10 feddans each (Ayeb 2012).

The detrimental impact on small farmers resulting from economic liberalisation is also highlighted in Morocco. The pattern of decline for the agricultural sector in general, and small farmers in particular, can be traced to the last 50 years of government policy. That policy has failed to promote either food security or export-led growth that might have generated revenue for development more generally. The promotion of what has been called 'reckless free trade' has failed to raise rural living standards because

> Headline structural problems [...] remain: deficits in production and productivity; trade deficits; insufficient and inadequate funding; infrastructure deficiencies; omnipotence of weather hazards; limited natural resources in constant degradation; archaic and counterproductive land tenure structures; weak farming systems poorly coordinated with the rest of the economy; poverty and widespread illiteracy; and an even more onerous food import dependency (Akesbi 2014, 169).

Moroccan agricultural policy changed in the mid-1980s. Up until then, government supported infrastructural growth, provided production subsidies and intervened in the market with cropping and distribution intervention. The policy from the 1960s was called the '*politique des barrages*' or politics of the dams with an objective of irrigating one million hectares before 2000. The strategy to favour large project development absorbed 60 per cent of the agricultural sector's resources and 30 per cent of public investments (Akesbi et al. 2008, 43). The strategy favoured large farmers with export-oriented capability and resources. There were some benefits from dam development in the 1970s but they were uneven in terms of revenue creation, working conditions and rural livelihoods.

Moderate land redistribution of 'reserve' land and of former colonised land in the early 1970s served as a vehicle for political reconciliation. Coup attempts and political unrest probably helped to accelerate a limited 'agrarian revolution' but land distribution of just 320,000 hectares to only 24,000 beneficiaries, just 2 per cent of farmers, did not relieve rural poverty or improve services like health care, education and transport (Akesbi et al. 2008, 46–47). Additional attention had also been given to trying to redress the imbalance between state support for irrigation and relative absence of support for rain-fed agriculture of small-scale farmers.

Structural adjustment led to the privatisation of veterinary services, water supply for irrigation, seed provision and ended management of cropping patterns. The liberalisation of the internal agricultural market exposed small farmers to the vagaries of private entrepreneurs. Moreover, state regulation of export markets through the Office de commercialisation et d'exportation ceased.

The World Bank aided the Moroccan agricultural vision, which, since the mid-1960s, had emphasised the twin aims of 'modernisation' and 'productivity' (Akesbi et al. 2008). According to the census of the mid-2000s, 13.4 million from a total population of 29.9 million live in the rural areas. An estimated 45.8 per cent of active working population is engaged in agriculture nationally, a figure that rises to 80.4 per cent in rural areas. Yet like elsewhere in MENA, there is rural exodus and little accuracy in rural unemployment figures.

Morocco's second SAP ended in 1997 with a World Bank evaluation report noting 'fatigue of adjustment'. A series of ministerial policy initiatives were considered in the 1990s but it was not until April 2008 with the Green Morocco Plan (Le Plan Maroc Vert) that rural development was pushed into the policy arena. The plan had two key pillars. The promotion of competitive modern agriculture, with market-based private investment and poverty reduction by boosting incomes of the poorest farmers in most peripheral areas (ADA 2018; Akesbi 2014, 171).

The desired outcome of the Green Moroccan Plan is to boost agricultural GDP and rural household income. The mechanism for so doing is to directly address the livelihoods of family farmers. This is to be done by a process of 'aggregation'. This means investors and agricultural managers with resources of land and income will work with smaller farmers to promote economies of scale. The plan is that over a 10-year period, almost a thousand projects, at a cost of EUR 6.8 billion will benefit 560,000 farmers. Second, the 'human face' of the project will focus on assisting small family farmers to move into more profitable crops. As many as 860,000 farmers may be targeted with 545 projects costing EUR 1.8 billion (Akesbi 2011; 2014).

After years of neglect the Green Moroccan Plan begins to reconsider the role of farmers and rural development, but there are a number of critical points to consider. Not the least among these is the absence of any prior consultation with farmers and rural communities. The critique in fact is applicable to other regional country examples in the period of neo-liberal reform. The approach taken in Morocco is very much driven by the concerns of productivity and a technocratic response to perceived underperformance of small marginalised farmers. Small farmers were not consulted about the plan even though in Morocco 99 per cent of farms are managed by family farmers; a little less than 12,000 farms covering just 3.2 per cent of (best?) agricultural area is run by managers (Akesbi 2011, 28). There is little mention of the complex and integrated pluriactivity of farming and farmers, and despite the rhetoric, the Plan seems not to consider boosting food security or a more nuanced notion of food sovereignty. The prioritised food chains seem to be fruit and vegetables, olives and olive oil.

It is with the idea of aggregation, however, that many pitfalls are evident. Aggregation jettisons any possibility of a redistributive land reform and instead tries to incorporate family farming into 'commercialised' and largely corporate-driven forms of production. The model in Morocco may be an attempt to expand the idea of success of special productive areas: tomatoes in the south, strawberries in the north and the continued protection of companies linked to the royal family like the COSUMAR group for sugar cane production, refining, distribution and export, at a time of rhetorical liberalisation of foreign trade. The absence of engagement with the agrarian question of land has led planners to assume that much land is empty and unused. The plan alienated small farmers who have perceived the schemes linked to it as mechanisms for redistributing the limited resources of family farmers to economic and political elites. More than 40 per cent of small farmers have been characterised as inefficient (Mahdi 2014). The Plan does not engage with the concerns of perhaps as many as 60,000 landless labourers, and there is little attempt to engage with rural petty trade and pastoralism.

Elsewhere, in the Maghreb, economic reform and structural adjustment led to what have been called the 'politics of prices' and a deterioration of the material and social conditions of small farmers (Bessaoud 2004). In Algeria the pitfalls of liberalisation are similar to those of Morocco. Economic liberalisation in Algeria of the 1980s and 1990s was a response to production shortfalls in fertilisers and food processing, failure to meet increased urban demand for food and the abandonment of agrarian reform. Liberalisation took the form of reducing state control after 1976 of the co-operative sector and the end of land nationalisation. An increase in the prices of fertilisers and other agricultural inputs after liberalisation, however, reduced their usage and agricultural output. Between 1983 and 1987, state-led land redistribution stopped and private entrepreneurs and the previously termed 'socialist agricultural domains' were dissolved. In 1990, and not dissimilar to Egypt's Law 96 of 1992, the beneficiaries of Algeria's long-standing agrarian reform programme were required to return land that had been redistributed to them 15 years earlier. Informal markets emerged between family farmers who were able to access farming resources and traders. Land fragmentation accelerated. The average farm size in Algeria is 4.7 hectares and 80 per cent of farmers own less than 10 hectares.

After years of declared reduced public sector agricultural involvement, in 2000 a new state-driven national programme emerged. The state did not revoke the period of neo-liberal market reform. Instead it recognised the importance of state intervention to manage 'reconversion of soils' up to 3 million hectares of land to move away from cereal production to increase production of fruits, livestock and wine.

The National Programme for Agricultural Development has delivered since 2000 more than 40 billion Algerian dinars a year to the rural area (about US$40 million) – four times more than average investments during 1995–98 and 10 times the amount delivered after the start of structural adjustment in agriculture in 1993. While on the surface there seemed to have been a major and critical shift in Algerian state policy, the impact on small farmers is likely to be limited (Bessaoud 2007). This is because the idea of the small farmer and the organisation of agricultural production is unrelated to the realities on the ground. Few small farmers have formal property rights; those who do cannot access credit and have little representation over rural development policy. At least one-third of 12 million rural Algerians are categorised as poor, 42 per cent of the unemployed live in the countryside and women's access to land and credit is especially limited. There has been a programme to introduce seasonal interest-free loans, *Rfig*, and to increase support for providing farm inputs, but the results of this are uneven and patchy.

Economic reform in Tunisia is intimately and inextricably linked to environmental transformation and thus we deal with it in the next section and in further detail in Chapter 4.

Environmental Crises

Almost all discussion of the environmental dimensions to MENA's crises begins with the premise of the region's ecological limits. MENA is 'the most water-stressed region in the world with 7 per cent of the world's population but only 1.5 per cent of its renewable freshwater supply' (Joffé 2016, 55; Michael et al. 2012; World Bank, 2008). Water scarcity drives the response to climate change and the regional government's hydro-politics (Allan 2001). Population growth up to 2025 may lower per capita water availability by 30–70 per cent but this assumes there will be no additional access to renewal water, which is unlikely (Sowers 2014, 1). MENA's hydro-politics, which is greatly aggravated by geopolitical conflicts and imperialist interventions, is also strongly influenced by the considerable expansion of irrigation in increasingly intensive agricultural sectors, which are largely export-oriented. Intensely extractivist hydraulic and hydro-agricultural policies that have multiplied irrigated areas by 10 (15 in some countries in the region) in less than 30 years. From Morocco to Saudi Arabia through the whole of the Maghreb, Egypt, Syria and occupied Palestine, the hydraulic choices have become the main pillars of agricultural and food policies. The aquifers, generally non-renewable, are depleted and thus accelerate the salinisation of the soil. Ongoing climate change exacerbates destructive successions of long droughts and devastating floods (Ayeb 1998, 2009). Hydro-politics is a cipher for the pattern of agricultural modernisation of the 1960s and 1970s. It has continued in the neo-liberal period further marginalising the region in the third food regime. State-led development merges with and drives agro export agriculture also marked by infrastructure expansion in dams and irrigation. It is a modernisation that repeatedly neglects rain-fed agriculture and relies more and more on cereal imports.

Hydro-politics is an important dimension to the way governments in the region try and exercise power over their riparian neighbours dependent upon one of the region's three main river systems. The first of these is the Tigris-Euphrates, which rises in Turkey and discharges in the Persian Gulf. Turkey generates hydroelectric energy and irrigation water from the Greater Anatolia Project, which is the largest river basin project in the world. Syria is 85 per cent dependent for its renewable water from the Tigris-Euphrates and Iraq is 100 per cent dependent upon it (Tsakalidou 2013, Ayeb 1998, 2011b). Dam projects in Turkey limited Iraq's water supply in the 2000s that were exacerbated by years of drought.

The second river system that shapes water availability in MENA is the Upper and Lower Jordan River Basin. This includes Lake Tiberias and the Yarmouk River providing water for Jordan, Syria and Lebanon (FAO, 2013). Water access is determined by Israel's occupation in Palestine that sucks water out to illegal settlements accelerating regional underdevelopment (Hass 2016). Finally, the River Nile, possibly the world's longest river (cf the Amazon) is the drainage basin for 11 countries providing most of the fresh water for Sudan and Egypt.

The status quo of access to Nile water has been thrown into doubt with the development of the Ethiopian Renaissance Dam. At an estimated cost of US$5 billion, it is Africa's biggest and most ambitious dam – 1,800 meters long, 155 meters high with a capacity of 74 billion cubic metres of water (165 billion cubic meters of water for the Aswan Dam). Such an enormous catchment jeopardises Egypt's historic access to 55.5 million cubic meters of water (against 18.5 for Sudan). The Nile waters agreements of 1959 had guaranteed Egypt and Sudan these levels of access. However, that agreement was always declared unacceptable by Ethiopian governments. This was because the 1959 agreement did not give any water rights to Ethiopia. This was despite the fact that the Blue Nile, which carries almost 80 per cent of the total Nile water, comes from Ethiopian territory. The agreement was cancelled by the Entebbe Agreement in May 2010 when neighbouring countries, pushed by Ethiopia, refused to honour historic colonial agreements. The conflict between Egypt and its neighbours over the building of the dam and Nile water access is legendary. Cairo policymakers deem any restriction on its access to Nile waters to be an issue of national security and to be severely detrimental to the country's economic development (Halawa 2015). Addis Ababa politicians, in contrast, claim water rights and renegotiation of the 1959 agreements. They also claim there will be no negative consequences for Cairo or Sudan despite Khartoum's worry about the loss of fertility to its soils. This latter would result from sediment retention at the head of the dam and Cairo worries about increased salination in the delta as the dam is likely to take up to 5 years to fill with reduced water flows to Egypt (International Rivers, 2017, Ayeb, 2008; 2011b).

Regional water constraint leads to calls for targeting more efficient water use like drip rather than flood irrigation. Hydro-politics has favoured the persistence of large-scale farming systems rather than small farmer techniques that may have adapted and worked with local conditions. It has also led to a view that moves towards regional food self-sufficiency are flawed with insufficient water and local resources to feed a growing population. For one commentator, agriculture consumes as much as 80 per cent of the water supply and therefore instead of trying to boost farm production, 'the focus should be on more efficient water management in order to stabilize that production' (Woertz 2017, 15). The regional stalemate is partly because oil rents have enabled autocratic regimes to offer only limited economic diversification as windfall revenue continues to provide income for food purchase on global markets. Saudi Arabia uses large fiscal balances accrued from oil sales to import 70 per cent of its food needs and in 2013 spent US$24 billion so to do (Karam 2014). Revenue from oil has facilitated a subsidy programme for household access to food and is used as a mechanism to also reduce political dissent with dynastic rule. Similar huge fiscal balances in Gulf States ensure continued access to imported food. One estimate is that the Gulf Cooperation Council (GCC) food import bill will be US$53.1 billion by 2020 (Deulgaonkar, 2017). This import dependence, fueled by both population growth and demand for wheat and meat, has made it common for Egypt, Qatar and Saudi Arabia to grab land in the region, and beyond, as a hedge against subordination to international food chains. These countries also have a growing national agribusiness sector.

The emerging contradiction for the majority of oil-producing states, notwithstanding US withdrawal from global climate change initiatives in 2017, is that environmental limits to the use of fossil fuels in the Global North will curtail the fiscal balances and the continued ability to purchase food on global markets of MENA countries. Economic crisis for the oil states will jeopardise the stability of social contracts that form the basis of regional rentier politics. Although the region as a whole is a relatively low carbon dioxide emitter, many of the region's oil producers have generated carbon-intensive lifestyles. In fact, 'per capita emissions in many MENA countries are 60% higher than the average among developing countries' (Nakhood et al. 2013, 1). Resource-poor Yemen, plunged in war by Saudi and Western military intervention, and Djibouti, have some of the world's highest levels of poverty, as does resource-rich Sudan and South Sudan. A recent report noted that there was a reduction in nitrogen dioxide over the Middle East after 2010. While there had been a steady increase in this noxious emission from the mid-1990s, it declined as a result of political and economic crisis, especially in Egypt but also in Saudi, Iraq and the Gulf. Although the index for the short-term changes was only air pollution emission inventories, they were noted as a (temporary?) counter to gloomy environmental debate (Lelieveld, Beirle et al. 2015).

As we have noted, the largest amount of water in the region is used for agriculture and the high dependence upon rainfed agriculture makes family farming, under existing policy constraints, vulnerable to climate change (Sowers et al. 2011; Chenoweth et al. 2011; Droogers et al. 2012). More than half of all arable land in Algeria, Iraq, Jordan, Lebanon, Libya, Mauritania, Morocco, Sudan, Syria, Tunisia and Yemen is rainfed. In Sudan and Yemen, up to 80 per cent of cereal production is rainfed. The region will become drier and hotter with the possibility of rainfall decreasing by 10 per cent by 2050 (FAO 2013, 60–61). Worsening water scarcity resulting from falls in groundwater resources and climate warming, under existing patterns of distribution and use, will lead to crop losses especially for small farmers. One estimate is that agricultural output may fall by 21 per cent by 2080 and the losses may be as high as 40 per cent in Morocco and Algeria (Cline 2007).

Agricultural strategy (and development policy more broadly), rather than an absolute scarcity, has accelerated an environmental and water crisis made more acute by climate change. The region's oil-fuel-water-agriculture nexus has placed structural and immediate limits to peasant agriculture. This is because cheap energy has, among other things, quickened the use of new water drilling techniques and capital intensification of farming. The policy has been to increase export-led growth of mostly high value, low nutritious foodstuffs rather than the production of local staples (Sowers 2014, 2). The drilling of deeper and deeper wells to access ground water aquifers has not allowed enough time for these sources of irrigation to be recharged. The consequence has been to mine the regions scarcest resource, limiting its social distribution.

Tunisia is an important illustration of how water policy linked to pressures of climate change was exacerbated during economic reform and the period of erstwhile dictator Ben Ali. Small farmers and agro pastoralists were undermined by the promotion of private agricultural projects that accompanied economic reform after 1982. Economic liberalisation intensified competition over agricultural land, water and rural resources between the Sahel region of Tunisia (northeast) and the rest of the country. This led to additonal conflict between small- and medium-sized farmers and agricultural private investors. Competition over water resources, minerals and wealth from agricultural products like olive oil intensified. Farmer surplus was increasingly transferred to the northern Sahel for processing where value added also accrued. Agriculture represents about 12 per cent of Tunisia's GDP and most of that production is located outside of the Sahel region (Ayeb 2012).

The transformation of Sidi Bouzid is illustrative of the processes of rural dispossession and wealth transfer. Sidi Bouzid is a semi-arid area where the local population has practiced semi-nomad pastoralism and extensive rainfed agriculture. This included sheep and camel farming together with olive, almond and cereal production. The region now captures a key contradiction, evident in other countries in MENA: high agricultural production *and* high rates of poverty, 42.3 per cent of the population living on less than US$2 a day in 2011. This 'green mirage' (Ayeb, 2013) is the result of a farming strategy that has excluded small farmers. It exemplifies an ideology of food security based upon maximising local water resources and mining the soil. Tunisia's Fifth Five Year Plan (1977–81) confirmed the end of collectivism and asserted an export-led role for agriculture intended to boost food security. Expansion of irrigated agriculture by investors from outside the region increased irrigated farmland from 2,000 hectares in 1958 to almost 50,000 in 2011 (Ayeb and Bush 2014). The entry of private investors from outside the region increased conflict. Private capital funded new irrigation techniques, electrification and plantation development. Increased displacement and dispossession of small farmers as a result of this strategy led to the reintroduciton of the term *colon* previously reserved for French settlers.

The impact of global warming accelerates constraints of water availability (World Bank 2010; Shetty 2006). We have begun to indicate that resource availability and distribution is shaped by political and economic forces that benefit the status quo. Drought in Eastern Syria between 2006 and 2010 destroyed an estimated 800,000 livelihoods, killing 85 per cent of livestock leading to the abandonment of more than 150 villages (Minio-Paluello 2014).

There is considerable variation in the projections for rising sea levels. The projections are politically charged. Sea levels in the Nile Delta may rise between 50 and 200 centimeters by 2100. Climate prediction indicates that there will be greater warming in the southern and eastern Mediterranean than the world as a whole (Sowers 2014). With half a meter rise in sea level in Alexandria, Egypt might lead to the loss of 15 per cent of high-quality delta agricultural land resulting from sinking and salinity. By 2030 the loss of agricultural value might be US$6 billion and enormous job losses (Fawaz and Soliman 2016).

The climate change debate has focused on strategies for mitigation and adaptation. A UNDP report suggests that mitigation relates to mainly energy concerns and suggests the imperative for 'collective action' (Waterbury 2013), although this mostly seems to be the Global North proposing that the Global South forget or downplay its developmental needs (Green 2012). Mitigation puts an emphasis on the need for equity in a way in which climate change impacts on the MENA and the Global South. Yet the needs of the Global South and family farmers within it are clearly uneven, and are socially as well as geographically differentiated. Climate finance has been almost entirely restricted to a small number of large projects with little reference to the impacts on family farming. The donor support for clean technology funds is more than US$701 million of which 80 per cent are for mitigation and not adaptation needs of water conservation and food security: Egypt and Morocco receive 80 per cent of approved climate funds in the MENA – 11 countries receive no funds at all (Nakhood et al. 2013, 1).

In contrast, adaptation to climate change is used to describe issues relating to the impact that occurs in the agricultural sector. Policy decisions will be shaped by welfare implications because more than a fifth of regional total employment is in agriculture and 'political leaders may find themselves asking the poorest in their societies to bear the costs of adaptation' (Waterbury 2013, 8). Adaptation and vulnerability have become two ideologically charged terms. Vulnerability relates to the tendency to be impacted by crises whereas climate changes are mediated by current vulnerability (IPCC 2012, 5 cited in Mason et al. 2014, ix). A wide-ranging report on climate security in the Jordan River Valley highlighted the shortcomings in the literature and the limited analytical heft of debates on vulnerability and community and household adaptive capacity (Mason et al. 2014). The scales used to analyse vulnerability are often pitched only at a macro level with little focus on community and propensity. There is often an absence of discussion that links national strategies regarding climate change with trans-boundary issues. This is a shortcoming that fails to consult or engage with small farmer strategies to deal with climate change, rising sea levels and soil salination and deliverability of alternative farming strategies.

Second, the debates about vulnerability tend to be pitched at a level that assumes political neutrality yet we have already seen how, in the MENA (and other?) contexts, debates about family farming, its limitations and opportunities is politically charged and in the case of much of MENA, it is shaped by intense militarisation, violence and uncertainty linked to occupation. There is also little crossover between debates regarding vulnerability and the political economy of water scarcity (Mason et al. 2014, 7–9). Scarcity is often seen as an absolute concept and not one that is shaped by differentiated use, renewal and transformation. It is also important to add that while the term vulnerability is much used in the debate regarding climate change so too is the idea of *resilience*, the much-vaunted mantra that the dangers of everyday life need simply to be adapted to, that people can learn to live with the experiences of climate change and will benefit from so doing by developing new ways of managing, (not radically transforming) their (often appalling) life chances (Evans and Reid 2014; Duffield 2007).

As in other regions of the world, there is much to applaud in the coping and survival strategies of family farmers. Strategies like changes to cropping and seed mixes, adjusting the planting calendar as rainfall appears late or is disrupted compared to previous years and in promoting access to off-farm income, travelling further to reach different markets and moderating diet and so on. These are strategies that differentially affect farmers of different land sizes and resource access and women more than men. Yet this 'adaptability' does little to reverse or counter the reasons why usually poorer family farmers are the first to experience crisis and why crises intensify rural poverty. Adaptability at best seems a strategy to take farmers back to pre-crisis levels of social organisation and production. Yet this is precisely the condition from which it was difficult to avoid entry into crisis.

It is now well known, and documented, that the poor are the first to suffer the impact of 'natural' disasters and hazards. When the term 'adaptation' is used, therefore, it is important to interrogate who in fact is being asked to adapt and with what kind of consequences (Malm and Esmailian 2013). It is also important to consider what the historical antecedents are to the ways in which climate change impact family farmers. How has agricultural policy, or its absence, intensified the consequences of climate change? Adaptation in Egypt, for example, to rising sea levels seems to be mostly concerned with how it will impact tourism and real estate development on the northern coast, and not how family farmers need to be protected to reduce their displacement and to manage potential new patterns of cropping and employment.

Family farmers have in fact resisted the linked implications of the policies of economic reform and recent consequences of climate change. They have done this in the context of the Arab uprisings in Egypt, Tunisia and Yemen, and elsewhere too. A UNDP report on the political economy of climate change, distinguished by the absence of political economy, is reluctant to engage critically with regional development strategies. Although the failures of policymakers to act decisively with regard to climate change and other issues is legendary in the MENA region, not least because of rentier politics and the frailty of social contracts between rulers and ruled, the UNDP report suggests that 'Radical departures are not warranted nor feasible' (Waterbury 2013, 8). This might be interpreted as a vote of confidence in the persistently authoritarian regimes in the region rather than suggesting the need to explore new possibilities in the aftermath of the Arab uprisings.

The persistent feature of debate on family farming in MENA is the absence of farmer voices. Even during the heyday of decolonisation and the state-led strategies to break from the dominance of dualistic agricultural structures, family farmers were seldom consulted about strategy, reforms and linkage between the countryside and the town. Agricultural policy without family farmers is a theme that runs through all our cases in the same way that our cases are all impacted by systematic and often routinised violence: dispossession from land and water resources, inadequate and too costly input prices and poor access to local marketing.

In Yemen farmers have experienced the flooding of markets with cheap grain as a result of trade liberalisation and the absence of state support for rainfed agriculture not least with inadequate support for infrastructure, terracing and transport. And policies that have failed to reduce gender-based poverty and exclusion, illiteracy and poor health provision are the result of a failure in rural development policy more broadly. These problems in Yemen are an acute illustration of the impacts of economic reform. They are also a consequence of the failure to understand the dynamics of 'subsistence' farming. One of the features of the region, not just in Yemen, is the heavily skewed levels of land holdings. Small proportions of large landowners and foreign companies own and control access to land compared with the high proportion of small holders and near landless. Policy measures and debates, in Yemen and elsewhere, tend to focus on the needs to increase the productivity of small holding farmers and to do that, as we have seen, by market-driven mechanisms. But as has been noted in the case of Yemen, 'Rain-fed agriculture is targeted by technical solutions dedicated to increase productivity' and raise incomes. But this means 'implicitly increasing production for a market wherein local rain-fed production will never be competitive without strong political support and protection' (Mundy and Pelat 2014, 17; Mundy et al. 2014).

Conclusion

We have traced in the many different cases of the MENA region how rhetorical policies to raise rural incomes in support of family farming has taken place in the context of conflict, economic liberalisation and climate change. Attempts to view the difficulties faced by family farming holistically with a view to addressing structural concerns of access to resources and the need therefore to address social inequality, and how that inequality is *reproduced*, have not been very extensive. NGOs, for example, may address issues of climate and water access and gender inequality but do not have the political clout to persuade governments to address policy failures that link sectoral issues with broader-based concerns of social differentiation. Policy reform has taken place in the context of enhanced internationalisation of the food regime where family farming, in even the remotest areas of MENA, are impacted by agribusiness and international trade arrangements in grain and other agricultural products.

Fundamentally, it is important for family farmers and farming to be seen to be important, for what they do and how they do it, for them to be viewed as significant and integral to development, broadly defined. This means valorising indigenous farming knowledge and techniques. This will involve penalising the actions of investors and speculators who may take land and other resources out of production of food. It also means thinking about agricultural extension in a different way. For family farming to be secured and its value understood, with all the consequences that can follow from that, namely a slowing of rural to urban migration, as rural work becomes more secure, agricultural extension needs to be orchestrated by family farmers themselves.

The conclusion therefore is that while a shopping list of recommendations is easy to boost regional and national food security, the deliverability of reforms that will affect family farming positively is far more difficult. A list that addresses financing and investment; land fragmentation without addressing inequality in land holding; youth and gender support; concern with climate change and so on will do little to change the status quo that has generated the crises of family farming which we have identified (FAO 2014, 2–3).

The shopping-list approach to family farming reform is understandable: it does not challenge issues of power, resource distribution and access to land. The shopping list of everyday IFI reforms that governments and agencies can agree on, and usually at a glacial pace of implementation and debate, will ensure the continued marginalisation of family farming and, among other things, the continued hegemony of global grain markets.

A research agenda that tries to think beyond the immediate dealing with host governments will need to address the structure of the reasons why family farming has been so underdeveloped. This will involve understanding the relationships of power that have emerged historically to enmesh family farming in patterns of uneven and deleterious incorporation of agrarian policy. There have been many common patterns in the MENA that have been identified and many country specificities particularly linked to overarching patterns of conflict, economic reform and climate change. Analysis and research that may address persistent agrarian underdevelopment will need to identify inter alia where the production and distribution shortfalls occur and why and with what kinds of social consequences. In other words, research and policy inter-vention will need to be *dynamic* and *differentiated*. This is because it is neces-sary to understand who is affected by shortfalls in production and how, what groups and social categories exist, particularly households distinguished with varied resource endowments, age and gender compositions and with different relationships with owners and so on.

This will require analysis of specific units of food production and patterns of self-provisioning. At the village and community level, further specification is needed of social and class differentiation and supportive or exploitative relations between different household units. Here, an analysis of mechanisms of mutual support, survival, storing and for tackling emergencies is important together with an understanding of the environmental balance and challenges, fragility of ecology and so on. These dynamic, actual and potential fault lines need exploring in detail and by case investigation rather than generalised policy invective. It will require a view of policy that is inclusive, based on informed ethnographic investigation rather than on urban-based agricultural extension and there is a need to identify what might be 'normal' relationships and what might be sources of cyclical crises, droughts, pests, economic and political. These cyclical crises can then be set alongside long-run trends of encroachment, dispossession and water scarcity. Only by doing this will it be possible to identify which family farmers have inadequate access to means of production cyclically or permanently. Chapter 3 begins to do this by looking at the rural roots of regime change in Egypt and Tunisia.

Note

1   Gamal Abdel Nasser was the second president of Egypt, 1954–70. He had led the Free Officers in the 1952 overthrow of the monarchy. The early land reforms were a key element of his programme to promote a radical transformation of Egyptian politics and society.

Chapter 3

THE AGRARIAN ORIGINS OF REGIME CHANGE

Assuming a hierarchy of demands where the 'economic' is portrayed as narrowly defined and less inclusive on the one hand and reformist and less revolutionary than the 'political' on the other is historically and theoretically without base and only stands to serve the interests of the capitalist state and its agents (Abdelrahman 2012, 615).

The Revolution has not changed the system but it has changed the people (*Cairo Graffiti* 2011).

Salah used to tell me that the Egyptian people are like running water under a stable bed of mud. On the surface it looks tranquil but underneath runs a stream of flowing water. That is why they will revolt again. The Egyptian people will never be shattered (Maklad quoted in Radi 2016).

Introduction

This chapter explores the social, economic and political origins of the revolutionary process that toppled Ben Ali from power on 14 January 2011 in Tunisia and Hosni Mubarak on 11 February 2011 in Egypt. Their ouster shook the foundations of other regional autocracies. Unlike most commentary on the uprisings in Tunisia and Egypt, we focus on the role played by rural-social classes, peasants and the near landless.

Before December 2010, almost all observers who thought they knew the countries of the region and their various difficulties and problems were well aware of the risk of spontaneous or organised violent protest. There had been, for example, the bread riots in Tunisia in 1984 and protests in phosphate mines in the south of the country (Seddon 1986, 1, 14; Daoud 2011; Bachta 2011, 11). And there had been bread riots in Egypt in 1977 and among other demonstrations, working-class protests in the textiles towns north of Cairo from 2006 (Toth 1998, 76; Ireton 2013; Beinin 2011). Despite this, the events of late 2010 and early 2011 came as a surprise to almost everyone. This was because they were the culmination of long historical processes of struggles by the poor and disenfranchised that had often gone without notice. In Egypt the resistance of the peasants against the agrarian reform of 1992 led to their expropriation by landed interests of agrarian capitalism and the birth of movements of struggles for democracy, especially among the middle classes. The *Kefaya* movement, for example, and the 6 April movement built on the history of industrial action especially in the textile towns of Mahalla and the long strikes of 2007 (Beinin 2016).[1] And the 'we are all Khaled Said' movement announced the inevitable explosion – 'expected in Egypt, even if it surprised 'foreign observers' (Amin 2011, 140; Achcar 2013; Bal 2014).

The eruption of protest to poor conditions of existence for the overwhelming majority of Egyptians was foregrounded by the outbreak of street protests in 2000. That protest signified a new dimension of opposition to the Egyptian dictatorship that linked local NGOs with transnational protest movements (Abdelrahman 2011). It also ushered in the development of new networks of opposition that were fluid, multidimensional and created new ways for opponents of dictatorship to resist and promote alternatives to persistent economic immiseration. The acceleration of protest in rural Egypt shook the idea that the *fellahin* can and will withstand anything the dictatorship threw at it.

The term 'revolution' has been widely used since 2011 to describe the tumultuous months at the end of 2010 and the start of 2011 (Abdelrahman 2015; Alexander and Aouragh 2014; Allal and Geisser 2011; Bal 2014; El-Mahdi 2012). We do not talk about revolution, however, because to do so suggests radical change not only in the political system or the removal of a head of state, but in the way in which society and economic production is organised. A revolution involves the transfer of power from one class to another that leads to 'fundamental change'. As Tariq Ali noted, the size of the crowd or the uprising is not the determinant unless those in the majority have a 'clear set of social and political aims' (Ali 2013, n.p.). If the crowd does not have a set of clear aims, it will be easy for them to be outflanked by 'those that do' or by the state. In Egypt it was the *feloul* or the remnants of the old regime that quickly recaptured lost ground. The irony and contradiction in Egypt, and also in Tunisia, is that while it may be argued the success of the uprisings were due to the fact that they were spontaneous, without an organised leadership, reliant instead on a combination of a long history of anger, it was the lack of a strong organisation or single party that enabled the persistence of the ancient regime. It had been advantageous for the success of rebellion that there had not been a single entity that the secret police could penetrate and undermine or a membership that could be identified and imprisoned. However, it was also precisely that spontaneity and lack of formal organisation, representation and programme for change that enabled the old guard to return – in fact it never went away.

We indicate that there was a complex process in both countries that led to the toppling of the dictatorships. In the words of one commentator in Egypt, 'We did not witness the demise of a revolution but the reconstitution of an authoritarian regime' (Albrecht 2012). Understanding the revolutionary processes requires an account of the multiple political and social, as well as temporal and spatial, dimensions that underpin any particular moment. In helping to inch towards this understanding, we introduce the idea of socio-spatial class analysis (Reynaud 1982, Harvey 1973; 2006). This adds an important dimension to the analysis of the revolutionary processes in Tunisia and Egypt. We begin to highlight the role that social and spatial inequality and injustice played in creating conditions for radical transformation. The idea of socio-spatial classes explores uneven geographical locations of poverty, unequal access to resources and services, and helps see the role of the geographical distribution of surplus extraction that shaped uneven and combined capitalist development in Tunisia and Egypt. The close observation of the revolutionary processes highlights a question regarding how to explain that these processes started in the most marginalised regions in Tunisia and Egypt. Prior to 2011 commentators asserted, almost unanimously, that the risks of uprisings could only come from urban marginalised spaces where inequalities were seen to be deeper and more visible. The majority of observers and scholars commenting about Tunisia expected the revolution in the surroundings of Sidi Bousaïd (rich bourgeois neighbourhood in Tunis) and yet in fact it began in Sidi Bouzid, the rural city, where Mohamed Bouazizi committed 'suicide'. And while the focus in Egypt was upon the crowds and demonstrators in Tahrir Square, there were years of rural struggles and regional dissent that foregrounded the Cairo protests.

Arab Springs and Jasmine Revolutions?

Confronted by what were described as extraordinary events in Egypt, several commentators and experts (Mitchell 2002) could not avoid Orientalist, Eurocentric or neocolonial and modernist representations of the political events after December 2010 (Shihade 2012, Allal and Geisser 2011). Two expressions were particularly visible. These were the notion of 'The Arab Spring' and 'The Jasmine Revolution'. These two catchy phrases remain in the mainstream. These expressions spread very quickly, particularly in Tunisia, the 'sweet', 'stable' and 'middle ground' country that smells of jasmine (Allal and Geisser 2011, 62), and in Egypt (and elsewhere), a 'Spring' to express 'surprise' and astonishment of witnessing a general popular uprising.

For a long time, the evolution of the political regime characterised by an 'authoritarian stability' in Tunisia and Egypt was expected by only one of two possibilities. The first was a coup d'état, or a palace strike which would come from within the regime. The second was through a controlled political 'transition' (Camau 1999) to some form of 'democratisation', which did not endanger the foundations of the political system.

Furthermore, there is a narrative that Tunisian society was an undifferentiated mass of people who had accepted a 'security pact', proposed by the Ben Ali regime. Tunisians were subjected to a duty of obedience in return for which they received security against the risks of forced Islamisation or any other 'brutal' political change. This pact of security was intended to maintain and consolidate the legitimacy of an authoritarian regime. It had been elaborated by erstwhile President Bourguiba and was subsequently consolidated by his successor Ben Ali to maintain an 'authoritarian stability' accepted by the people. The security pact established an exchange between the state and the people (Hibou 2011, 6). In return for protection and delivery of consumption goods for many (not all), the provision of credit and controlled prices, the population was required to grant the regime legitimacy. The supposed combination of the 'peaceful and obedient people' and the authoritarian regime, legitimised by its role of protector against risks and dangers through the 'security pact', provided the political foundation of 'authoritarian stability' (Daguzan 2011, 22). This made any popular uprising leading to a radical change in the political system and regime unlikely. Authoritarian stability, however, was generated increasingly by the privatisation of the state. This was because 'in a society where the state is a central actor and where there is a very strong demand of state, a demand seeking inclusion, well-being and or protection, the "privatization" of the state' – in which a small group monopolises the state as if it were a private object – 'was seen as an intolerable hold-up [...] the supreme theft is undoubtedly that of the state itself!' (Ghérib, 2012, 33).

The use of reductive and Eurocentred expressions, such as Jasmine Revolution and Arab Spring were too superficial to grasp the ways in which the state in Tunisia had become so privatised. Commentators were ignorant of some of the complex local realities because they persisted with Orientalist and colonial representations.

A similar corporatist relationship was seen to have been established by Abdel Nasser with the Egyptian masses and was continued by Hosni Mubarak (Bianchi 1986). At the political level, while Mubarak's regime was authoritarian and unrepresentative and repressive of workers and farmers, the assumption was that a certain freedom of speech existed as long as there was no overt criticism of Mubarak and his family. This broke down with the uprising of

2011, and one of the reasons for the breakdown was an increased role of social networks like Facebook and Twitter. Social media was granted a real actor status confusing the function of a tool – 'a tool and space for activism' (Alexander and Aouragh 2014, 891) – with the role of the actor who used it (Khader 2012). Thus, on 25 January 2011, Radio France International (RFI) published an article by its correspondent in Tunis saying;

> This is an internet revolution to the point that here in Tunisia, people prefer to talk about a Facebook revolution rather than the jasmine revolution, a term considered unfit especially a little folkloric (RFI 2011).

Recalling when the Egyptian authorities cut internet communications (after 25 January 2011) in order to deprive activists of their main means of communication and mobilisation, the latter had no difficulty in continuing to mobilise a mass of people in squares protesting the regime and demanding the departure of Mubarak.

> In fact, despite the media hype about 'Facebook Revolutions,' the Egyptian activists we interviewed rightly reject simplistic claims that technology somehow caused the 2011 uprisings, and they say it undermines the agency of the millions of people who participated in the movement that brought down Hosni Mubarak (Alexander and Aouragh 2011, 1344).

Behind the narrative developed by Western analysts, but also by 'Arab' liberals, who read local phenomena through Western commentary, there is always a three-dimensional orientalist, Eurocentric and neocolonial framing. Whether it is Jasmine, Spring or Facebook and other social networks, any change that occurs from Arab countries 'must be due to, influenced by, or aided by Western ideas, thought, and technology' (Shihade 2012, 62). Even the 'peaceful' side of the revolution in Tunisia and Egypt can only be explained, according to the same narrative, by the fact that some individuals involved in the revolution came to the United States for training and learning the methods of 'non-violent activism' (Shihade 2012, 62). The 2011 Egyptian uprisings are seen as a youth, non-violent movement in which social media played an important role. The idea here is to say that 'these "middle-class" educated and modernized youth hold the same values as "us" (the democratic West), and finally use the same tools (Facebook and Twitter) that "we" invented and use in our daily-lives' (El-Mahdi 2011).

We emphasise that one of the major actors in the uprisings, the Tunisian and Egyptian peasant, has been totally ignored and made invisible by the vast majority of analyses. This was despite the fact that the first catalyst to provoke the long-term crisis in Tunisia was Mohamed Bouazizi who came from a peasant background and, as we will see, was driven to self-immolation because of debt and land dispossession (Ayeb, 2011a, Fautras 2014).

The Peasantry and the Uprisings

Workers and peasants have been largely erased from the long processes that created the conditions for the Tunisian and Egyptian uprisings (exceptions would be, Bush and Ayeb, 2012; Beinin 2016; Achcar 2013). We will now highlight how the struggles for 'bread, dignity, social justice' during the years that preceded the 'explosion' after 17 December 2010 in Tunisia involved peasants and rural poor. We also highlight the dynamic of regional struggles especially within Tunisia.

We begin by showing the claim that the processes that yielded the collapse of the two dictatorial regimes of Ben Ali and Hosni Mubarak were much longer in the fermentation, and more complex, than simple immediate protests that lasted only a few weeks or days but which captured most of the media attention between December 2010 and February 2011. The protests had their origins in the unequal policies of de-development, particularly in the agricultural sector. These were historical processes that have been part of the incorporation of Tunisia and Egypt into the international economy and which continued since independence. GoT and GoE policies intensified the pattern of underdevelopment, particularly in the agricultural sector after the adoption of neo-liberal policies from the 1980s. Economic reform in both countries resulted in social exclusion, marginalisation and impoverishment of the most fragile fringes of society. There was marginalisation of both social classes and geographical spaces, or territory and rural poor became increasingly abjected from development and often pushed into urban fringes and poverty.

The concept of socio-spatial classes (Reynaud 1982) helps to explain why the uprisings started from the rural marginalised areas rather than the towns and industrial areas where there were greater concentrations of the working class. Understanding the significance of rural class action in the toppling of both dictatorships provides insight into why there should not have been such surprise by commentators that the regimes fell when they did, and that the peasantry was a driver of the uprisings. Understanding the importance of rural class struggle and different forms of resistance also indicates why the new 'democracies' have found it so difficult to transform the national political economies away from dependence upon economic rent, uneven incorporation and Western government collusion with repression.

The importance of the episode that occurred from 17 December 2010 to 11 February 2011 lies in what it reveals about the complexity of the mechanisms and processes considered in their temporality and their spatiality, scales of time and of space. The beginning of this cannot be situated simply at a specific moment in time and neither is it appropriate to declare an end moment. As Bourdieu noted, we need to try and put 'the extraordinary event back into the series of ordinary events, within which the extraordinary event explains itself' (Bourdieu 1984, 210). While this chapter examines the reasons behind the regime changes in Tunisia and Egypt, it argues that understanding the ousting of Ben Ali and Hosni Mubarak is only possible by understanding 30 years of political resistance and economic crises in both countries. We are making two points here. First, the revolutionary processes did not start on 17 December 2010, even if we affirm clearly and we recognise that the 'suicide' of Bouazizi constituted an extraordinary moment of tremendous, though unexpected, acceleration of these processes. The suicide was the product of a long accu-mulation of privations, exclusions, humiliations and dispossessions, and also resistance. Second, the social and 'geographical' origins of the revolutionary processes in Tunisia as well as in Egypt are in isolated regions, the impoverished countryside, the popular layers, including peasants, the dispossessed and the abjected. We are, therefore, more interested in the 'alfa grass revolution' than in the 'jasmine or facebook revolution' (Ayeb 2011).

How do we begin to (re)establish and map a spatial chronology of the processes that emerge to generate the uprisings in Tunisia and Egypt? Are there particular moments and dates to remember and what criteria do we consider in exploring the ways in which the uprisings emerged? Although the writing of every narrative of history is risky, the reconstitution of a coherent analysis around social movements that preceded December 2010 is crucial. It will contest the common view at the time that Arabs could not promote their integration into the 'free and democratic world' by replacing the old authoritarian and corrupt regimes with democracy aligned with the rules and norms of the declared free and globalised market. We note that the wide-spread celebration of the Tunisian revolution is only a celebration of limited liberal political reforms, which become a model for successful 'revolution'. In contrast, we will see that while the outcome of the Tunisian uprisings is far more successful in liberalising and deepening democracy than in Egypt, regime change remains limited. Moreover, social transformation for the socio-spatial classes that promoted the toppling of Ben Ali remains stagnant.

The social and economic demands of protesters for 'bread, dignity, social justice', uttered in the slogans in Tunisia in Sidi Bouzid, Bourguiba Avenue, La Kasba and which reached Egypt's Tahrir Square, lie at the heart of the uprisings. Yet they were foregrounded 30 years earlier in 1984 and 1977, respectively, when there were bread riots in Tunisia (see Chapter 5) and Egypt (see Chapter 6). Egypt's unrest culminated at that time with the assassination of President Anwar Sadat by Islamists in October 1981. Sadat had overseen a reversal of Nasser's land reforms that had attempted to promote redistributive justice. With the support of large landowners, Sadat enacted Law 69 of 1974 that abolished the state's role of custodianship of land. The speed with which Sadat reversed Nasser's reforms indicated the extent of entrenched landlord power. It also highlighted the politicisation of land that continued into the contemporary period.

The desire for better livelihoods, and the struggles against the processes of impoverishment and social marginalisation, constitute the link between the different social movements of the late 1970s and early 1980s, and the years 2010 and 2011. Two other dates, or more accurately social processes linked to an earlier period, are important to reinforce our view of the longue durée of struggle. The first was 1992 in Egypt with the adoption of Law 96 of 1992. This legislation, as we further detail in Chapter 6, set new liberal rules in the agricultural real estate market and new relationships between owners and tenants. The second was 2008 in Tunisia with the outbreak of the labour strikes in the mining basin, southwest of the country between January and June.

Why were the peasants and rural citizens often in the leadership of resist-ance movements that led to the collapse of the two regimes? Far from any deterministic thoughts or idealisation of the rural and peasant communities, we think that the answer lies in farmer reaction to the 'modernist' and urban model of development. Farmers were angry that the mechanism of modernity was exploitation of rural and agricultural resources for the benefit of the city. In these policies of forced modernisation, considered as an objective rather than a means to an end, the rural communities and peasants were considered a constraint and a break on development. 'Backward' farmers and their com-munities were assumed by policymakers not to fit and adjust to modern devel-opment policies built on technical modernisation. Farmers were seen instead to have an undue attachment to the traditional tribal or family structures and to inherited 'non-expert-approved' practices.

It is precisely this double social and spatial marginalisation which explains why revolutionary processes started in these marginalised and dispossessed regions. Thus, the analysis of these processes and of their socio-spatial chron-ologies requires the consideration of the two driving factors. These are the social classes and the spatial dynamics that underpin them, hence the useful-ness of the concept of 'socio-spatial classes' (Zemni and Ayeb 2016; Reynaud 1982). It is by associating the social and the spatial over time that one can deconstruct the revolutionary processes to identify the mechanisms, the actors and the sequences of the revolutionary processes between December 2010 and February 2011. That then enables the opportunity to establish the geography of the uprisings.

The fall of the Ben Ali and Mubarak regimes is celebrated as a success story. The fall of Ben Ali is especially seen through a liberal prism to mark a democratic transition. This is reified as the key instrument to measure any kind of R-evolution from one political situation to another. As Dakhlia points out, 'Every democratic revolution is henceforth supposed to take a single, imposed path, which is one way at a time and indistinctly democratic and liberal or neoliberal' (2016 n.p.).

The agricultural policies adopted since independence, except for the Nasserist period in Egypt (1956–70), were aimed to suppress the roles and presence of the peasantry. The strategy in both countries was to foster the birth of a capitalist, modern, productivist and export-oriented agricultural sector, designed to provide a surplus and support to other economic sectors. It was a strategy intended to promote an agricultural system without farmers. Stigmatised, dispossessed and marginalised, the peasantry were intended to become progressively more invisible and unreported.

Egypt

Coverage of the Egyptian uprising in 2011 tended to ignore previous episodes of political protest thereby ignoring any sense of historical experience (Badiou, 2014). The dominant narrative was urban, and the role of the youth and demands for political rights were seen to be at the heart of the uprising (Amin, G. 2014, cf Korany and El-Mahdi 2012). Admittedly, during the first reported demonstration of 25 January 2011 in Tahrir Square, there were an additional 40,000 other demonstrations (El Nour 2015a, 203). The Tahrir demonstration was originally planned against police repression: a 'day of rage'. Demonstrators came together to specifically denounce the murder of the young Khaled Said in Alexandria on 6 June 2010 by the police. He had been arrested the same day and his murder led to the massive outcry and movement, 'We are all Khaled Said' (Abdelrahman 2012, 616; Gelabert 2013, 13; El-Chazli and Rayner, 2011). The early Tahrir protesters were mostly urban youth and activists of the *Kifaya* ('enough') movement. Between 2004 and 2006, *Kifaya* had grown to oppose the persistent renewal of Mubarak's tenure as president. It had also opposed Israel's occupation in Palestine and the possibility that Mubarak was preparing to establish a dynastic presidency by installing his son Gamal as head of state (Abdelrahman 2015, Beinin and Duboc, 2013, El-Mahdi 2012). But starting from 28 January, millions of people of all social and professional backgrounds, among which were peasants and workers, gathered to protest in Tahrir Square as well as in all streets and villages throughout Egypt.

The social unrest and the widespread movements that led to the resignation of Mubarak in February 2011 began in 1992 after the beginning of the counter-agrarian reform Law 96. Although there was a five-year transitional period before the legislation was to be fully enacted, there were a series of strong peasant protests. Protest continued into the contemporary period, with the resistance seldom covered by the media (Ayeb and Bush 2014; Ayeb 2010; Saad 2002).

Law 96 addressed two main issues. First, it announced the end of tenancies in perpetuity that had ensured security for tenants who would otherwise be landless. Second, it liberalised the price of agricultural land (both sales and lease prices). Most significant of all, however, it aimed to effectively confiscate land and water resources for irrigation by dispossessing small-scale farmers who were seen as an obstacle to the country's economic development. That dispossession was achieved through a multitude of legal and economic mechanisms to facilitate the entry of big producers (Wang, et al. 2012, 194).

The first implication and consequence of Law 96 after its full implementation in October 1997 was the immediate cancellation of all tenancies. They were replaced with new contracts (and often without formal contract at all) of limited duration and at free market rates that were around five times higher than the previous average rents. A dramatic humanitarian situation quickly emerged with 904,000 tenant families overnight denied access to the land. They became destitute with only minimum access to food, having lost their livelihoods after dispossession from land that in some cases had been farmed by families for generations (Ayeb 2010; El Nour, 2015b).

Farmers resisted dispossession in ways reminiscent of their parents and grand-parents in 1919 and from 1944 to 1951 (El Nour 2015b, 206). Peasant resistance aimed at defending what they saw as their legitimate right to land and their need to secure a minimum of household food security. They were confronted by an aggressive range of security forces that defended and promoted the interests of landowners many of whom had lost land in Nasser's reforms and now had no legal right to access land that was not part of Law 96. The resistance was largely ignored by the media, national and international observers, journalists, researchers, politicians and activists. In the first few months of the application of the reform in October 1997, the results of repression were already heavy. According to World Organisation against Torture (OMCT 2006, 7), the implementation of the law resulted in extensive violence committed by state security forces against tenants in more than a hundred villages. During the first few months after the application of the law

(October–December, 1997), about a hundred tenants were killed, a thousand injured and more than a thousand arrested. In 1998–99, violence led to 87 deaths, 545 injuries and 798 arrests (a total of 187 deaths, 1,545 injured and 1,798 arrested, between 1997 and 1999). From 1992 to 1998, farmers and some social movements organised protests that led the security forces to randomly arrest and torture farmers (OMCT 2006; LCHR 2002; El Nour 2015a; Ayeb 2010).

There were several activists who were, however, sensitive to peasant causes. One of the most vocal and long standing was Shahinda Maklad (1938–2016), whose life had been dedicated to defending peasant and landless interests (Bush and Ayeb 2014). And there were some academics, NGOs, such as the Land Centre for Human Rights (LCHR), Awlad al-ard (The Children of the Earth) and a few members of political parties, especially from *Tagammou*, who made remarkable and sometimes courageous efforts to support the peasants who experienced the consequences of Law 96 of 1992. Protest failed to prevent the law from being implemented. There were around a hundred conferences and gatherings with lawyers and activists critiquing the proposed law. A petition to the government with 350,000 signatures was ridiculed by the Ministry of Agriculture for being full of bogus names, and there were hundreds of demonstrations across Egypt fearful of the impact that the legislation might have (El Nour 2015a, 59). Although there was some support from progressive journalists, party militants and human rights activists, in general, peasants remained isolated from the rest of society during their struggle (Zemni, De Smet and Bogaert 2012, 6). The relative invisibility and inaudibility of peasant struggles is accounted for by the rupture between the city and the countryside. There was a collective and individual insensitivity of the political, cultural and economic elites to peasant livelihoods, to the food question in relation to natural resource rights and the use and access to environmental consequences of intensive agriculture.

A new normal developed as part of the context in which Law 96 of 1992 emerged. It is significant that economic reform in Egypt's countryside prefigured the economic adjustment of 1991 agreed with the IMF and World Bank (Bush 1999). But the adjustment programme in 1991 created the conditions for the Egyptian parliament to dispossess small farmers. The coalition of businessmen MPs from the ruling NDP, old landed families and political elites accused the *fellahin* of holding landlords to ransom. Parliament, with the blessing of the IFIs and USAID, asserted that tenant farmers and peasants more generally had taken advantage of the favoured position created by President Nasser. Neo-liberal ideology was used to accuse farmers of laziness and inefficiency and the Law 96 of 1992 was part of a strategy of agricultural modernisation necessary to boost food security (Saad 1999; 2002).

Neo-liberal policy of dispossession, liberalisation of tenancies, agricultural inputs and credit intensified rural conflict.

The revolutionary process, which put an end to the dictatorship of Mubarak, began in the mid-1990s and it began in the countryside before it expanded into the cities. We can similarly affirm that from the countryside to the city, the content of the initial protest was to resist government attacks on social and economic conditions of rural livelihoods. These objections to the state preceded the more obviously political opposition to the Mubarak dictatorship and the attempt to prepare the presidency for Gamal Mubarak. The 25 January uprising was foregrounded by an escalation of class conflict: working-class unrest, strikes and sit-ins and rebellion within the state-run trades unions. The ouster of Mubarak was also driven by persistent groundswell of rural dissent. Both types of opposition emerged especially after 2004 when Prime Minister Ahmed Nazif aggressively advanced a campaign of privatisation of public companies.

It is significant that the persistence of rural struggles and networks for change in Egypt's countryside after the 1990s were more fluid than those centred in urban struggles (Bush 2011). There emerged an important network of social resistance to state brutality that was orchestrated through the mix of security forces, police and military in the countryside. Landlords colluded with security forces attacking farmers, claiming back land, hiking rents and disrupting rural markets. The security forces arrested leaders of the broad front, National Committee for the Defence of Farmers that had been short lived, and which had linked rural and urban activists in 1997. Some of the most intense conflicts unsurprisingly took place where landlords tried to reclaim land in Bani Suef, Kafr al Shaykh and Abu Nassar in El Faiyum governorate. Major conflict also occurred in Dakahlia where land density was high. The celebrated case of conflict was in the village of Sarandu in 2005 but which had been at the centre of conflict between farmers and the large landowning Nawwar family since the 1950s. The family evicted hundreds of farmers from land over which the family had no locus standi harassing families who had accessed land since the 1950s. The conflict in Sarandu became a catalyst, bringing urban and rural activists together to oppose what was seen as the horror of landlordism. It reinforced the entrenchment of a network of activists around the Adala (Justice) Centre for Political and Social Studies, the Hisham Mubarak Law Centre and other rights-based organisations. The struggles in Sarandu also added further credence, if any had been necessary, of the significant persistent struggles in the village of Khamshish where there had been a continuous struggle with landlordism (Ahmed and Saad 2011).

Egyptian farmers engaged in struggle across a range of activities and made links trying to forge new social networks to resist landlord repression and the exigencies of market reform. Rural resistance had always been susceptible to being undermined and disrupted by state security. Rural locations were ripe for intimidation and violence, imprisonment and torture and harassment of the poor. But this did not prevent resistance, direct action and even the use of the courts to try and hold landlords to account and to at least slow the return of feudalism

Tunisia

The urban and rural poor suffer from marginalisation and mechanisms and dynamics of neo-liberalism that reduced their income and resources and slashed service provision. The urban poor are proletarian because they were dispossessed of access to the means of production. They have been additionally marginalised through individual and collective stigmatisation that created the representation of them as a dangerous social group. They were repeatedly attacked in the media and by government because of their increased levels of criminality, drug use, prostitution and Salafism (Lamloum and Ben Zina 2015). The inhabitants of the peripheral and rural areas (south, central and northwest of Tunisia) are subjected to a process of abjection as follows: (1) social marginalisation and stigmatisation that also affected the residents of the popular neighbourhoods of the big cities (2) the extractive dispossession of regional resources for the almost exclusive benefit of the 'centre' – Tunis and coastal areas. Whether it is water, human resources, agricultural products or raw materials (phosphate, minerals, oil, gas, etc.), everything is extracted from peripheral regions and conveyed to the centre, where the resources are processed, consumed or exported. It is remarkable that there is hardly any 'local' accumulation of wealth (if only to the benefit of a few), as most investors reside in the coastal towns and 'manage' their investments from there (Zemni and Ayeb, 2016).

January 2008 is a crucial time in the long revolutionary processes in Tunisia's history. One of the companies particularly impacted by structural adjustment was the Gafsa Phosphate Society. Restructuring led to large-scale job losses. From over 14,000 workers in the 1980s, CPG employment shrunk to around 5,500 workers in the period 2007–8 (Zemni, De Smet and Bogaert 2012, 5)

Local unemployed youth expressed anger following a recruitment competition for work where jobs were offered to candidates from other regions. In protest, the unemployed occupied the offices of the UGTT (General Union of Tunisian Workers), which had co-organised the contest. The protesters were then joined by their families and they set up tents for a sit-in. Quickly, thousands of policemen lay siege to the city and, in order to prevent the media from jumping on the situation, the authorities forbid access to journalists and various national and international outlets. Heavily repressed, the movement that had spread to Redeyef, Oum Lares, Metlaoui and Feriana ended with three people being killed and tens injured. It was the trigger to the start of the struggles for economic and social rights and against the repressions and corruption that finally led to the downfall of Ben Ali (Allal 2010, Ayeb 2011a, Zemni, De Smet and Bogaert 2012). The result was a five-month popular protest movement that was broken in June, when police and army units brutally attacked the town of Redeyef and arrested many activists (ibid., 5), as Adnen Hajji, one of the local unionist leaders declared:

> In 2008, the announcement of falsified results for a highly anticipated recruitment of workers at the CPG, the Gafsa Phosphate Company, shattered the social movement in the four mining towns. In Redeyef, a hunger strike begins at the local UGTT. My comrades and I decided to supervise this hunger strike and to negotiate with the sous-préfet of Redeyef, and with the governor of Gafsa (local and regional authorities) [...] Through this action, we have sent the message to Ben Ali's regime that we cannot continue living in this misery and that the state should intervene to develop our region, to create things that allow people to live humanly. Finally, the police intervened to stop this movement and fired on the demonstrators: 3 dead, 34 wounded and more than 300 people arrested in the region (*Solidaires International* 2012, 106).

In December 2008, 38 unionists were called to appear in court: five were released, the rest of them were sentenced from two years imprisonment with conditional sentence to ten years in jail. During one of the trials qualified by activists as a 'justice parody', the six leaders of the movement, who were accused of 'leading protests troubling public order in which the police was attacked with stones and Molotov cocktails', were sentenced to the maximum penalty. A strong international mobilisation imposed the revision of the case in the Court of Appeal. But in February 2009, the Court of Appeal of Gafsa slightly changed the first ruling against the detainees and condemned them to heavy sentences. Adnen Hajji, the spokesperson of the movement, who became a deputy after the fall of Ben Ali and Bechir Laabidi, had his sentence reduced from 10 to 8 years of confinement (Ayeb 2011, 473, Ayeb 2017, 94).

While the regime used repression to try and put a temporary pause to these strikes and protest movements in the mining basin and its surroundings, new hubs of resistance and other struggles emerged. Resistance to the regime erupted throughout the country, particularly in the rural areas such as Sidi Bouzid and Ben Guerdane. The chronology and Map 3.1 follow closely the

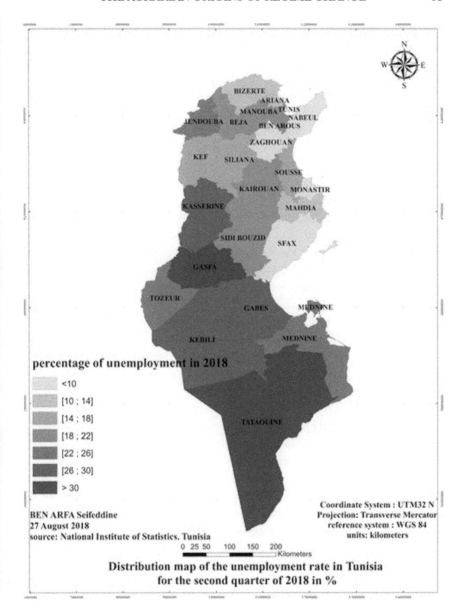

Map 3.1 Poverty and Revolution in Tunisia, 2008–11.

Source: Habib Ayeb.

magnitude, timing and the geography, and the evolution of the struggles and especially their continuity over more than two years.

In August 2010 riots broke out in Ben Guerdane, a town located in the southeast near the Libyan border. The immediate cause of the riot was because of the closure of the frontier with Libya. The official version explains this decision to close the frontiers as the need to control the very active informal trade between the two countries. It was a trade that fed hundreds and even thousands of families, either by creating informal jobs, usually precarious and on the margins of legality, or by offering the local population various products, including food, much cheaper (up to 50 per cent) than through formal commercial channels (Ayeb 2016).

Cross-border trade included motor fuel, foreign currency, Chinese imports, food products produced in Tunisia or Egypt and sold in Libya at highly subsidised prices. This trade took place in the regions near to the Libyan border in the east and the Algerian borders in the west. An example of this informal trade was the way a can of tomato produced and manufactured in Tunisia was exported to Libya at half its selling price in Tunisia. The same can would then be re-imported and sold at almost 30 to 40 per cent of its regular price. The border closure had a considerable effect on increasing levels of conflict that reflected the extent of local poverty and the weakness of the regional economy and government neglect. However, the decision to close the frontiers was due to what became known as the Trabelsi mafia. At the end of 2010, some 220 businesses connected to Ben Ali and his extended family accounted for 21 per cent of all annual private sector profits in Tunisia. This was about US$233 million, or more than 0.5 per cent of GDP (World Bank 2014, 338). Ben Ali and the Trabelsi family acquired 50 per cent of the businesses in Tunisia. The 'financial sector was the most affected' (Gani 2013, 3). The Trabelsi, also known as the Ben Ali 'clan', family and in-laws of the president were part of the privatisation of the state. There were also a number of influential personalities who took advantage of their relationship with the presidential couple to establish themselves as unavoidable intermediaries in illegal customs clearance operations, transit and money transfer (Meddeb 2012, 108; see also Zemni, et al. 2012; Hibou 2011, 18). The Trabelsi mafia and the Ben Ali clans increasingly recognised that they were missing out from the cross-border trade and now wanted to control it (Meddeb 2012, 205–6). Their plan was to transfer these informal activities from the frontier to the region of Sahel (coast) by opening a direct maritime line between Tripoli, the Libyan capital, and the Tunisian port of Sfax. Riots that broke out in Ben Guerdane in August 2010 lead to scores of arrests. People were tortured, dragged before tribunals and given heavy sentences (Meddeb 2011, Zemni and Ayeb 2015, Ayeb 2011a; 2016, Hibou 2011).

Class and the Uprisings

Chapter 1 indicated the importance of a materialist analysis to understand the dynamics of rural Tunisia and Egypt. The importance goes against the grain of predominantly elite-based commentary (Tyler 2015, 497) where issues of social class are jettisoned in favour of notions of social stratification based on income or status. Yet one commentator in an early case study of rural Tunisia in Testour noted:

> In order to understand the behaviour of individuals, one must understand the mental universe in which these individuals evolve. There are two possible explanations for each behaviour or each situation. One explanation associates them with the mode of production and with the economic base, while the other is based on the conceptions and definitions of the situation that are shared among the persons concerned. The first operates at the level of the society, the second at the level of the individual, as a member of that society (Hopkins 1983, 10–11).

Paraphrasing Karl Marx, the response as to how social classes mobilise, develop consciousness and become a class for themselves, promoting collective class interests, emerges from

> a social group in conflict with the class that is dialectically opposite to it [...] formed of an aggregate of individuals whose lived experience has been formed, first, by working conditions, and then by struggle; in sum, individuals whose common perception of their material interests has been forged through easy and frequent contact and a consciousness that presupposes a terminology or a vocabulary to express its symbols. In other words, each class needs to have a structure and a discourse, a means of representing its consciousness, that can articulate the conflict (Hopkins 1983, 53).

The largely rural solidarity expressed by the people of Sidi Bouzid with regards to Bouazizi's self-immolation corresponds to the construction that Hopkins indicates with regards to social class. Class as an analytical category informs how the capacity of labour is realised and it highlights the (exploitative) character of social relationships in production (Campling et al. 2016). Class also helps us understand how social actors mobilise collectively to promote their own interests.

Discussions and interviews with peasants from the Sidi Bouzid region highlighted conflict with investors, the majority of whom came from the cities of Sfax or Tunis and other coastal cities. The investors were accused of being 'racist'. Other, often larger absentee, investors were called 'foreigners' or settlers (referring to the French colons) despite the fact that they were indeed Tunisian but from wealthier northern regions. There were several reasons for the developing resistance seen through the prism of class voiced by peasants. Among these was the competition over land and water but a larger oft-repeated complaint from respondents was that instead of employing local labour, investors would bring workers from their own regions (especially from Sfax and Sousse). This was done for the labour-intensive seasons, such as the olive, fruit and vegetable harvests. The pretext for this was that the people of Sidi Bouzid were lazy. Local workers were told that they did not know how to work properly and were untrustworthy (Ayeb 2013, 2017).

Socio-Spatial Marginalisation

The geographic (spatial) route helped to drive the process of the uprising by marginalised social classes. This started in 2008 in the mining zones south-east of the country. This was followed by the important phase of 2010 in Sidi Bouzid, and finally the uprising emerged in 2011 in Tunis and the big coastal cities. The geographical and spatial dynamic highlights the wave of resistance from the marginalised areas, border areas, rural spaces, slums and other popular zones before arriving to the cities and especially Tunis where political and economic power is exercised. These are revealed in Maps 3.2 and 3.3, which indicate the geographical dimensions of poverty and unemployment in Tunisia. For decades, the processes of social marginalisation that was at the heart of what happened was paired with strong patterns of territorial and spatial marginalisation. The two processes converge and complement each other within the mechanisms of accumulation through dispossession (Harvey 2003; 2005). This suggests that the term social class might be enlarged to include a new spatial dimension as indicated earlier in this chapter and to use the expression or concept of 'socio-spatial class' (Zemni and Ayeb, 2016; Ayeb 2017).

The social and economic marginalisation of individuals, social groups and communities in the 'peripheral' rural areas is overlaid by a spatial and territorial marginalisation. This is the result of the extractive economy that dispossesses most of the country from its natural resources for the benefit of central regions. The centre takes over the resources of the periphery, whose integration into the national and global economy is achieved only by the capture of local natural resources without any return and compensation in terms of equipment, infrastructure, jobs and services. The Ben Ali clan and Trabelsi mafia gained financially from raw material rents extracted from the mining areas and surplus value accruing from wage and agricultural workers. The country of riches is dispossessed of its resources for the benefit of the country

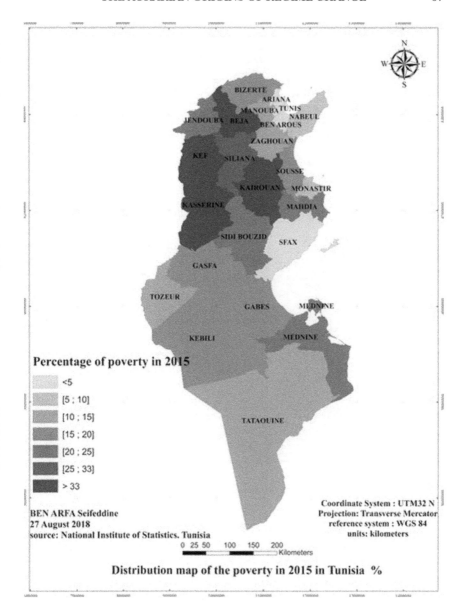

Map 3.2 Percentage of Unemployed, Tunisia, 2018.

of the rich, which monopolised political, economic and financial wealth. The monopoly gains accrued to the 'centre', Tunisia's north and coastal areas, while the south became an entrenched 'periphery' (Amin 1974a).

This system of central domination over geographical spaces was generated by the historical patterns of unequal exchange between the centre and the

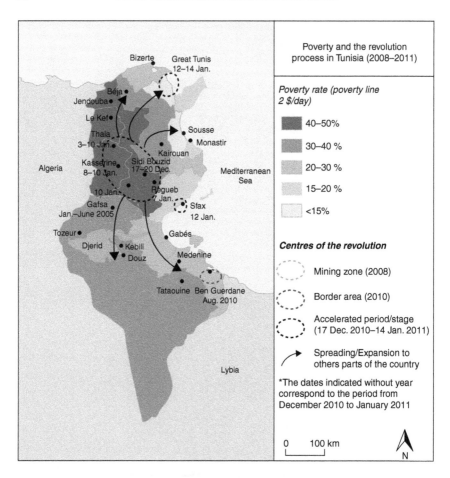

Map 3.3 Percentage of Poverty, Tunisia, 2015.

periphery. The dominance of the socio-spatial class in Tunis and the coast, and its impact on the south and northwest is visible to any observer who travels through Tunisia. It is similar to the contrasts between Egypt's Delta and Upper Egypt and the holiday resort fringes of Sinai and the southeast and dominance of the Cairo military and industrial-financial elite. The dependency and surplus extraction that benefit the northern and coastal elite in Tunisia result from 'non-reciprocal relations' and the domination of a social class or group by another (Reynaud 1982, 40). In this case the social group is revealed by its largely spatial location.

Despite the obvious political, social and historical differences, Egypt and Tunisia have similar socio-spatial class configurations. There is also a dominating centre in Egypt that harnesses the resources of its periphery rich in natural resources, particularly the fertile agricultural land and water, but maintained in a flagrant level of economic and political marginality. This partly explains the prevalence of rural poverty. According to a World Bank report, 78 per cent of the poor live in the countryside (Arab Republic of Egypt and World Bank, 2007, El Nour 2015a, 52).

A specific example seems to highlight the relations of domination and dispossession between the centre and the periphery. While the state supported the development of a large intensive, productivist, capitalist and export-oriented agriculture in the Egyptian desert, especially on the fringes of the valley and the Nile Delta, stimulated through free water access, subsidies and financial incentives on imported inputs and exported products, almost 4 million peasants (about 20 million, if we include family members), have less than half of the cultivable agricultural land. In 2002, 91 per cent of Egyptian farmers owned less than 5 feddans and shared 50.5 per cent of the agricultural land, while 3 per cent of farmers owned 10 or more feddans and shared 33.5 per cent of the agricultural land.

The absence of widely available new agricultural censuses since the beginning of the 2000s deprives us of updated comprehensive data, but we fear an aggravation of this inequality between the smallest and the biggest producers (Ayeb 2010). In addition, the available volume of irrigation water has decreased. This is despite the fact that peasants pay for water by volume used and receive virtually no state subsidy or support (Ayeb, 2010; 2011b). These farmers, as we note in Chapters 2 and 6 are witnessing a crisis of water access for irrigation. Paradoxically, while geographically, historically and hydraulically, the Nile valley and delta and its peasants were at the centre of the agricultural sector, the focus of Egypt's agriculture is gradually moving towards the desert. Those who have become the new farmers and investors, producing for mostly export markets and not domestic consumption, are connected and favoured by the political and economic military and elite in the urban centre of the country.

Bouazizi's Immolation and Class Solidarity

The mainstream narrative around the awful death of Mohamed Bouazizi highlights how social class is buried in place of descriptive moral narrative. He is described as a young graduate practicing the informal activity of a fruits and vegetables seller in Sidi Bouzid's market. He was harassed and humiliated by a policewoman who allegedly slapped him in public because he refused to abide by the law and stop his informal merchant activity. Yet this description is insufficient to explain why there was such a mass involvement around his fate. Why was there such a protest of this suicide when over several years there were up to 250 suicides of people who were in many cases similar to Boazizi? Why had those suicides not led to a collective outcry? Our explanation is that Boazizi's suicide generated a social class solidarity and demonstrations of the people of Sidi Bouzid, symbolically directed against the state and its official local institutional representation, the local government buildings and offices.

We know, today, that Mohamed Bouazizi, whom almost nobody knew outside his immediate circles, was not an unemployed graduate as had been claimed, and that he had not been slapped by the policewoman. One could understand the reasons and the political objectives of this invented story and could even accede to such a use. And we cannot deny its formidable effectiveness since that narrative helped to overthrow the dictatorship. Perhaps the real story would not have done that. However, we continue to think that despite its undeniable effectiveness and its historical importance, Bouazizi's constructed history has dispossessed the peasants of Sidi Bouzid, and of the rest of the country, of their stories of struggles and resistance, stories with which the real history of Bouazizi fits perfectly (Ayeb 2017).

To understand why the suicide of Bouazizi created the conditions of the general uprising, we must recontextualise this action, within the longer scale of the revolutionary processes. There were many individual and collective actions of resistance that preceded the Bouazizi suicide. One of significance was the sit-in organised in June–July 2010 in front of the governorate building of Sidi Bouzid, which gathered tens of small local farmers and peasants. Among the demands and claims, the most significant were: drinking and irrigation water rights, farmland, subsidies, and agricultural inputs, whose prices had risen considerably, not to mention the behaviour of the 'foreign' investors, who were seen as aggressive and disdainful (Ayeb, unpublished interviews and notes during fieldwork in Sidi Bouzid 2012, 2014 and 2017). But there was also the huge problem of peasant-accumulated debt, which prevented small local farmers from securing their food and incomes from their own land: credits with the BNA (National Bank of Agriculture), as well as their unpaid dues for water to SONEDE (National company of water management) and electricity used for pumping irrigation water to the STEG (Tunisian Company for Electricity and Gas). The indebted peasants were threatened with lawsuits, or were already involved in them, and risked losing their land. Twenty debtor families had already lost the lands through procedural debt recovery by the BNA (Ayeb 2017, Gana 2012a). The reason behind the sit-in was, partially, to express solidarity for Bouazizi's family after they were dispossessed of their land (Fautras 2015). This had happened through mechanisms of debt and mortgage loans well-crafted by the BNA in 'mafia-like' complicity with investors in quest of land to grab. The participants in the sit-in also came to express their fears of suffering the same fate as the Bouazizi family. Participants in the sit-in in front of the governorate building indicated Mohemed Bouazizi had been strongly involved in the mobilisation of peasants and was present at the sit-in (Ayeb, 2017 and unpublished interviews and notes during fieldwork in Sidi Bouzid 2012, 2014 and 2017). While demonstrating peacefully, the protesters were violently attacked and forced by police to disperse. The protesters associated the police and security forces with the state and the defence of investor interests, not the interests of the family farmer and the increasingly indebted and landless.

Five months after Bouazizi committed suicide, as an act of resistance to long- standing humiliation and deprivation, peasants rallied to protest in the streets. Support was spontaneous. It expressed a movement of class solidarity towards one of their active members. These demonstrations involved, in particular, hundreds of young people in the region. Many of them were the sons of impoverished peasants, who felt excluded from the agricultural development that they could see but could not benefit from; they had lost all hope for their future (André et al. 2014).

There is a clear link between these peasant 'mobilisations' of summer 2010 and those that followed Bouazizi's desperate self-immolation. This is, in our opinion, what explains the fact that, unlike many others, the suicide of Mohamed Bouazizi caused the huge momentum of solidarity that promptly transformed into the massive popular uprising that began in Sidi Bouzid on 17 December 2010, spread throughout the centre and the south of the country, and ended on Avenue Bourguiba in Tunis in the major demonstration of 14 January 2011 (Ayeb 2017). The rapid progress of this uprising between 17 December 2010 and 14 January 2011, in what we might label the accelerated phase, as well as longer revolutionary processes (from January 2008, see Map 3.1), bears witness to an obvious class consciousness that goes far beyond the peasant world. It reached the entire rural and urban population (Ayeb, 2011; 2017). This is undoubtedly a case of class solidarity (Hopkins 1983) by the inhabitants of the region directly concerned, such as Bouazizi, by the many dramatic economic, social and environmental consequences of a top-down development model: limited access to land, irrigation water and other agricultural resources. This class solidarity gives evidence of a certain class-consciousness that went beyond the peasantry to reach the entire rural and urban 'poor' (Ayeb 2011; 2017).

Peasants felt the individual humiliation they experienced from the state as a collective ordeal. As an uncle of Mohamed Bouazizi noted, about the real reasons that pushed Bouazizi to set himself on fire and why the suicide was followed by such huge demonstrations throughout Tunisia;

This land [referring to the land of the family which an investor had acquired through the NBA that the institution had confiscated and sold to cover up the unpaid loan dues of the Bouazizi family] was the only resources for the whole family, a source of life, and Mohamed did a lot of work here, on this land. In fact, you can see him in the photos taken during the sit-in in June and July 2010. When the Sfaxian grabbed their land, Mohamed started selling fruit and vegetables at the market. So you could say that his family's dispossession was the indirect cause of his burning himself. Some people say a policewomen slapped him, others not. In any case, she humiliated him, whatever she did. And he got revolted, really revolted. So he went to the [headquarters of] the governorate, they turned him away, he was completely furious, and he set himself on fire. In any case, the reason he did it is because the land was taken away. It's all linked. I want you to understand the link (Fautras 2015).

The poor peasants and landless in Sidi Bouzid wove a fabric of solidarity in their conflict with the local and national ruling class of land investors and merchants. The solidarity went beyond affinity of family and tribe to affirm a new and larger framework of social class. It is within this framework of conflict and solidarity of classes that the struggles were led, and which resulted in their climax in December 2010. This large and spontaneous mobilisation, including several individual and collective actions, fits into what Asef Bayat calls 'the social non-movement':

In general, non-movements refers to the collective actions of non-collective actors; they embody shared practices of large numbers of ordinary people whose fragmented but similar activities trigger much social change, even though these practices are rarely guided by an ideology or recognizable leaderships and organizations (Bayat 2013, 14).

In other words, the process is initiated 'spontaneously' by the rural population. Among these are the peasants, since the mid-2000s, before intersecting in late December 2010 with the middle-class population that aspired to more individual and collective freedoms and to a larger space for political expression and participation.

Social Change and Class Conflict: The Case of Sidi Bouzid

The region of Sidi Bouzid highlights the social and spatial changes in rural areas in Tunisia during the last 30 or 40 years. During this time a new modern agriculture was born over an extensive and semi-pastoral arid land. Sidi Bouzid highlights the dynamics that underpin class formation and conflict and the appropriateness of the term socio-spatial classes in explaining the origins of the revolutionary processes in Tunisia and in Egypt. Sidi Bouzid is an exemplar of the ways in which a spontaneous solidarity movement in the periphery of Tunisia, in the country's south and centre is managed to generate surplus for Tunis city and the urban centres of the coast.

Even though the region of Sidi Bouzid has become, in a very short time, the first agricultural region of the country, in terms of investment and production, the region still occupies the fourth place in the list of the poorest regions of the country.

The irrigated agricultural area has doubled in Sidi Bouzid between 1993 and 2011. It rose from 25,000 ha in 1993 to 47,000 ha in 2011 (21,000 ha in 1987, 8,700 in 1974 and 2,000 ha in 1958) (MEDD and PNUD 2006, 67). In 2018 it constituted about 10 per cent of the total useful area for agriculture in the region. This is the result of the increased role of capital flows from outside the region in mobilising the underground water for irrigation, particularly in the region of Regueb (a district of Sidi Bouzid) and the concentration of investors in agricultural projects requiring significant investments. Around 80 per cent of agriculture land in Regueb is irrigated from surface wells (9,524 wells). They exploit the deep water table, and the irrigated sector accounts for 50 per cent of the total production (irrigated and non-irrigated) in the region and it accounts for 10–15 per cent of total national vegetable production (unpublished data provided by the CRDA (Regional Commissariat of Agricultural Development) of Sidi Bouzid in September 2011). In contrast, the general 'development' of irrigation, the exceptional investment in agricultural activities, particularly private investments, since the period 1980–90, have not helped reduce regional poverty. Poverty levels of the centre-west of the country were above 32.3 per cent in 2010, against 9.1 per cent in greater Tunis, 10.3 per cent in the northeast, 8 per cent for the eastern-centre (INS 2012, 16). According to the Ministry of Social Affairs, the poverty rates were even higher in the region of Sidi Bouzid with 42.3 per cent in 2011 compared with 13.4 per cent for Tunis and 24 per cent as a national average (Touhami 2012, 7; Riadh and Sghaier 2013, 12–14).

The uncontrolled extension of the irrigated area shrunk the volume of underground water. 'In the plain of Sidi Bouzid, the drawdown has reached several meters in some places, leading to the intrusion of salted water coming from the aquifer borders' (Daoud, 2011). Furthermore, the open access to water resources for private use provoked a competition among different users, especially between local peasants and agricultural enterprises, which continue to extend their irrigated areas. The free access to water resources for large private farms provoked a competition between the different users and particularly between the local peasants and the agricultural companies which constantly extend their irrigated areas, while small farmers (under 10 ha), lack financial means, experience a deep crisis, exclusion from irrigation and economic opportunities (Jouili et al. 2011). The various incentives for irrigation development and the spectacular proliferation of wells have led to overuse of groundwater. From the mid-1990s, deep-drilling irrigation began to spread, mainly in the Regueb district. The strong and growing demand for agricultural land in some areas of the district created economic dynamics that were driven by a category of investors with large financial resources. These resources were made in other economic sectors (trade, tourism, industry). The investors were the only group that could afford the costs of modern irrigation schemes: purchase of land, drilling, equipment, electrification, irrigation network and plantations (Daoud 2011)

The investor grab of local resources (water and soil) for agricultural production only marginally benefitted the local population and the region. There was scarcely an addition to employment as a large number of workers came from other regions and local markets of fruits and vegetables. The capital investors came essentially from the Sahel, and particularly from the region of Sfax, the closest big city, and from Tunis (Fautras 2017). When it is not directly shipped abroad, the major part of the production is channelled to the markets of Tunis and other cities for transformation plants in Sfax (for olives to produce olive oil) or Cap Bon (for tomatoes to produce tomato paste) that are then partly exported. A consequence of the drive for a modern capital-intensive and water-heavy agriculture is environmental degradation and the squeezing of small peasants unable to compete with big investors. The small farmers have difficulty protecting their resources and struggle with indebtedness that increase their vulnerability to sell land and exit traditional agriculture.

Conclusion

This chapter has highlighted the role played by peasants in the uprisings in Tunisia and Egypt. It has done so by tracing the historical context in which the uprisings took place, the persistent role that farmers played in the political economy of the two dictatorships and the different types of struggle over water, inputs and especially land. Indeed, we have highlighted how land has been a persistent feature of contestation in both political economies. Both social formations have been overdetermined by the politicisation of land. The policy debate about agricultural reform, modernisation and transformation of the peasantry in both countries has been central to the ways in which the peasantry and rural poor have tried to deal with acute hardship, uncertainty and dominance of landlord classes. The peasantry has been excluded from decision-making and the consequences of that is highlighted by the flow of rural resources to urban centres. Our next chapter (Chapter 4) details how the debate about food security has shaped the conditions of Tunisia and Egypt's countryside.

Note

1   Kifaya was the grassroots Egyptian movement for change. The 6 April Youth Movement was established in early 2008 in solidarity with workers and strike action in the textile and industrial town of El Mahalla El-Kubra.

Chapter 4

FOOD SECURITY IN EGYPT AND TUNISIA

Introduction

This chapter examines the debate in Egypt and Tunisia about food security. It highlights that there is only a very limited and restricted debate, other than among small groups of activists and some academic activists. When these alternative voices are raised, they are often at the risk of personal safety in criticising government policy. Government media and policy 'debate' is regulated and constrained, where it exists at all. It is restricted to compliance with time weary IFI discourse regarding the importance of neo-liberal free markets and open international trade as vehicles for agricultural growth and prosperity. The common feature of all government pronouncements is the assumption that crops can grow without farmers, unless they are large-scale capital-intensive investors, often with little farming experience if they have farmed at all.

We broaden the debate about food security away from macro-economic concerns of trade in food on international markets and the ability of states to purchase food on global markets. We pursue our concern to place small-scale farmers at the centre of the action needed regarding food availability and consumption. We also affirm the importance of food security becoming an integral part of national (and regional?) strategies of rural development. For too long food security has been divorced from the development of links with the producers of food. The debate has remained focused on the interests of big capital, direct foreign investments and export crop production. We will indicate how food and agricultural policy has helped shape politics and under-development in Egypt and Tunisia. We highlight how a rhetoric of export-driven growth and the failure to engage by governments with food producers has repeatedly failed to safeguard national food availability at affordable prices for the poor and ensure well-being for small holder farmers.

Our discussion of food security further advances our critique of the contemporary world food regime. We begin to allude to the importance of an agenda of food sovereignty and how a strategy to promote that will necessarily have to understand the contradictions that emerge from the food regime and the ways in which food is produced in our two case studies. We detail the farming systems in Egypt and Tunisia in Chapters 5 and 6. First, however, we need to explore what is meant by food security and why we think the dominant formulation of that term undermines the possibilities for advancing the economic, political and social interests of family farmers.

Food Security

The MENA region imports more than 50 per cent of it grain and cereal consumption. Commentary focuses on impending regional gloom resulting from rising population, dietary change and limited natural resources (Breisinger et al. 2010, 3). And the critique extends to regional historical preoccupation with flawed import substitution, industrialisation and state intervention. For the World Bank, USAID and others, a more sustainable strategy for food security and economic growth is to give stronger encouragement to the private sector and limit state intervention to help facilitate investment (World Bank 2017).

Dependence upon food imports makes the region extremely vulnerable to global price fluctuations and shocks. The upward trend in global food commodity prices since 2000 and especially after 2007 led to the characterisation of 'agflation' (McMichael 2009, 283). Overall world food prices in 2008 were 83 per cent higher compared with 2005. The price of wheat rose by 130 per cent and rice doubled in the first three months of 2008. An 'integration of energy and food prices' (Patel and McMichael 2009) exacerbated balance of payment crises for oil importers, and critical scholars argued that the world food price spike in 2008 indicated the end of cheap food (Moore 2010). Mainstream commentators asserted that the 2008 crisis would be short lived and temporary but global food crises have been persistent and continuous (UNDESA 2011, 62; Bush and Martiniello, 2017).

One of the consequences of the trend of persistently high food prices has been the systematic and systemic presence of political protest. Often simplified in the description as food riots, the political struggles that emerged in many parts of the Global South were an indication of much deeper opposition and resistance to capitalism and its crisis (Bush and Martiniello 2017). Between 2007 and 2008, more than 25 countries globally experienced food riots (Schneider 2008) as the poor became increasingly unable to access enough cash to buy food. Deaths in bread queues in Cairo might have given a strong signal to the erstwhile Mubarak regime that political turmoil was emerging, but the poor's food crisis was met with increased political repression. We know the social turmoil and outcome in Egypt and Tunisia at the end of 2010 and beginning of 2011 resulting from persistent hunger, political protest and state inaction, for instance, the toppling of dictatorship, although in Egypt only short lived. Authoritarian regimes are unable and unwilling to meet the peaceful complaints of the poor when governments fail to ameliorate hunger. In Egypt in 2017, a major general in President Sisi's security services told Egyptians to stop complaining about their hunger and poverty. The poor and hungry were told to 'sacrifice their dinner for the sake of Egypt' and this at a time of mounting unrest in bread queues in Upper Egypt's Minya and in Cairo's poor and working-class area of Imbaba (Diamante, 2017).

Food security was defined after the second World Food summit in 1996 as:

When all people, at all times, have physical and economic access to sufficient safe and nutritious food that meets their dietary needs and food preferences for an active and healthy life (FAO 1996).

The FAO and the IFIs concentrate their work on food security on the ability of countries to purchase food on global markets. They advance the need for countries in the Global South to liberalise domestic and international food markets and get local prices right (World Bank 2016). Even the poorest country is encouraged to raise income from trade to purchase food on international markets and promote comparative advantage. This policy suggests that the real indicator of whether a country is food secure or not is if a country 'exports enough goods and services to finance food imports' and a measure of this is ratio of total exports to food imports (Breisinger, et al. 2010,2; Breisinger et al. 2012). MENA countries on average use 11.5 per cent of exports to cover for the importing of food (178 country average is 11.3 per cent) with only three – Kuwait, UAE and Iran – having a higher than average ratio. The difficulty for MENA countries is that most of the export revenue accrues from energy or mineral exports and value from manufacturing are weak.

The uneven sectoral balance and the structure of MENA economies increase their vulnerability to food import dependency (Kadri 2014). The mainstream focus on food security is paradoxically, given its neo-liberal bias, state centric: national economies can import food and do not need to try and meet all their food needs by producing locally. Self-sufficiency is discouraged and historically, after the collapse of import substitution industrialisation, and the legitimacy of state intervention, economies in the Global South were encouraged to embrace trade policy that promoted comparative advantage. This meant reverting to or simply continuing with colonially inherited patterns of export resource dependency, and to purchase food on international markets.

The IFIs assert that food security can be attained with an efficient production and circulation of food through global commodity chains linking producers with consumers. This is an analysis of food security that suggests technical and productivist solutions (Bush and Martiniello 2017). This is technical because of the need to finely tune connectivity between the production of agricultural commodities and global demand, something over which southern producers have little control. It is productivist in that solutions offered, as we will see in the case of Egypt and Tunisia, suggest the need to boost local production with no reference to the relations of production or ownership of the means of production, notably land and also access to water and irrigation. It is a policy that has encouraged Gulf food-insecure states to promote land grabs in Africa and further afield (TNI 2012; Land Matrix 2017).

Saudi businesses already have more than US$11 billion of investment in countries as diverse as Brazil, Canada, Ukraine, Poland, Ethiopia and Sudan (The Middle East, 2013, 2; Lippman 2010; Cooke 2016). The large-scale investments have at least two significant consequences for the host countries. First, increased agribusiness involvement in food production disempowers small-scale farmers and the deliverability of an alternative to food security, namely food sovereignty. This is developed further in Chapter 7 (Borras and Franco 2012; McMichael 2013; Wittman et al. 2010). Second, globalisation of food production undermines and inhibits the possibilities of countries with structural food deficits and recurrent famines, like Sudan, and Ethiopia, to promote engagement with local farmers and pastoralists to boost production for local consumption. Failing to enhance and defend the interests of small-scale farmers has the knock-on effect of jeopardising rural wellbeing, nutrition and education or rural development more broadly defined.

Trade-based food security continues to promote an idea of comparative advantage for family farming and large-scale agriculture. 'MENA countries have a comparative advantage in producing fruit and vegetables – provided that domestic institutions and regulation allow efficient marketing chains' (World Bank 2008, 1). The World Bank has suggested the need for improved techniques for buying cereals to avoid price impact of market volatility. And the Bank has noted that its funding is channeled to support for upstream sectorial analysis, help with reducing rural-urban divides and focusing on community projects that address rural poverty in Morocco, Yemen and Tunisia (World Bank 2008, 3). The driver for this is the private sector and there is little by way of recommendation for food-insecure farmers other than that farmers must be able to respond to market prices more effectively. Getting the prices right is a familiar neo-liberal mantra. Regional governments and IFIs have emphasised, since the 1970s, that the drivers for agricultural reform are not family farmers but foreign direct investment, agribusiness and large-scale investors. This at a time when the paradox continues: the first to experience food shortfalls and dietary constraints are the producers of food or near land-less rural dwellers.

There is also persistent, albeit at times only residual, Malthusianism to food security policy. This is expressed in IFI and other literature that the problem of food security is that there is simply not enough food for a growing population. This leads to potentially sinister debates about surplus populations, refugee crises, rural to urban migration and the need to control population and the mobility of people. There is little, if any, debate about the need to understand issues of power and control and how people who are hungry might be able to develop the means to access food (but cf Bauman 2004; Duffield 2007).

Issues of power and uneven access to food and land is restricted because the international food regime, which we referred to in Chapter 1, is unques-tioned and seen to be unchallengeable. The international food regime is seen as the solution to food crises and not the cause of them. This is because of the twin axis, and quasi-monopoly, of World Trade Organization rules and the power of agribusiness transnationals to shape food policy discourse (Patel and McMichael 2009, 24). Although in later chapters we indicate the ways in which small farmers have resisted food insecurity, the IFIs are hegemonic gatekeepers of food security issues, refusing to critically engage with agrarian crises that underpin persistent hunger.

Egypt

The GoE declared in the late 1980s that improving food security entailed the need to promote deregulation of agriculture. The economic reform of agri-culture began in 1987 before an agreed programme of structural adjustment lending with the IFIs in 1991. The erstwhile minister of agriculture, Yusuf Wali, promoted economic liberalisation under the claim that it was neces-sary to improve Egypt's agricultural self-sufficiency ratios. He was minister for 22 years from 1982. He was also a large landowner in Fayyum and was finally sacked from his ministerial position in 2004 because of corruption charges. He was possibly just a scapegoat at a time when political agitation for reform mounted. It seems even the notoriously corrupt regime of President Mubarak wanted to try and indicate it was not quite as crooked as evidence overwhelm-ingly indicated (Kifaya n.d.). Policy for economic reform accelerated in the 1990s as poor oil prices and the end of the cold war reduced Egypt's geostra-tegic rent (Bush 1999). At the start of the liberalisation programme, the state regulated production, pricing and marketing of cotton, wheat, rice, sugar cane, winter onions and beans. By the mid-1990s only cotton and sugar cane were regulated. The state also reduced its subsidy programme as a percentage of spending from 15 per cent of spending in 1980 to 6 per cent in 1997 (Woertz 2017) but the private sector, seen as a replacement for the state, failed to boost production and food insecurity remained.

The World Bank and other IFIs asserted the need for strong and vibrant national economies as a prerequisite for food security. As one influential research group has noted,

> Economic growth that raises people's incomes is the single most important driver of food security. Rapid economic growth and transformation of rural and urban sectors will thus be key for future prosperity and food security (Breisinger et al. 2010, 5).

But here is the paradox. Egypt had high levels of per capita growth – at least 3 per cent per annum over a decade before the uprisings in 2011. Yet this did not guarantee food security or sustainable development. This was because at the same time as there were high rates of growth, there were also increases in the numbers of Egyptians living in poverty on less than US$2 a day. Egypt's growth was based upon rentier income and cronyism, extractives, land speculation and rural underdevelopment (Bush 2014; Achcar 2013). These elements of neo-liberal reform were especially evident after 2004 when Ahmed Nazif was appointed prime minister. It was also a time when political resistance and opposition to neo-liberalism and authoritarianism increased (Abdelrahman 2015; Beinin 2016).

Contemporary Food Security

Food security got worse after the 2011 uprisings. Egypt has some of the highest levels of agricultural productivity in the world for many of its crops, but crop production needs to always be set alongside the ability of households to access food, purchase it in markets at affordable prices and to ensure that well-being can be positively enhanced.

We deal with some of these themes in the context of food sovereignty in Chapter 7. For the moment it is important to be reminded of the contradiction between Egypt's level of per capita growth in the 2000s and the persistence of poverty, particularly in rural poverty. While the veracity of all data needs to treated with caution, it is alarming that the World Food Programme and the Egyptian state's Central Agency for Public Mobilisation and Statistics (CAPMAS is an organisation renown for it poor data collection and especially the under-reporting of poverty levels) reported an increase in food insecurity from 14 per cent in 2009 to 17.2 per cent (13.7 million people) in 2011 (WFP 2014). This increase was directly driven by increases in poverty as well as global capitalist crisis and policy failure after the 2011 uprisings. Between 2009 and 2011, 15.2 per cent of the population moved into poverty, 12.6 per cent were deemed to be chronically poor. The number for chronically poor shoots up to more than 50 per cent for people living in rural Upper Egypt compared with the national average of 25.2 per cent. This was roughly in the same time frame, 2005–10, that Egypt's economic growth was recorded to be an average 6.2 per cent. Poverty was no longer, if it had ever been, only a rural phenomenon, with more than 15 per cent of town dwellers living on less than US$2 per person per day.

Egypt imports more than half its wheat needs. National consumption is about 18 million tons of which 9–10 million tons is imported annually (WFP 2014). The difficulty for the GoE has been the high cost of importing wheat, which increased significantly in 2016/2017 after the Egyptian pound was devalued by 48 per cent following its flotation against the dollar (*The Economist* 2016; *The Guardian* 2016). Egypt's foreign reserves in 2017 were US$36 billion but the average for 2003/2017 was just US$22 billion. That was barely enough to meet the wheat import bill for three months, and the use of the country's strategic wheat reserve further jeopardised food security.

While there has been a gradual upward trajectory in food production in Egypt since the early 2000s, it only noticeable for vegetables and fruit; rice and maize has fallen and wheat production has been pretty much stagnant. Wheat is susceptible to shifts in global prices; farmers in 2009/2010 planted *bersim* (clover) for livestock fodder as wheat prices were low and the GoE was often slow to intervene in the market. In 2016/17, Egypt imported 12 million tons of wheat, over a million tons more than the average for the preceding 5 years. This coincided with 42 per cent annual food price inflation, the highest for 30 years. The Egyptian Food bank, a large charity that feeds the poor, increased its 'handouts' by 20 per cent, extending their reach to 'middle-class' families.

Figure 4.1 highlights the national Egyptian figures since 2000 for food deficits and changing position in macro imports and exports. Food deficits increased as a percentage of total deficit. Food exports increased but so too did food imports as a per cent of total imports. The impact of the global food crisis in 2008 highlights a boost in food exports and a spike in food imports.

The GoE responded to increased food insecurity and complied with stringent IMF conditions for a US$12 billion loan, by mobilising the military to distribute one-off items like sugar and rice at half price. President el-Sisi told Egyptians in October 2016 that the GoE measures were tough but that Egyptians had to endure them and be patient (Egyptian Streets 2016). The GoE raised the prices of sugar for ration card holders by 40 per cent, doubling it to LE10 for unsubsidised sugar. Rhetorically the state clamped down

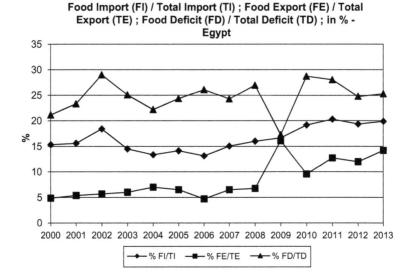

Figure 4.1 Egypt: Food Security.

Source: World Bank various tables. Compiled by François Ireton.

on hoarding, which led to, among other things, the well-publicised ludicrous arrest of a man in Cairo for possessing a 10-kg bag of sugar (Al Ahram 2016).

The GoE has continued to persist with two flaws in its agricultural strategy. The first is to remain wedded to a trade-based view of food security driving investments in attempts to increase production of high-value and usually low-nutritious foodstuff for export. And second, linked to this, has been the refusal to dialogue with small-scale farmers.

The productionist and trade-based formulae have two elements to boost agricultural exports. The first of these is to continue favouring large-scale agriculture that accelerates moves away from support for small-scale farmers. An example of this is the continuing investment with Toshka and newly planned land reclamation schemes. The Mubarak era 'pyramid in the desert' is the Toshka pumping station and irrigation canal that has linked the river Nile with the south Western Desert. It has been called 'Egypt's hope for the twenty first century' (Water-technology n.d.). It is a scheme that has sucked in almost all of Egypt's available investment liquidity. One estimate is that the financial cost since the 1990s has been US$90 billion (Schilling 2013). Toshka was intended to generate high levels of production of agricultural crops for export funded by Gulf and Saudi finance. Neither has happened to any significant extent. This scheme was also intended to attract large numbers of migrants from the densely populated delta. The projection was for some 16 million to migrate into new towns creating 2.8 million jobs on 1.5 million acres of newly reclaimed land. And it was a scheme that had never had a detailed environmental impact study (Weir 2015).

The second feature of the productionist model is highlighted by President el-Sisi's recently declared strategy to reclaim more of Egypt's land area for agricultural production and in so doing reduce dependency upon imported wheat. El-Sisi announced a plan in 2015 to reclaim 1.5 million feddans of land in the New Valley Governorate (Western Desert) near Farafra. He had initially announced that his government intended to reclaim 4 million feddans. In doing so, the president seemed unaware or unwilling to understand the historical limitations of land reclamation and the environmental costs of so doing. One estimate is that the 1.5 million feddan scheme will draw upon 25 per cent of Egypt's groundwater supply, and the newly formed Egyptian Rural Development Company, formed to manage the scheme, has been given LE8 billion capital (approximately US$440 million) (Mada Masr 2015; Mukhtar 2016). Crucially, too, there seems to have been very little discussion as to how the reclaimed land will be distributed and to whom. The balance between large-scale agricultural investors and small-scale family farmers is moot and the proposed interest rate for GoE loans to farmers of 5 per cent over 8 years seems to be at odds with what is realistic for poor farmers (Dardeer 2017; Ramadan 2016).

The resurrection of land reclamation to improve food security runs alongside rhetorical policy announcements regarding the need to improve agricultural technology and the use of higher yielding seeds. There has long been a fierce debate in Egypt about the health standards of genetically modified seeds and agricultural commodities. There have been many cases where produce has been impounded and rejected at Egypt's docks for fear that there is just insufficient knowledge regarding the health and well-being consequences of genetically modified organisms (GMOs). But despite many protests from the GoE and civil society representatives, Egyptian legislation does not formally prohibit GMOs (Library of Congress 2015; Hussain 2013).

Two different ministers of agriculture in January 2017, first, Essam Fayed (sacked for corruption) and then his replacement Abdel Moneim al Banna stressed the importance of reducing dependence upon imported strategic crops (Mitwally 2017). There was a slight departure from previous policy rhetoric as the importance of liaising with farmers was announced. The new minister said he was committed to supporting farmers, to understand more clearly the character of farming cycles and to try and reduce the exploitative practices of merchants and middlemen (Al-Noubi 2017).

The context in which these statements were made was persistent anger and rural resistance to merchant market power that had driven and increased market liberalisation. Rhetorical policy statements had not delivered improvements in productivity of strategic crops and it had certainly not improved or tried to develop increased liaison or even basic exchange of information with small-scale farmers. This is the second persistent flaw in the GoE agricultural strategy: the absence of linking with or trying to understand more clearly what it is that drives small farmers and how their interests, even broadly defined, like regular and guaranteed access to land, water, agricultural inputs and markets, can be secured.

The new 2014 Egyptian constitution had a clause, inserted following farmer petitioning, mobilisation and surprising representation at the constitutional assembly, affirming the significance of 'food sovereignty'. At the time it was hailed by NGOs and other civil society organisations and parties to be a significant departure from the ways in which farmers and farming was conceived. It has subsequently had little impact.

Tunisia

Tunisia has also pursued a trade-based strategy for food security. As we highlight in Chapter 5, Tunisian agricultural policy, notably after the early 1970s focused on capital-intensive agriculture. Like the experience in Egypt, the rhetoric for promoting food security neglected consultation with farmers and was driven by patterns of capital accumulation for large-scale national and foreign investors. There was also in Tunisia an acceleration of combined and uneven development. This was exemplified by development of the richer Sahel region in the north of the country at the expense of the south highlighted in part by uneven access to water and land. And like Egypt, there was a view that economic growth during the years of dictatorship would improve all living standards including those in rural Tunisia. However, as the IFIs and other international agencies noted after the toppling of Ben Ali in January 2011:

> Tunisia's aggregate growth per capita and social indicators masked the rising resentment against injustice and worsening governance. The top-down character of the former regime allowed for the organized capture of rents by the ruling elite, a trend which increased during the last decade in tandem with the economic liberalization of the country (AfDB 2012, 12).

Tunisia's food trade balance was negative from the late 1980s with persistent and chronic dependence on cereal imports that account for about 40 per cent of the country's total food imports. About 35 per cent of the country's population is rural based, and like Egypt, there are large disparities in the size and productivity of land holdings: 54 per cent of farmers have less than five hectares, about 11 per cent of the total area. Only 3 per cent of farmers have holdings of more than 50 hectares accounting for 34 per cent of farmland (Jouili 2009, 5).

The World Bank has suggested that superficially the country's agricultural sector has been vibrant, or at least it has appeared to be vibrant. It noted that in 2010 it accounted for almost 8 per cent of GDP and almost one-tenth of total exports. Significantly the sector accounted for 20 per cent of employment. Over the years, however, the World Bank has given mixed signals to Tunisian policymakers regarding the development of agriculture and how food security and the need for the sector to more effectively meet its 'potential' (World Bank 2006, 7). The World Bank has noted that one of the difficulties of agriculture in Tunisia is poor productivity highlighted by the unusual phenomenon, for a middle-income country, of simply employing more labour to the same area of land. Between 1993 and 2002, agricultural employment grew by 20 per cent without a trend increase in productivity. For the IFIs the difficulty with food security is that growth in the agricultural sector, before the ouster of Ben Ali, was a product of government subsidies and protection, especially in beef and dairy production. Tunisia's major export market is the EU but its competitive advantage in fruit and vegetables has not been delivered (World Bank 2006).

As with the Egyptian case, the impact of the international food crisis in 2008 in Tunisia is evident from Figure 4.2. So too is the persistent food deficit as a percent of total deficit.

The paradox here is that the World Bank in its dealings with Tunisia since the 1980s has repeatedly advanced the mantra of trade liberalisation as a vehicle for boosting Tunisian agricultural growth and food security. This was the strategy that Ben Ali pursued. The implementation of the structural adjustment programme in 1986 may have been uneven, and Ben Ali and his family retained control of major sectors, especially in manufacturing, car sales, real estate and land sales and gifts (Reuters 2011). Yet the state edged unevenly towards applying market prices for agricultural commodities and the consequences for small farmers was calamitous. Economic liberalisation reduced farmer subsidies, including access to important lines of credit (Jouili 2009). The withdrawal of state support for marginalised small farmers added to rural social differentiation as the number of farming households working less than 5 hectares rose from 133,000 in 1961 to 281,000 in 2004. Small holder farmers were caught in a vicious grip of the consequences of economic reform on the one hand and large landowner predation accelerated by small holder indebtedness on the other.

The neo-liberal agenda of market reform and state allocation of agricultural resources followed decades of collectivised agriculture between 1964

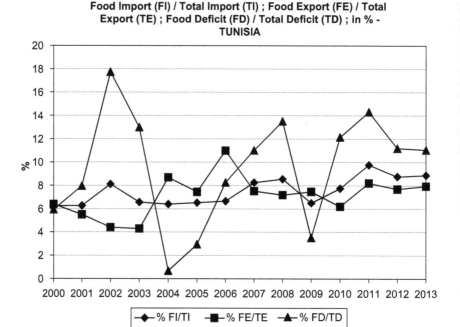

Food Import (FI) / Total Import (TI) ; Food Export (FE) / Total
Export (TE) ; Food Deficit (FD) / Total Deficit (TD) ; in % -
TUNISIA

Figure 4.2 Tunisia: Food Security.

Source: World Bank various. Compiled by François Ireton.

and 1970. The Fifth Five Year Plan (1977–81) advanced market liberalisation and the enhanced role for private investors. This was also a period of environmental devastation with consequences that are felt into the twenty-first century. State land was converted into private holdings owned by mainly northern elites. The focus was not on growing wheat and other cereals for staple local consumption but olive oil and vegetables for export. Irrigated wheat accounted for less than 15 per cent of the total area planted for wheat (FAO 2017). Production tended to be from inland, from the south and centre of Tunisia, where environmental chaos was promoted as the wealth accrued from sales was held in northern enclaves. Even the World Bank noted, after the uprising against Ben Ali, reflecting on a strategy that the IFI had encouraged:

> *Despite notable achievements and progress, Tunisia's pre-revolutionary development model failed to generate inclusive growth in its most comprehensive sense. A deterioration of economic governance and pervasive elite capture during the decade preceding the revolution undermined the country's social progress, hindered further economic*

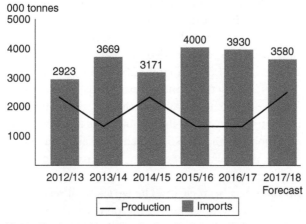

Notes: Total cereal includes rice in milled terms, Split year refers to individual crop marketing years.

Figure 4.3 Tunisia: Cereal Production and Imports.

Source: FAO Global Information and Early Warning System.

development and ultimately fed the social discontent that culminated in the 2011 fall of the regime (emphasis in original, World Bank 2012, 1).

Sidi Bouzid, as we have already indicated, was an area where the impact of uneven development was most acutely experienced. It was also the site of the catalyst for the 2010 uprisings (see Chapter 5). Debt and depeasantisation resulted from, among other things, the increased spread of private investment, especially in irrigated farmland from just 2,000 hectares in 1958 to 47,000 hectares in 2011 (Ayeb 2012; Fautras 2015). Sidi Bouzid is the fourth poorest governorate in Tunisia with more than 40 per cent of people living on less than US$2 a day in 2011 (Touhami 2012; Szakal 2016). Cereal production (see Figure 4.3) was always outstripped by food imports. It seems the strategy of market liberalisation did not deliver the sustained boost in agricultural production that could deliver food security.

Contemporary Food Security

It is significant that the uprisings that toppled Ben Ali began in the underdeveloped regions of Tunisia. We detailed some of the reasons for this in

Chapter 3 and are developed further in Chapter 5. As a reminder, the rates of poverty in Tunisia's central and southern regions in 2010 were estimated to be 32 per cent with more than 20 per cent unemployment – this does not consider rates of underemployment. In contrast, poverty and unemployment rates in coastal areas were 9 and 11 per cent respectively (Mestiri 2016). While the World Bank and IMF had heralded the years of Ben Ali as a 'role model' for Africa, the IFIs in 2014 noted that the liberalising had not gone far enough (World Bank 2014). In fact, continued restrictions on the economic participation of Tunisians had 'caused social exclusion', dampening economic performance. In contrast, we argue throughout that it was not the restrictions on market exclusion but the ways in which Tunisian farmers were unevenly incorporated into the liberalised economy that ensured accelerated poverty and underdevelopment.

The World Bank has been clear: 'The agricultural sector plays a key role in the Tunisian economy especially in the poor rural areas of the interior' but it also notes that 'Tunisia does not really have an agricultural policy but has instead a food security policy that in fact hinders the development of its agricultural sector' (World Bank 2014, 260). The issue for the World Bank is not that food security is being delivered albeit in a way that it does not think is developmentally sustainable, but that Tunisia has continued to rely too heavily on state intervention, frustrating the free market and encouragement of private entrepreneurship. In the process Tunisia has focused on growing the 'wrong' crops. We can agree the cropping patterns may have been less than productive and efficient in the way they were supported by the state. This does not mean that the public sector has no role in agriculture and especially that the coastal-land-owning elites and owners of food processing plants should have benefitted from state policy in the ways that they did.

The World Bank has argued that 'Tunisia has a comparative advantage in crops with greater labor intensity and a disadvantage in crops with high land intensity' (World Bank 2014, 260). The implication of this is that Tunisia should focus on olive, tomato and out-of-season vegetables for export. Although soft wheat is profitable in the north and northwest, dependent upon good rainfall, the World Bank now argues against the production of wheat, barley, beef and milk because their efficiency is dependent upon large government subsidy. A feature of Tunisia's agricultural malaise is that while it is the world's second largest olive oil producer, production stagnates while global demand since 2000 has boomed.

The IFIs are now critiquing in large part a strategy that they have overseen. It is entirely in keeping with 'bankspeak' (Moretti and Pestre 2015) to continue pressing the mantra of free markets and private investment as a mechanism for economic growth. The IFIs in fact concede that the Tunisia model of public-sector-led development in the 1970s was effective, sustained state-led growth and reduced poverty. The crisis for Tunisia in the 1980s was seen as a result of persistence with the public-sector-led model rather than of international capitalist crisis (World Bank 2014, 300). The figures for 'inclusive growth', however, and income per capita growth are misleading. Tunisia's per capita economic growth in the 1990s was the second strongest in the MENA region and to use the World Bank's language of modernisation, economic growth did not lead to a 'take off'. In fact, unemployment remained high – more than 13 per cent in the 1990s – and wages were low and predominantly in a mushrooming insecure informal sector. The consequence was an economy and political dictatorship shaped by rentierism and corruption underpinned by international support craving continued regional political stability.

The parallels with Egypt are stark although the process of democratic liberalisation and democratic deepening has been more extensive in Tunisia than Egypt. The IFIs have called for a 're-engineering' of institutions to facilitate greater market entry for private investors in cereal production and in the promotion of that recurrent neo-liberal trope: land titling. But while in value terms agricultural production increased by 67 per cent in the 10 years after 1990 and was heralded, 17 per cent of this value accrued from beef and milk production that received large state subsidy. Rather than this being seen as a strategic state investment, the state's role is now advised by the IFIs to be limited to facilitating 'a regulatory framework'. This framework is intended so the market for agricultural goods, and the promotion of food security, is not impeded by inefficient government intervention.

The discussion of food security is once again limited to the interests of large agricultural producers: policy is divorced from the welfare and well-being of small-scale farmers. The market is reified in the language of 'unleashing the potential of agriculture to boost growth' (World Bank 2014, 259) rather than an arena in which powerful landed and coastal elites once again will be allowed to benefit at the expense of small holders.

In early 2017 the GoT announced a new Five Year Plan for agriculture and it is likely the IFIs were pleased with what they read and heard. There was a policy concession that crops favoured by small farmers would be supported in a strategy more broadly of rural development. However, there was little recognition that historical patterns of rural marginalisation and small farmer abjection would be effectively redressed. And there was little recognition that there would be any change in the way large-scale farmers and landowners had benefitted from government policy during dictatorship.

The newly declared agricultural policy had another shopping list feel to it. Land problems would be addressed as part of a focus on natural resources to promote production and sustainability, improve knowledge dissemination and decision-making in farming (Kapitalis 2017). The GoT announced a proposed increase in agricultural investment of more than 55 per cent from 5.8 billion dinars (US$2.3 billion) 2011–15 to 9 billion between 2016 and 2020. There was little mention, however, of the way this investment would be divided between the private and public sectors.

Conclusion

This chapter has traced the debates in Egypt and Tunisia relating to food security. It has indicated the similarity in the way in which trade-based views of food production and import have shaped agricultural policy in both countries. It has also reinforced our argument regarding the impact of uneven and combined agricultural underdevelopment and the spatial dimensions to that. We have indicated how the long history of IFI involvement in both countries has failed to deliver the declared promises of agricultural reform. IFI and government policy in both countries have assumed that food security is possible without small farmer involvement and engagement. The next two chapters (Chapters 5 and 6) look at the consequences of this in more detail. We indicate how small farmers have attempted to reject state and IFI interventions and why food sovereignty, detailed in Chapter 7, is the only solution to rural poverty and food insecurity.

Chapter 5

FARMERS AND FARMING: TUNISIA

The peasantry has always been considered, in its vast majority as a force of inertia, blockage, as a brake on the modernization of agriculture. On it crystallize all the deficiencies, the weaknesses of the traditional society. The peasantry can truly be the subject of its own future only if it is radically transformed. For this she must be educated, guided, oriented, helped. What it is: its history, its culture, its social organization, its relationship to space, its know-how, is of no interest. Agriculture, as an economic sector, has always been enslaved (in the cybernetic sense of the term) to a logic of operation, to economic objectives that were external to it and derived from the development strategy implemented (Gachet, 1987, 149).

Introduction

Two processes have shaped Tunisia's food and agriculture sector. The first has been an increase in food dependence, which has become structural and exceeds 50 per cent of the country's food needs. The second has been the general impoverishment of the peasantry, which in large part is now unable to supply and ensure its own food security.

This combined situation of food dependence and peasant poverty is far from being a simple cyclical crisis and is instead the culmination of more than a century of anti-peasant government policies. These are the result of decision-makers during both the colonial era and since independence, to integrate Tunisian agriculture into the global market and the global food system (Friedmann 2005; Friedmann 2016; Friedmann and McMichael 1989). The reliance on the global food system and the global market results in high exposure to the risks of unstable international prices for agricultural and food products. This was highlighted during the 2007–8 global food crisis that hit the Tunisian economy dependent on imported cereals and vegetable oils. Cereals and vegetable oils account for 80 per cent of food energy availability, and imports constitute a significant part of the consumption: 75 per cent for the soft wheat, 20 per cent for the durum wheat and close to 100 per cent for the oils' (Ben Said et al. 2011, 37–38).

Peasants and Agricultural Land: A Source of Inequality

Access to land for small-scale family farmers has worsened since independence. This is because the political decisions taken by state holders fostered the interests and enhanced access for big agricultural landowners. Large landowners and wealthy absentee owners have been considered as the only stakeholders able to adapt to the challenge of modernity and guarantee integration in the global economy. A second explanation can be found in the set of neo-liberal policies implemented since the early 1970s, which disadvantaged peasant farmers. The third explanation lies in the state decision not to redistribute the colonial lands nationalised in 1964 to the heirs of previous owners. In so doing the regime continued the dispossession of small farmers of their lands by the colonial forces. State officials argued that land redistribution would fragment land holdings. Thus, the peasants who were dispossessed since the colonial era and who thought that independence would lead to the return of their land were surprised by government policy to annex land to the state's private domain. Farmer occupations since 2010 of previously colonised lands, linked to the state's domain after 1964, highlight that the heirs of the previous dispossessed landowners never lost hope in recovering 'their' lands. The case of the occupation in 2012 of the oasis of Jemna in southern Tunisia is a particularly representative example of that protest (Ayeb 2016).

By 2010, Tunisian land had several different statuses. The first was private lands that had been previously consolidated in 1885 by the French administration through the adoption of the cadastre system: 4.7 million hectares are covered by this private status. Second, collective lands were established in 1901 by colonial legislation that incorporated the concept of tribal land. In 1964 tribal communities got exclusive rights to some land and some collective land was converted into 'forest lands status' (Poortman et al. 2006, 63).

Since independence, 3 million hectares of collective (tribal) land have been converted either privately or under the forest regime. Third, state lands (or what is referred to as public domain) resulted from the nationalisation of colonial lands in 1964. The total area of state lands was 820,000 hectares. In the mid-2000s, this category of land still covered 500,000 hectares of very fertile land. It included managed pilot farms, and agricultural cooperatives under the supervision of the State Land Office (Poortman et al. 2006, 63).

The available data, especially based on the Surveys on the Structures of Agricultural Farms,[1] shows a gap between the smallest agricultural producers (less than 5 hectares) and the biggest with more than 100 hectares. Table 5.1

shows the structural characteristics of Tunisian agriculture with a high level of inequality in agrarian structures since 1960 to the mid-2000s. The smallest farmers (less than 5 ha) represented 41 per cent of the producers and shared 6 per cent of the agricultural area in 1961–62. They represented 53 per cent with 9 per cent in 1994–95 and 54 per cent with 11 per cent of the Useful Agricultural Surfaces (UAS) in 2004–5. Those whose farms were 100 hectares or more represented 2 per cent with 29 per cent of the agriculture land in 1961–62, 1 per cent with 25 per cent in 1994–95 and 1 per cent with 22 per cent in 2004–5.

When we widen the scope to analyse and compare the access to land for the two categories of landholders with less than 20 hectares (small and medium peasantry) with those of more than 100 hectares (big land owners and agricultural investors), the inequalities are striking and alarming. In 1961–62, less than 1.5 per cent of farmers cultivated 29 per cent of the area while 82 per cent (less than 20 ha) cultivated 33 per cent of the total area. In 1994–95, 1 per cent disposed of 25 per cent of the land while 88 per cent cultivated 29 per cent of the total area. And finally, in 2004–5, 1 per cent of the farmers exploited 22 per cent of the land while 88 per cent shared 39 per cent of the total area.

Table 5.1 reveals the extreme inequalities in the access to agricultural land. It highlights both the origins of the Tunisian long agricultural crisis and the magnitude of food dependence. The crisis covers the whole country and especially the most vulnerable peasant families (who own less than 5 hectares per family) which was estimated at 281,000 families in 2004–5.

It is also important to note that the agricultural area available per inhabitant has dropped between 1961–62 and 1994–95 from 1.2 hectares to 0.6 hectares. In 2004–5, the average declined more moderately and reached 0.5 hectares per inhabitant (MARH[2] 1962; 1995; 2005; Elloumi 2006a, 8). The average size of the agricultural farms has also slightly dropped between 1961–62 and 2004–5, from 15.97 hectares in 1961–62 to 11.25 hectares in 1994–95 and to 10.21 hectares in 2004–5. However, the gap between the average size of the smallest farms of less than 5 hectares and that of farms of more than 100 hectares remained in the scale of 1/100: 2.39 hectares for the smallest and 299.8 (1/125) for the biggest in 1961–62, 1.87 hectares and 325.25 hectares (1/173) in 1994–95 and finally, 1.98 hectares and 281.75 hectares (1/142) in 2004–5.

We also want to highlight that the number of peasants holding less than 5 hectares has more than doubled during this period from 133,000 in 1961–62 to 251,000 in 1994–95 and 281,000 in 2004–5 (which is more than twice the amount between 1961–62 and 2004–5). In contrast, the share of this category of the arable land has only evolved modestly growing from 318,000 hectares

Table 5.1 Evolution of Agrarian Structures (Number, Area, Area/Farmer) 1961–62, 1994–95 and 2004–5 (Tunisia)

Size	Survey 1961–62					Survey 1994–95					Survey 2004–5				
	Numb. (1000)	%	Area 1000 ha	%	Average	Numb. (1000)	%	Area 1000 ha	%	Average	Numb. (1000)	%	Area 1000 ha	%	Average
-5 ha	133	41	318	6	2.4	251	53	471	9	1.9	281	54	556	11	2
5–10	73	22	531	10	7.3	92	20	643	12	7	109	21	757	14	6.9
10–20	64	19.6	887	17	13.9	71	15	986	18	13.9	71.4	13.8	964	18.3	13.5
<20	270	82.6	1736	33	6.43	414	88	2100	39	5.07	461.4	88.8	2276	43.3	4.93
20–50	42	12.9	1388	27	33	43	9	1249	23.4	29	40.7	7.9	1216	22.6	29.9
50–100	9	2.7	583	11	64.8	10	2	645	12	64.5	10	2	651	12	65.1
+100	5	1.5	1499	29	299.8	4	1	1301	25	325.3	4	1	1127	22	281.8
Total	326	100	5206	100	16	471	100	5295	100	11.2	516	100	5271	100	10.2

Source: Study on the structure of agricultural farms. 1961–62, 1994–95 and 2004–5, Ministère de l'Agriculture et des Ressources Hydrauliques (MARH) (Various years 1962, 1996 and 2006). Direction Générale des Etudes et du Developpement Agricole. 'Enquête sur les Structures des Exploitations Agricoles' and Jouili (2008, 244). 2004–5 (Jouili 2008, 244) and MARH various years.

to 417,000 hectares and to 556,000 hectares for the three successive periods (hardly 57 per cent more between 1961–62 and 2004–5). If we take the category that own less than 20 hectares, the most important element to highlight is the evolution of the average area of the farms that evolved from 6.43 hectares per farmer in 1961–62 to 5.07 hectares in 1994–95 and 4.93 hectares in 2004–5. The number of farmers in this category rose from 270,000 in 1961–62 to 461,400 in 2004–5.

With holdings from 20 hectares, the general trend is relatively homogeneous. The farmers and agricultural producers that have more than 20 hectares represent only 10.9 per cent of the total number in 2004–5 but they own 56.6 per cent of the total agricultural area. In 1961–62, they used to represent 17.1 per cent of the total number and owned 57 per cent of the area.

There has been a strong concentration of agricultural land between 1961–62 and 2004–5. If we look at the category of those who own more than 100 hectares, the inequalities of land access are stark. The number of producers disposing of a surface between 100 and 200 hectares was 3,000 in 1961–62, representing 0.9 per cent of the total number and disposed of 427,000 hectares in total, which was 8.5 per cent of the total usable area. Those owning areas between 200 and 500 hectares are 1,500 producers and represent 0.5 per cent of all farmers. They own 468,000 hectares, which is 9.3 per cent of the total area.

Finally, only 600 people controlled farms of 500 ha. They represented 0.2 per cent of the total number of farmers but owned 554,000 hectares or 11 per cent of the total used area. This concentration of land in the hands of the biggest owners, after independence, show that the collectivisation of land in 1960 did not touch this category of big agricultural owners since it continues to dominate 22 per cent of the total usable agricultural area in the contemporary period.

Irrigation as a Tool of Dispossession

The total irrigated area in 2004–5, reached 418,800 hectares and represents 8.6 per cent of the total area of cultivable land estimated at 4,884,800 ha. Almost half the irrigable area is in the north of Tunisia which also receives the most rainfall. Thirty six per cent of the irrigable land is in the centre semi-arid region and 14.4 per cent in the arid and desert South (Table 5.2).

The distribution by number and size of the farms of irrigated areas also highlights a strong inequality in access to irrigation. Table 5.3 highlights that among other things the farms of more than 10 hectares cover more than half of the irrigated land, while 44.8 per cent of irrigated land are for owners of less than 10 hectares and only 16 per cent is the share for farmers with less than 5ha.

The inequality in access to irrigation exacerbates differences between large and small-scale farmers. Five hectares of irrigated land are not comparable in

Table 5.2 Evolution of Public, Private and Total Irrigated Areas (in ha) 1956 to 2005 (Tunisia)

Years	Public Schemes	Private Schemes	Total
1956	3,000	62,000	65,000
1972	49,500	70,500	120,000
1976	64,500	80,500	145,000
1981	70,300	156,100	226,400
1985	93,060	150,500	243,500
1990	114,000	174,000	288,000
1997	161,610	210,400	372,010
2000	190,090	187,240	377,330
2005	217,250	201,550	418,800

Source: Hassaïnya (1991, 65) until 1981 and Jouili (2008, 437).

Table 5.3 Distribution of Irrigated Areas according to the Size of Land, Tunisia, 1994–95 and 2004–5. (Units 1,000 ha and %)

Size of the land piece	Survey 1994–95			Survey 2004–5		
	Area	%	Irrigated area/ Cultivated area	Area	%	Irrigated area/ Cultivated area
<5 Ha	71,9	24.4	17,1	82,6	25.0	16,0
5–10 Ha	52,3	17.8	9,7	65,6	19.8	9,8
10–50 Ha	99,7	34.0	5,9	108,8	32.9	6,3
50–100 Ha	19,0	6.5	4,2	20,9	6.4	4,5
>100 Ha	50,9	17.3	5,7	52,6	15.9	6,4
Total	2,938	0	7,5	330,6	10.0	7,8

Source: Ministère de l'Agriculture et des Ressources Hydrauliques (MARH) 2006.

terms of productivity and profitability to 5 hectares in rain-fed farming. While in rain-fed farms, a minimum of 20 hectares is necessary to secure the livelihood of a peasant family to a reasonable standard of living and food security, this level is attainable with just 5 hectares in the irrigated sector with good conditions of access to water. In other words, the producers who own more than 5 hectares of irrigated land can be classified as medium producers (5–20 ha) or big producers for those with more than 20 hectares. This is not the case in rain-fed farming.

The difficulties of access to land for poor farmers increases in areas where there may be dam development or possibilities of irrigation. The price of land in these circumstances increases dramatically and limits small owner access. Irrigation is a highly speculative sector and the competition between big investors (who are generally exporters of agricultural products) and peasants very rarely ends up benefiting the latter.

Table 5.4 Percentage Distribution of Irrigated Areas between the North and the South of the Country

Year	North + South	(North/Total)×100	(South/Total)×100
	ha	%	%
1965	78,800	68.8	31.2
1979	211,690	56.7	43.3
1985	243,530	57.3	42.7
1990	288,600	54.6	45.4
1997	372,010	52.3	47.7
2000	377,330	50.9	49.1
2006	427,250	50.8	49.2

Sources: Data extracted from Table 5.6.

Table 5.4 shows the evolution of the different irrigated areas in the north and south of the country between 1965 and 2006. It highlights that irrigation in the north where rainfall is greater accounts for 68.8% of the total irrigated area. This is a result of the colonial inheritance which invested in the intensification of northern agriculture where rainfall and water resources were more plentiful. Table 5.4 also highlights an intensification of irrigation in the south. This shows specifically that the political choice favoured a groundwater-based irrigation in the south to develop and intensify export oriented agriculture. That became based on early vegetables and fruits (including dates) that could be easily exported to Europe and the Gulf countries.

The irrigated and intensive agriculture in the south benefited from very low labour costs fuelled by poverty and high unemployment. The conditions generated quicker returns than were received in the higher rainfall agriculture in the North of Tunisia. Favourable climate conditions and state incentives for investors provided permanent and secure access to deep underground water since 1990.

We can now begin to understand how the unequal patterns of land holdings and resource access emerged. To do that we need a sense of what the character of colonial transformation looked like and where the patterns of continuity and discontinuity lay with the postcolonial agricultural policy.

Land: Reform and Dispossession from Colonialism to Neoliberalism

Since the beginning of colonisation and until the contemporary period, the evolution of the Tunisian agriculture is marked by profound technical and social transformation. This has been the outcome of policies for modernisation that have had four outcomes. First, aggravation of processes of dispossession and impoverishment of the peasantry, worsening of the unequal access to agricultural resources (land and water) and, consequently, land consolidation in the hands of wealthy owners. Second, a set of technical changes: mechanisation, land registration (cadastre), extension of irrigated areas, big hydraulic projects, agriculture intensification through the use of chemical pesticides and fertilisers. Third, agricultural and food dependence towards the global market, food insecurity of peasant families and social injustice. Fourth, the exhaustion of agricultural natural resources, deterioration of the environment and decline of biodiversity. These four processes are directly and mechanically linked.

There are two important sequences of colonial transformation that should be highlighted. The first are the early years of colonisation from 1881 to 1920. During this first period, local peasants and farmers were dispossessed from their land. The beneficiaries were French and European settlers to which the colonial state gave incentives and facilities to invest in agriculture to create a capitalist and mechanised sector. This was dedicated to establishing the French presence in Tunisia and to provide the French market with agricultural goods. It initiated colonial agricultural capitalism in Tunisia. The second important colonial period was between 1920 and 1930. That involved accelerated mechanisation of colonial agriculture, starting as early as 1930. It was the first to create a new market for French industry especially in the context of the 1936 economic crisis. But this period is also significant for farmer and worker resistance to dispossession. The new landless refused to collaborate with the occupiers and many openly rebelled against French occupation stimulating the first movements for national independence.

Geographically, agricultural colonisation took place in three different regions characterised by specific advantages and potentials that correspond to the objectives set by colonial policy. The first involved the installation of settlers, including the winemakers and the supply of the French market in agricultural products, especially wine, cereals, mostly soft wheat that was not grown in Tunisia, and olive oil. While the lands of the plains of the north-east were 'allocated' to the installation of French winemakers little was consumed in Tunisia. Ninety per cent of the total production was exported. The higher rainfall areas of the north-west, including those of Beja, Mateur, Le Kef, Jendouba and Seliana, were intended for the production of cereals, soft wheat, durum wheat, barley. Wheat was also exported to France. In addition, arboriculture, mainly olives, were developed in the centre and south of the country where rainfall as we have noted is lower than in the northern regions (Sethom 1993, 112).

Although the French colonial power claimed to be colonising settlements,

much of the land was in the hands of large colonial companies and large settlers. For example, before 1981, there were four large colonial companies with 156,000 hectares, almost one-fifth of the colonial land (Sethom 1993, 111).

The grabbing of agricultural land widened during the rest of the colonial period culminating at independence to reach a total area of 800,000 hectares held by 3,750 settlers. That is to say an average of 213 hectares per settler and about 16 per cent of the total agricultural area (Sethom 1993, 110–11).

To facilitate the colonisation and settlement of French and European settlers, the occupying power adopted a law introducing the concept of a cadastre into legislation. The 'Torrens Act' was named after the English colonel Robert Torrens, who instituted the system of real-estate records in Australia in 1858. Now in effect in most countries, the cadastre or land registry at first permitted the dispossession of indigenous populations in the colonies. Even in contemporary Tunisia the registry requirement has the effect of privatising collective tribal or family land. The aims of the 1885 legislation were to establish private property and facilitate the 'privatisation' of collective / indivisible lands, to develop mortgages and land transactions; develop credit instruments; legalise doubtful title deeds previously acquired by Europeans on *melk* lands or private properties (Ayeb 2017, Jouili 2008, 117).

In addition to private land (*melk*), which is actually easy to acquire from the moment it is registered in the land register as required by the 1885 law, the colonial state took an interest in habous[3] land, which was in principle inalienable and indivisible. The habous is a private or public land tenure status that makes the land 'inalienable', indivisible and non-transmissible 'common' property. The process of liquidation of habous land started with colonial legislation in July 1885 and by a decree of May 23, 1886 that transformed habous public land in enzel land (land with perpetual rents) for the benefit of settlers for an unlimited period (Jouili 2008, 116). By a Decree of 13 November 1898, the Jamaïa (local association) was subject to the obligation of making 2,000 hectares per year of habous land available to the State for exclusive colonial use (Jouili 2008, 116).

Dispossessed of its lands and without sufficient resources, a large part of the local peasantry living in the northwest migrated to coastal towns including Tunis in search for wage labour. As Sethom (1979, 119) wrote;

'the destruction of traditional agrarian structures and the sudden eruption of mechanized colonial agriculture inaugurate a rural exodus resulting of colonial control over one of the most fertile regions of the country, the expropriation and the proletarianization of its inhabitants'.

Modern mechanisation of agriculture certainly made it possible to increase yields and boost cereal production. Yet it also considerably accelerated rural exodus that the processes of dispossession had, in large part, initiated or, at least, strongly favoured. Industrial development and mechanisation of colonial agriculture began to create a working class separated mostly from its pre colonial contexts (Hopkins 1983, 47).

1956–64: The Postcolonial State and Early Agrarian Transformation

Tunisia gained independence in 1956. The early years after independence were spent establishing the new State, its different institutions as well as in stabilising the political system that was put in place by the political elite around President Bourguiba[4] to strengthen his domination and engage his political project (Chouikha 2010, Camau 1984). In other words this first short period was devoted to the establishment and the consolidation of the power of the President. His arrival as head of the state gave rise to strong opposition and protest. That was led by his first opponent Salah Ben Youssef[5]. He challenged both the independence agreements signed with France, particularly the clause that kept the port city of Bizerte under occupation, the populist, liberal and pro-Western orientation of Bourguiba and the domination of his friends in the new State institutions. Gradually, Bourguiba silenced the left opposition by the double tactics of oppression and co-optation. Thus, 'the interval 1956–60 appears as an interim period, a brief but necessary parenthesis with regard to what will succeed him, a propaedeutic to action' (Krichen 1987, 273).

Bourguiba not only had to eradicate fundamental opposition, including within his own party, The Socialist Destourian Party, but also had to undo the aim of the General Union for Tunisian Workers (UGTT) to organise a socialist opposition party from scratch. By the end of 1950s, the dangers of opposition had been eliminated and an open party co-opting newly emerging elites was established under the benevolent aegis of the president. 'He placed and replaced his lieutenants at will, for though they might represent different currents of opinion, none had any independent source of power that escaped the control' (Dawisha and Zartman 1988, 81).

One of the first questions faced by the new elite concerned the countryside and the rural populations access to land. In its quest to consolidate his power and marginalise its political opponents, Bourguiba could not ignore the high expectations of the rural poor and those who had been forced to migrate. If expectations were not met it was likely to manifest as discontent against the new government and foster yousséfisme[6]. That which was already largely rooted in the poorest regions of the country, particularly the interior regions. Agriculture was the country's leading economic sector and it was in crisis. The Head of State was soon engaged in a policy of agricultural reforms with three main objectives. The first was to show that the government was attentive to the demands and expectations of agricultural and rural populations to limit social and political vulnerability. The second was to increase the State's agricultural income and finally to foster the development of agricultural capitalism. In this strategy, the issue of agricultural land quickly became the first political and social emergency and conflict and struggles over access to it were a major obstacle to any new policy. At the same time, the political symbolism of the land provided Bourguiba with a unique opportunity to deny accusations of proximity to French interests, or even treason (Bessis and Belhassen, 2012, Belkodja 1998).

One of the first issues the Tunisian postcolonial state had to try and resolve related to colonial land. There were three potentially explosive dimensions to this. The first were how to deal with the legitimate claims of the heirs of the former owners, who had been dispossessed of their lands by colonialism. The second, were the risks that this question posed for maintaining good relations with France to which Bourguiba had committed himself. And finally, the state had to deal with the short-term risks of sudden falls in agricultural production, and the considerable economic consequences posed by a too rapid transfer of colonial lands to Tunisian farmers. 'In 1958 French colonial lands used to produce 42 per cent of cereals, 54 per cent of fruit and vegetable products, 20 per cent of oil, almost 30 per cent of Tunisia's total production' (Hubert 1960, 934).

Before independence, fearing the rise of the struggles for national independence in Algeria and Tunisia, some settlers got rid of the land they cultivated (40,000 ha in total) by selling or renting to Tunisian landowners. This benefitted and supported the agrarian capitalism of the large Tunisian landowners, particularly in the cereal growing regions in the north west of the country (Elloumi 2013, 6; Makhlouf 1966). In 1957, the colonial lands still covered an area of 785,000 ha, including 600,000 hectares of direct use and 115,000 hectares leased to Tunisians, or about 10 per cent of the Tunisian arable area, which extended over 7.45 million hectares. French farmers in Tunisia (owners, tenants and sharecroppers) numbered 2,200 in 1957, among which 1,800 were owners (Hubert 1960, 934). According to Poncet (1976, 52), in 1961–62 there were still a total of 3,000 European settlers cultivating between 500,000 and 600,000 hectares.

To recover settler land the Tunisian government begun a difficult round of negotiations with the French state. On May 8, 1957, the two governments signed an agreement for the return of the colonial lands located near the borders with Algeria if compensation was paid to the settlers. More than two hundred properties covering a total of 127,000 hectares were transferred to the Tunisian government (Elloumi 2013, 7). A few years later, France rejected the Tunisian authorities demand to resume negotiations for the transfer of the rest of the colonial lands. To show its displeasure Paris unilaterally suspended financial aid to Tunis. In response, Tunis issued the law of May 12, 1964, which nationalised all the farmland held by foreigners. By this law, 300,000 hectares passed into the domain of the Tunisian state (Elloumi 2013; Hubert 1960, 952).

The Tunisian government had made the risky political decision not to return the land to the legitimate heirs of the former owners, depriving them of their pre colonial rights. By doing so the state denied farmers access to land needed to improve their production conditions and their incomes. Consequently, the nationalisation of the colonial land had no real impact on the structure of land ownership and access. Nationalisation meant only a transfer of property to big landowners and the public or cooperative sector (Poncet 1976, 52). The transfer of nationalised lands to the state made it the largest owner of agricultural land which continues to the contemporary period. However, a part of these colonial lands were 'sold' or generously 'given' to private owners, often members of the Destour ruling party, companions of Bourguiba during and after the fight for independence and other political clientele. Many of these were absentee owners not working the land directly but managing it in a form of tenancy or 'sharecropping' (Gachet 1987)).

State officials had a large appetite for land. In addition to the old colonial lands, the state grabbed the habous lands which constituted a kind of common good, at least of community goods by abolishing private and mixed habous status and the annexation of whole public habous lands to the domain of the State. About 180,000 hectares of public habous were transferred to the state and re-attributed, by a new law, issued in 1974, to the *enzel* (fixed perpetual annuity) or *kirdar* (perpetual annuity with variable rate) (Elloumi 2006a, 4).

1960–70: Collectivising the Private and Privatising the Collective: The Dramatic Phase of Collectivisation

During the 1960s, the Tunisian peasantry was subjected to a policy of massive dispossession of their lands. The new Minister of Planning and Finance, Ahmad Ben Sala,[7] wanted to recover the small farmers' land to constitute large Cooperative Production Units, directly managed by state officials. Their main objective was to accelerate the mechanisation and modernisation of the agricultural sector and to facilitate the transfer of agricultural capital to other sectors of the economy, especially industry, considered as the strategic engine and the condition of overall economic development.

Contested by wealthy owners, Ben Salah found in Bourguiba, at least initially, a supporter and defender who publicly advanced his political line endorsing his 'socialist' reform plans for the collectivisation of the entire national economy. Accordingly, the president declared in June 1961: 'I am personally responsible for the [collectivization] plan I cover with my authority. From now on, the plan will be the work program of the party' (Belkhodja 1998, 55). In June 1963, during a speech delivered in Sfax, Bourguiba repeated his full political support by criticising the opposition: 'to those who defend individual freedom, private sector and free enterprise, we say that the plan serves everyone's interest. In our situation, only collective action is efficient' (Belkhodja 1998, 57).

In 1961, the Secretariat of Ministry of Planning and Finance adopted and published a policy report entitled 'The Decade Perspectives for Development 1962–1971', based on the Economic and Social Report of the UGTT (1956). In it, Ahmed Ben Salah specified the global direction of his project: 'Tunisian planning is socialist' and its objective: 'the promotion of man, the defence of his concrete freedoms: in a word the humanization of society'. This first document of economic orientation, endorsed by Bourguiba's party, announced the political decision to carry out a broad reform of land and agrarian structures and the creation of agricultural cooperatives (Cooperative Units for Agricultural Productions (UCPA)). The document presented the general framework and the philosophy. It also set the objectives and the method as to how they would be delivered. The different stages of execution were to be detailed and specified by roadmaps at every step. The three-year plan (1962–64) and the five-year plan, drawn up in 1964, were the first concrete translation of the collectivisation policy. 'This is a turning point in the emergence and extension of the power of planners. Allied to the new generation of technical and bureaucratic staff [...], they will engage resolutely in the cooperative way' (Gachet 1987, 159).

Legislation in May 1963 stipulated the establishment of the system of cooperatives and the creation of UCPA, binding on all agricultural producers to 'modernize agriculture and at the same time to achieve the objectives inherent in the education of the people [sic] and social progress' (Ben Salah 2008, 130). The law specified that the 'cooperatives are imposed on all owners of land inside the UCPA area, each land owner that is not able to be a member of the cooperative shall either sell or lease his piece of land to the society (UCPA)' (Le Coz 1975, 55).

Ben Salah[8] defended his policies by noting, 'Agriculture used to contribute with the biggest share to the national GDP, since it accounted for almost 32 per cent, and used to provide, so poorly, 70 per cent of the population on the eve of the 1960s' (Ben Salah 2008, 55). He evoked the problem of agricultural land fragmentation ranking it as the number one cause of the sector's crisis and something we pursue later in the chapter.

Land fragmentation is the bitter result of the escape/migration of the small farmers to the cities after they sold land pieces that could not feed them anymore. It is the fruit of the inheritance laws which heavily contributed to the deterioration of agriculture (Ben Salah 2008, 110).

He continued,

It was necessary to 'abolish borders' and build viable spaces at the socio-economic and technical levels. These viable spaces varied in areas with the nature of agricultural speculations. It is thanks to these spaces, we think, that the important investments in the agricultural field could be profitable from the socio-economic point of view. Thus modernization, credit could become necessary and impose itself for the benefit of development and growth (Ben Salah 2008, 119)

Tens of thousands of small and medium-sized peasants were forced to integrate into cooperatives, dispossessed of their land and their means of production to become poorly paid agricultural labourers. In January 1969, there were 1,500 basic cooperative units, comprising about 370,000 'cooperatives' (including all economic sectors), including some 700 agricultural cooperatives covering 600,000 hectares. A third of the total area was accounted for by the contribution of 37,500 small farmers who had less than 6 hectares per family. The rest, about 380,000 hectares, came from State lands. The contribution of the big landowners was almost nil (Poncet 1970).

The obligation of small farmers to integrate into cooperatives was experienced by them as a form of spoliation and dispossession, all the more so as it rapidly resulted in a process of widespread impoverishment of all the co-operators. Their conditions were reported by several observers of the time, including the French agronomist Rene Dumont who wrote about the co-operators:

They were not treated as true co-operators, as real 'co-owners' of their enterprises, but rather as employees with very low pay, invited to obey, to follow without discussing the prescriptions of the authorities. But those who had been hired by settler farms soon realized that they had been earning less, and sometimes much less, since their recent 'promotion' (1971, 124).

Detailing the incomes of former peasants who had become co-operators without having solicited it, Dumont pointed out that the daily wage available per dependent would have been between 10 and 57 millimes;[9] in 50 per cent of cases, it was 25 millimes (i.e. the value of 340 grams of bread per day). 'We are abruptly reduced to the level of the poorest rural strata of India'. Nevertheless, in 1969, the Congress of the *National Union of Cooperatives* recommended the 'maintenance, reinforcement and extension' of the cooperative system [...] qualified as 'the only guarantee for the promotion of a balanced, and homogeneous society protected from class struggles' (Poncet 1970, 101). This declaration showed another aspect of the objectives of the forced 'cooperativisation'. First, the reinforcement of the domination of big land owners and their technical, political, financial and administrative allies and second the accelerated processes of dispossession of the peasantry.

After the fall of Ben Salah in 1969 and the announcement of the end of the cooperative system, a circular from the prime minister (2 September 1969) gave freedom to the cooperators to leave their cooperative with the land that they had brought to the cooperative as members. 'Consequently, most of forced co-operators left their cooperatives with their piece of land. Only former workers with settlers or holders of a plot, that was insufficient for their livelihood, remained' (Le Coz 1975, 56). Within a year, between 1969 and 1970, around 19,619 cooperators quit the UPCAs with less than 175,000 hectares (an average of 8.92 ha per quitting cooperator) (Le Coz 1975, 56).

Numerous small farmers, who became members of the cooperatives years earlier, had at that time, already sold their tools and animals (milking animals, cattle, plough, water pumps). Impoverished, they could not reinstate their old farms. Thus, when the lands were reprivatised, they did not have the means to afford buying new equipment, agricultural inputs, seeds, fertilisers, phytosanitary products and other inputs and assets. Taking loans from big landowners of the surrounding lands was then almost the only possible option, which many peasants took. But their situation gradually worsened through accumulation of debt that they could not pay. The road towards a progressive expropriation boosted indebtedness. Peasants were compelled, in the short or medium run, to sell their lands, to end up as *Khamméssa*[10] or workers in their own land, or they migrated to the big urban centres especially Tunis. The rural exodus and the 'migratory flows started to grow during the years 1965–1969' (Ruf 1975, 353; Gachet 1987). At the same time, the areas of big landowners increased. Big landowners had never been challenged by collectivisation as it had only been obligatory for small peasants. However, they now increased their efforts to extend their hold on agricultural lands and their influence on the decision-making in the state. The neo-liberal period that began in 1970 increases the room and opportunity for accumulation of wealth, especially land and the power that followed from it.

Table 5.5 highlights a number of shortcomings of the 1960s collectivist experience.

Table 5.5 Comparison of Tunisia's Planned and Achieved Agriculture Performance, 1971

Item	1961 Target for 1971	Achieved 1971	Per cent Achievement
	million dinars (1966 price and cost levels) Per cent		
Gross product	259.8	148.2	57
Value added	141	103.5	73
Intermediate consumption	118.8	44.7	38
Exports	27	24.6	91
Imports	17	48.4	285
Gross investment	59.6	21.7	36

Source: Daves and Warsch (1976, 40).

Economic liberalisation, was implemented in two distinct periods. The first, 1969–80 was a period of 'directed' capitalism, during which the state remained the first actor and unique planner. And a second period, inaugurated in 1980 and furthered by successive governments, which was marked by a declared period of state disengagement. At that time the state was used to accelerate economic reforms towards a progressively aggressive uncontrolled neo-liberalism. That period marked the use of the state to promote the interests of the leading politicians, their clients and power brokers in Tunis and in rural Tunisia.

Contrary to what the politicians suggested, this vague neo-liberal expression of 'state disengagement' concealed a radical change in its role. It was to more aggressively favour the economic interests of the dominant classes and elites. On the one hand, the state abandoned its social role in favour of the most disadvantaged strata and classes. On the other hand, the state mobilised all its means, especially financial, to serve the dominant economic and political groups. In agriculture this meant the end of support and subsidies for small farmers and peasant agriculture and the financial, fiscal and political support for agribusiness and capitalist agriculture oriented towards export.

Dispossession and Collective Lands

The counter-revolution to the postcolonial agricultural policies of Ahmed Ben Salah began in 1969. Until then he had tried to reorganise agriculture in a collectivist system based on the cooperative structures we have noted. The experience of collectivisation called the 'socialist experience', in Tunisia, was dramatic for small holders. A large number of farmers had been simply dispossessed of their agricultural resources in less than a decade. Yet while the contemporary agricultural crisis might be traced to the heavy handedness of those enforced reforms, the emergent neo-liberal period was to accelerate dispossession. The cooperatives had failed in large part because of

the absence of an efficient and representative organization of the peasants and favoured the domination over them. This is how the modernization of agriculture was conceived independently from the interests of peasants. This modernization, of the 'top down' type, is illustrated by the cooperative experience of the 1960s, which was simply improvised and imposed on the rural world (Bachta 2011, 7).

The top down strategy was entrenched further with the end of cooperatisation policy in 1969. The dismissal of Ahmed Ben Salah resulted from among other things an alliance of big landowners and the more liberal rightist leaning group of the ruling party. They mobilised around a free market ideology and the process of dispossession and accumulation of capital for large owners was accelerated despite rhetoric to promote policy to assist food producers more generally.

In the early 1970s, Tunisia experienced a fairly radical change in its overall economic policy. There was a switch from an attempt at state capitalism, which at its core had the system of cooperatives, to a controlled liberalisation, an attempt at a more expansive capitalism that paved the way for a long process of liberalisation from the mid-1980s. The regime relinquished part of its 'legacy' by selling or leasing large areas of its agricultural land. In 1974, the minister of agriculture announced that the state will limit its domain to a total of 330,000 hectares and that they will accelerate the procedures of liquidation and of privatisation of collective lands (tribal land). This was to reactivate the land market and reinforce the private sector of medium and big farmers (Gachet 1987, 163).

An important dimension to Tunisia's neo-liberal transformation was a 'land reform', often overlooked, that redefined the modes and conditions of access to agricultural collective land, coveted by the large owners. It did so by accelerating its privatisation. This reform introduced by Law 88, 5 of 8 February 1988, modified that of 28 September 1957. The legislation opened the door and removed the barriers that at least partially protected collective land from private appropriation. Prior to this legislation communities could farm collective land with the possibility of appropriating, individually land not intended for pasture and get the necessary funding for its development. The state now opened these protected areas to commodification, the land market and gains to agribusiness and the export sector (Jouili 2008, 238). The many irrigation schemes that flourish in the steppe lands of south and west are further evidence of these processes and their direct consequences.

From Bread Riots to Structural Adjustment and the Construction of Food Dependence

Bread Riots, January 1984

From the beginning of the 1980s, the government embarked on accelerating policies to liberalise the agricultural sector and the Tunisian economy as a whole. This was done to reduce the budget deficit and to increase the state's tax revenues. The latter had suffered, since the early 1980s after the decline in oil revenues and the rising price of imported food products (Bachta 2011, 11). An early aspect of reform was the liberalisation in 1983 of consumer prices for food products such as cereals, couscous, bread, pasta, which formed the basis for household food consumption. This led to a near doubling of prices and it led to widespread popular discontent. Protests erupted in the urban areas December 27, 1983 and January 6, 1984.

In the summer of 1983, the IMF and the World Bank approved the removal of food subsidies under the 'Economic Stabilisation Programme', which included other price liberalisation measures (Seddon 1986, 1). When the government introduced its measures in December 1983, prices immediately rose to spectacular levels: 'The price of the 700-gram flat loaf that is the basic staple for most poor people was raised from 80 millimes to 170 millimes. In the far south of Tunisia, it was the increase in the price of semolina (used for couscous) that created the main impact. As a resident of the South noted, 'A sack of 50 kilos of semolina went from 7.2 dinars to 13.5 and a kilo of flour from 120 millimes to 295' (Seddon 1986, 14). Demonstrations and protest at the high food prices spread throughout Tunisia. The confrontations led to 60 deaths and more than 100 injured. A state of emergency and a curfew were declared on January 3rd 1984. Public gatherings of more than three people were forbidden. But the demonstrations and street violence continued; on January 4th there were numerous clashes, and on January 5th the army and police fired on 'rioters' in Tunis, moving into the old medina to dislodge snipers. On the morning of January 6th, President Bourghiba appeared on television to rescind the price increases and promise the restoration of food subsidies (Seddon 1986, 1; Daoud 2011; Bachta 2011).

Structural Adjustment

Despite the deaths and violence resulting from an attempt to increase food prices the IFIs stepped up the pressure on the Tunisian government to accelerate market liberalisation (Murphy 1999, Hammouda 1995). The government conceded to the required reforms through a Structural Adjustment Programme, signed in 1986 with the IFIs. That included the rapid liberalisation of all markets, the devaluation of the Tunisian dinar and the reduction of various subsidies with the aim of definitively eliminating them in the medium term (Bachta 2011, 11). The agricultural sector was subject to a specific treatment through the specially designed 'Programme of Agricultural Structural Adjustment' (ASAP) (Jouili 2008, 175). One of the central objectives of ASAP was to re-launch agricultural production to re-equilibrate the agricultural trade balance, limit the increases in labour costs, stimulate private investment and increase the share of agricultural investment in relation to overall investment (Jouili 2008, 188; Boughanmi 1995, 128).

To deliver this programme the state opted for radical measures including the reduction of agricultural subsidies, the privatisation of state farms, the liberalisation of the agricultural market, the reorganisation of agricultural credit and the privatisation of food marketing networks. These policies were to boost large and absentee landowners as

the elimination of subsidies [has] affected the credit sector with the abolition of subsidized rates for agriculture and the introduction of investment subsidies, for irrigation water-saving equipment and finally for water and soil conservation works (Elloumi 2006b, 145–46).

In 1991 the 'state-owned' land reclamation programme was launched intended to consolidate agribusiness units that did not require additional support; the confirmation of Cooperative Production Units that have executed development projects and are managed in good conditions and the restructuring of state farms (UCP, agro-industrial complexes, etc.) that require investments or that have not achieved satisfactory results. These farms were to be identified and erected into companies of land reclamation and agricultural Development (SMVDA) or batched and assigned to technicians and young farmers. Finally the state sought to transfer small state parcels of land to former farmers, technicians or young farmers for a rental renewable period of 25 years (Jouili 2008, 240–241).

The ASAP in Tunisia limited the intervention of the state in economic activities including at the level of support and commercial policy. Cereal producer prices (durum wheat, soft wheat, barley) rose above international prices after 1986. Fertiliser, livestock, seed and herbicide prices were aligned with international prices through the phasing out of subsidies. Since 1992, subsidies for super 16, urea, corn and soybean meal were abolished. There was liberalisation of imports of milk powder, beef, corn and seed oils, as well as a partial liberalisation of domestic barley production, despite the application of an intervention price by the collection and storage agencies for the purpose of the acquisition. Other measures taken under the ASAP included the reduction in the average rate of agricultural tariffs, from 32 per cent in 1987 to 18.5 per cent in 1989 (Ghazi and Khediri 2001, 93).

Tunisia also opted for a policy of economic openness (*infitah*) to the outside world. It joined the General Agreement on Tariffs and Trade (GATT) negotiations, in 1986–94, and also signed a partnership agreement with the European Union in 1995, on the creation of a free trade area that excluded agricultural products (Ghazi and Khediri 2001, 93).

The (uneven) integration of postcolonial Tunisia in the global economy was promoted over two time periods in parallel with the evolution of the global food system (McMichael, 2009). The first period lasted until the mid-1980s, dominated by state planning and dirigisme exercising the dual function of 'public investor' and 'supervisor' of private investment. It was the period of directed capitalism. During this period, agricultural policy was conducted with the aim of achieving 'food self-sufficiency' and reducing food imports. The second period of economic liberalisation from the mid-1980s was marked by the transfer of the role of the state to the private sector and the shift towards the goal of 'food security'. This was through the development of a specialised agriculture and export orientation based on the principle of 'comparative advantage'. This period corresponded to what Friedmann and McMichael (1989) characterised as the third global food regime (see chapter one and Gana 2012c, 205).

From Food Self-Sufficiency to Food Security: A Paradigm Shift

As we explored in Chapter 5 the new liberal economic policy confirmed the paradigm shift from the discourse of 'food self-sufficiency' to 'food security'. This shift was based on the reorientation of agricultural, economic and 'natural' resources to the benefit of investment agribusiness agriculture. It promoted the interests of those who benefitted from that state investment in irrigation to the detriment of family farming. The political lexicon concerning the objectives of agricultural policy changed dramatically from the end of the 1980s. Far from being a simple play on words (jeux de mots) or a political slogan, this lexical change heralded a *gestalt* marked by a political change on a large scale. Tunisian agricultural strategy became no longer a focus on producing more to feed more who were hungry, and disadvantaged in either the countryside or the town. It was instead a strategy to produce more to export. This change in food strategy materialised 'ideologically' by the migration from food self-sufficiency to food security and was registered in the official government documents and specifically in the five-year plans. Thus, in the fifth development plan (1977–81), 'the objective assigned to the agriculture and fishing sector is to reach, on the horizon of 1981, food self-sufficiency materialized through the equilibrium of the trade balance of food products'. The Sixth (1982–87) and the Seventh Plans (1987–92) placed agricultural policy and in particular the cereals sector in the new objective of food security; 'The performances of the cereals sector cannot go unnoticed knowing the importance of this sector to food security as well as that of the trade balance of the country'. The Eighth Plan (1992–96) affirmed the position that 'agriculture has the role to contribute to reaching the foreign balance, the balance of public finance, the balance in employment and the regional balance as well. [...] Achieving food security would consist of assuring to the country the quality food, in sufficient quantities and without interruption, by an optimal combination between national production, import and export. The optimum will show through the sustainable equilibrium of the food trade balance, or even the realisation of a surplus to contribute to the recovery of the global economic balance' (Khaldi and Naïli 1995, 95).

The state radically changed the paradigm with these new policies. It promoted a shift in its development policies. This was to involve among other things, 'production at the lowest labour cost in order to maintain the only comparative advantage of which Tunisia disposes and which is the low cost of its labour' (Gachet 1987, 163). The first consequences of ASAP was probably the best evidence of this turning point. While exports of agricultural products, mainly early vegetables (fruits and vegetables, off-season), and fishery products increased, imports of commodities, especially cereals (55 per cent of requirements) and livestock feed (100 per cent of poultry feed and 40 per cent of livestock feed) were growing even faster, leading to a worsening of overall budgetary expenditure 'particularly since the 2008 shrinking capacity of the state to subsidize commodities' (Gana 2012b, 205).

The ASAP led to the removal of agricultural support (subsidy reduction and public investment, reduction of transfers to the rural sectors), stagnation in output prices, and increases in input prices. Consequently, this situation reduced the use of certain inputs, caused stagnation and often decline in the yields of certain crops and in animal production. Ultimately, natural resources declined under relentless pressure, and led to their rapid degradation. The degradation of rural households, particularly farmers and farm workers, seem to be the result of the degradation of exchange terms for agricultural products and a decrease in investment in the agricultural sector. These patterns partially explained the decline of the productivity (Elloumi and Dhehibi 2012, 3; Gachet 1987, 161).

Agriculture and 'Development'

The Tunisian agricultural sector has been in decline for many years increasing the country's food dependency. Deeply de-developed since the colonial era and heavily penalised by neo-liberal policy since the 1970s, agriculture has been undermined in relation to other economic sectors. As we noted in Chapter 4, agricultures participation in GDP is low. It did not exceed 9 per cent in 2016, compared with 20 per cent in 1960 and 14 per cent in the 1990s. It has steadily declined in favour of other economic sectors such as services (50 per cent), industry (19 per cent) and particularly growth in the informal sector (38.4 per cent) in 2010 (Gana 2012a, 2–3; Elloumi 2006a, 11).

According to the World Bank (2018)[11], the participation of Tunisian agriculture in GDP fell from 20.8 per cent in 1965 (at the beginning of collectivisation) to 17.03 per cent in 1970 (at the end of collectivisation) before continuing in mostly decline to 14.13 per cent in 1980, 15.72 per cent in 1990, 10.01 per cent in 2000, 7.54 per cent in 2010, 10.20 in 2015 and 9.2 per cent in 2016.

In 2012, 17.3 per cent of the active population was employed in the primary sector (agriculture and fishing) against almost half (49.6 per cent) in the service sector, and 33.1 per cent in industry (manufacturing and non-manufacturing) (ONEQ, 2013, 22). However, the proportion of agricultural employment relative to total employment has steadily declined since the mid-1970s. It went from 37.24 per cent in 1975 to 33.36 per cent in 1980, 17.57 per cent in 2010 and 15.3 per cent in 2013 (World Bank 2018). In parallel, the decrease of the share of agriculture in total government spending, has been spectacular; from 20 per cent to 5 per cent in 30 years (Santos and Ceccacci 2015, 35).

Pluriactivity

Within the context of changes to the composition and transformation of the agricultural labour force, two important issues emerged, and they are evident in our Egyptian case study too. The first is pluriactivity which we referred to in Chapter 1. Pluriactivity in agriculture can be defined by generating additional out-of-farm income by a household member as long as the main income continues to come from on-farm labour activity. This concept of pluriactivity, widely discussed in the academic literature, covers both part-time farming and diversification (Loughrey et al. 2013; Evans and Llbery, 1993). In Tunisia, the pluriactivity affects a large number of small producers but also some with larger farms. According to the results of the survey on farm structures 2004–5, (quoted by Marzin et al. 2017, 49), pluriactivity was practiced by 48.6 per cent of all agricultural producers with a significant difference between farmers with less than 5 hectares (55.4 per cent) and farmers with more than 100 hectares (21.4 per cent only). If for the first group, pluriactivity is an opportunity of coping with poverty, for the second group, it is a question of the diversification of the investments and the multiplication of the sources of income or profits. 'Similarly, the pluriactivity of farmers tends to increase from North (31.3 per cent) to the Centre (56 per cent) and South (58.4 per cent) of the country and is more common in dry rather than in irrigated farms' (Marzin et al. 2017, 10).

The pluriactivity of the small and medium farmers and the increasingly visible 'feminisation' of labour follow the same rationale and respond to the same processes of impoverishment and marginalisation of peasantry. When small farmers are threatened by dispossession they develop strategies of survival and resistance and try to secure land access and struggle to promote or retain their autonomy. Pluriactivity is one the first responses. Adults, and particularly men – whose mobility is socially easier – seek income earning opportunity that can be far from home and outside the agricultural sector. To compensate for the lack of male labour, women replace them raising their labour time and farm labour to fulfil everyday tasks in the absence of their husbands and adult sons.

Women's Labour

This leads to the second important theme that has emerged: the so-called feminisation of labour. Poorer female farmers may also sell their labour power to other, often larger farmers as day-workers especially in high production seasons. The women get paid a per-diem rate that corresponds to almost half of what men get per day. Thus, we see more and more frequently male peasants in construction sites or in other activity sectors and women peasants on their own land or working for other big landowners.

Feminisation of agricultural work is common throughout the Global South where small peasants cannot sustain themselves only through farming their own land. However, women have always been in one way or another, present in agricultural work (Ayeb and Saad 2013). We are therefore not witnessing a feminisation of agricultural work, but rather its increased visibility. Women have always undertaken activities that are crucial to the functioning of the farm, and household, although mostly in close surrounding spaces around the house. It is also clear that women hold land in their own right. In Tunisia, while they hold only 4 per cent of the total agricultural land, the number of peasant women have increased from 26,000 in 1994–95 to 32,980 in 2004–5, showing an aggregate increase of almost 25 per cent for the whole period (MARH 2006).

Another aspect is the wage labour of rural women, which reveals the dynamics of agricultural investments and of its corollary of the shrinking of family agriculture and the necessity for women to find new sources of revenue. For the poor farmer families who did not opt for migration to big cities, the waged labour with big absentee farmers, is the most practical and suitable regarding their farming knowledge. Women's agricultural activity is not recent, therefore but their paid work outside of the family farm is now more common. There has been an increase in the number and formal counting of women's participation in the total agricultural labour force. There also seems to be a preference of employers to hire women workers, supposedly more compliant and flexible and perhaps less demanding in terms of salary and social rights than men. As one large-scale farmer reported to us, 'Rural day-working women do not contest orders, do not form unions, do not organize strikes [...] and they do not count working hours'. This farmer had developed a large irrigated area in Gabes, South-East Tunisia employing a large number of seasonal workers. There is a 'feminisation' of waged agricultural labour and this has been one of the outcomes of, dispossession and impoverishment of Tunisia's small-scale peasantry.

The number of permanent female agricultural workers is estimated at 4,400 (which is 8.3 per cent of the total permanent agricultural work force) in 2004–5, among which 43 per cent are located in the North, 27 per cent in the centre and 30 per cent in the South. However, this is a gross under-estimation of the reality of women engaged as day workers in agriculture, as seasonal workers, or permanent but seldom declared workers. They generally receive meagre salaries, their working conditions are particularly tedious and are often subjected to different harassments, including demands for sex. As one women noted to us in a small village near the city of Jendouba in 2017, 'if I do not give him the quarter of an hour he demands, he will not hire me and will replace me with another woman, whom he will submit to the same harassment', On an indicative basis, in 2016, a woman worker earned around 8 Tunisian dinars (dt) per day while men could receive 14 dt per day.

Agriculture in Crisis

The decline in agricultural sector participation in GDP and employment is accompanied by a reduction in its contribution to agricultural exports. These were 14.65 per cent over the period 1997–2002 and 11.95 per cent in 2004 before recording a significant increase from 2005 with 14.63 per cent (Bachta 2008, 77).

The production and availability of cereals in Tunisia, especially wheat, is of extremely high strategic importance. Yet as we can see from Table 5.6 cereals production increased only very marginally while fruits and vegetables have increased significantly.

After a period of relative stability, import prices for agricultural commodities have increased dramatically. Between 2005 and the beginning of 2008, import prices were multiplied by 3.69 for durum wheat, 2.56 for soft wheat

Table 5.6 Export Growth Rate by Sector, Tunisia

Exports of Goods and Services	10th Plan (2002/6)	11th Plan (2007/11)	12th Plan (2012/16)
Agriculture and agri-food	12.7	9.0	10.2
Machinery and electricity	13.5	12.2	13.1
Textile and leather	3.1	4.4	5.4
Services	1.0	7.4	8.7
All goods and services	5.8	8.1	9.3

Source: Bachta (2008, 77).

Table 5.7 Agricultural Production, Tunisia 2000–2016 (in 000 tons)

	2000	2005	2010	2015	2016
Cereals (Total)	1,122	2,135	1,114	1,340	1,324
Wheat	842	1,627	822	913	927
Barley	242	465	237	364	328
Fruit	1,380	1,590	1,704	2,040	2,031
Oil crops, oil equivalent	129	238	198		
Pulses (Total)	57	78	83	81	107
Roots and tubers	290	310	370	400	440
Vegetables	1,710	1,825	2,542	3,123	3,004

Source: FAOSTAT, June 2018.

and 2.4 for barley (Table 5.7). Vegetable oils, which are entirely imported, rose in cost from 944 dinars per tonne in 2005 to 1200 dinars in 2007, an increase of around 27 per cent (Akari and Jouili 2010, 4). In terms of value, cereal imports almost tripled, rising from 599 MD (million dinars) in 2006 to 1438 MD in 2008. Those of vegetable oils almost doubled from 286 MD in 2006 to 560 MD in 2008. Thus, from an annual average of 1011MD in 2001–5, Tunisia's food imports increased to 1321 MD in 2006 and 2600MD in 2008. Over the period 2006–8, cereals and vegetable oils represented on average nearly 70 per cent of the value of food imports (Akari and Jouili 2010, 4–5).

Over the next ten years (Horizon 2020), projections suggest a significant increase in Tunisian food demand: + 27 per cent for cereals, + 34 per cent for oils, + 47 per cent for fruits and vegetables, + 47 per cent for milk and by-products, and + 59 per cent for red meats (Ben Said et al. 2011, 38). The coverage rate of agri-food imports by exports is over 80 per cent in the 2000s (Ben Said et al. 2011, 37–38) (Table 5.8).

Table 5.8 Foreign Trade in Agri-Food Products, Tunisia, 1990, 1995, 2000, 2005 (in percentage)

	1990	1995	2000	2005
Importations	100	100	100	100
Cereals	41.2	48.9	48.9	43.4
Sugar	16.5	8.3	9.5	10.9
Vegetable oil	12.4	13.5	13.3	22.4
Others	29.9	29.3	28.3	23.3
Exportations	100	100	100	100
Sea products	31.8	16.0	19.1	16.5
Dates	14.1	12.6	8.4	10.6
Olive oil	33.6	46.9	42.0	38.9
Others	20.5	24.5	30.5	34.0

Source: Bachta (2008, 77).

Exports were considered by the Eleventh Plan (2007–11) to be an engine of growth for the agricultural sector and as its main economic contribution to the national development effort. This objective of increasing agricultural exports was to be achieved by diversification of agricultural products and outlets and specialisation in products for which the comparative advantage of the country was evident. Export promotion was also to be achieved by upgrading farms by helping them acquire an 'export culture', that is, knowing export markets to better meet their requirements. These efforts aim to shift agricultural exports from 22 per cent of total goods exports, a performance recorded during the Tenth Plan (2002–6), to 33 per cent of this total during the Eleventh Plan (Bachta 2008, 84–85).

Several devaluations of the national currency have been made since economic adjustment. The policy intent was to boost exports. Moreover, and in accordance with the principle of a free market, the programme recommended the eventual elimination of any price support provided by the public authorities. To this end, a process of progressive liberalisation of all markets was initiated (Bachta 2011, 11).

These changes are the result of agricultural and food policies implemented since independence. In the first phase (from independence until the mid-1980s) policy had a declared goal of food self-sufficiency through important support measures for production combined with a significant subsidy of food prices (Table 5.9). Then, with structural adjustment and economic reform, policy focus shifted to the objective of food security, giving market mechanisms a growing role in meeting national food need (Ben Said et al. 2011, 37–38).

Table 5.9 Distribution of Subsidy Benefits by Class of Population (Poor/Non-Poor) (Tunisia)

Foodstuffs	Poor	Non-Poor
Semolina	14.5	85.5
Couscous	14.2	85.8
Pasta	12.1	87.9
Flour	8	92
Big bread	11.7	88.3
Baguette (French bread)	2.2	97.8
Industrial tomato	10.3	89.7
Milk	6	94
Sugar	11.6	88.4
Vegetable oil	12.9	87.1
Share of subsidies received by year	12	88

Source: Ben Nasr (2016, 5).

Conclusion

This chapter has explored the main trends that have impacted small farmers in Tunisia. It has done so by examining the ways in which agricultural policy in general and policy in relation to land in particular has undermined family farmers and farming. Under the guise of agricultural modernisation, first the colonial regime and then repeated postcolonial governments have accelerated patterns of rural social differentiation marked by extreme inequality in land holding, access to farming inputs and to markets to ensure a sustainable and effective rural standard of living.

We have traced how successive agricultural policy sought to privatise land by enclosing it and favouring through policy incentives to large-scale owners and absentee landlords. There was a memorable and important interlude of attempted collectivisation between 1960 and 1970 but this period, like the one that preceded it, and that followed, was clear in one thing: farmers did not have a voice to be considered, instead they were to be marshalled in the interests of urban elites and especially export-led growth of ostensibly high value commodities for European dinner tables.

We have noted how the characterisations of Tunisia's agricultural 'problems' was always made from interests that lay outside the countryside and one of the themes that has been a continuous feature of agricultural policymakers, not only in Tunisia but Egypt too, has been concerns with overpopulation and fragmentation of land holdings. For ideological reasons and for the self-serving interests of large-scale farmers this rhetoric has been repeatedly used to justify farmer marginalisation. Of course, land fragmentation is not solely a Tunisian phenomenon. It relates to factors like inheritance laws, collectivisation and consolidation processes, plot size and the shape of plots as well as how farm holdings relate to market access (Latruffe and Piet 2013; Ciaian et al. 2018). Land fragmentation was a justification for collectivisation in Tunisia as it was seen to be the reason why farmers left their land and migrated to the towns (Ben Salah 2008, 110). The debate about land fragmentation has continued (Boughanmi 1995,130; Gana 2012a, 2–3; Zaafouri 2010,6) and as we have noted the response to it was first a forced collectivisation and second neoliberal marketisation of land. We would argue, in contrast, that while fragmentation does indeed pose real issues of concern for planners, the bigger issue that needs to be addressed is the inequality in land holdings and the concentration of land holding for the benefit of large owners that we have detailed.

We will pursue some of these themes in the concluding chapter on food sovereignty in Egypt and Tunisia. We will see that there have been attempts, albeit very uneven and partial, to try and promote an alternative to both forced collectivisation and the hegemony of the market. In doing this, we will see that the attempts to promote an alternative rural development strategy, to engage with agroecological debate and small farmers taking control of their agricultural futures is linked to the view that land fragmentation may be an asset, and that land fragmentation cannot simply be linked to negative consequences (Latruffe and Piet, 2013; Ciaian et al. 2018). There may be positive correlations between land fragmentation and biodiversity on the one hand and food security on the other.

Notes

1   In Tunisia, there are no agricultural censuses. The only statistical sources for agriculture come from Surveys on the Structures of Agricultural Farms. All the figures mentioned in the following paragraphs come from these surveys.

2   MARH. 1962, 1995, 2005. 'Study on the structures of agricultural farms 1961/62 1994/95 et 2004/05'.

3   Dating from the beginning of Islam, and probably even older, the habous is well known throughout the Maghreb and elsewhere in the Middle East. As stated by Khalfoune (2005: 441–42) 'Habous is the legal act or the real property or realty, or from the State or private, it is a charitable or public interest organization. Often, the incomes of the habous lands financed the religious and social activities undertaken by the Djemaïa ("association") of the Habous. In addition to mosques, some hospitals and religious schools were funded by the same revenues' (Poortman et al. 2006, 63).

4   Habib Bourguiba (1903–2000), first president of the Tunisian Republic (1957–1987). A lawyer trained in France, a prominent politician, Bourguiba is one of the historic leaders of the struggle for national independence, which was officially proclaimed on

March 20, 1956 after long decades of political and armed struggle. Bearer of a liberal and 'modernist' political project, copied from the French political system, Bourguiba used to give, as examples to follow, Kamal Ataturk, founder of modern Turkey, and Mohamed Ali, the founder of the Modern Egypt. At the time of independence, which he had negotiated with the colonial state, he was violently confronted with other political leaders (Chouikha, 2010; Camau, 1984).

5   Salah Ben Youssef, another leader of the national movement and bearer of a project more 'socialist' and Arab nationalist and close to both Nasser in Egypt and the Algerian national liberation movement. He is assassinated by two men hired and mandated by Bourguiba in 1961 (Chouikha, 2010; Camau, 1984).

6   Yousséfisme is not a doctrine or a political party, in the true sense of the word. It is about a political movement born in 1955, initiated by Salah Ben Youssef, general secretary of the party of Neo Destour, and gathering several opponents to Bourguiba, first leader of the same party.

7   Ahmed Ben Salah, at that time a militant modernist with a 'socialist' inclination, former general secretary of the UGTT and ambitious young minister (35 years old in 1961), was charged by Bourguiba with the Ministry of Planning and Finance in 1961, after having been in charge of the ministry of health and social affairs.

8   The book is a reissue of a thesis that Ben Salah had presented at the Sorbonne in 1974, after his disgrace and his 'flight' to France where he remained in exile until the mid-2000s.

9   The dinar is the Tunisian currency. 1 dinar: 1,000 millimes.

10   The term Khammas comes from the word khamsa, which means five in Arabic. So Khammas is the one who works for the fifth of the harvest. The practice of khammas in southern Tunisia has long been practiced by black men, mostly from slavery. The contract between the khammas and the owner of the land is an oral contract, even moral ('orf). He assumes that the khammas must work exclusively with the contracting owner, otherwise the contract is cancelled. Thus, the khammas was a 'worker', even a 'servant' providing housework, who cultivated the land and whose remuneration was the fifth of the harvest, which induces a form of enslavement. Often indebted to his boss, the khammas could not end the contract.

11   Banque Mondiale: Agriculture, valeur ajoutée (% du PIB) https://donnees. banquemondiale.org/indicateur/NV.AGR.TOTL.ZS?end=2016&locations=TN&st art=1965&view=chart Accessed 20 July 2018.

Chapter 6

FARMERS AND FARMING: EGYPT

Introduction

One of the many slogans of Egyptian protesters against the Mubarak dictatorship in January 2011 was 'Bread, freedom and social justice.' This was similar to the slogans in Tunisia by protestors between December 2010 and January 2011. The presence of the word bread in the slogan marks similar origins and progression of the revolutionary processes in Tunisia and Egypt. In both cases, the issue of sustained access to affordable food was at the heart of the popular uprisings. It constituted the core of the claims of millions of demonstrators who, in a few weeks, were able to defeat two of the harshest dictatorships in the region that were thought to be untouchable and unshakable.

Focusing on the food issue as a central element of the revolutionary events in Tunisia and in Egypt emphasises three important aspects of the uprising. The first of these is the importance of a longue durée view of historical transformation. This contrasts with the naïve mainstream reading of the events that reduces the origins of the uprisings to issues of political rights and freedom and an objective of creating liberal democracy (Abdelrahman 2012; Mazeau and Sabaseviciute 2014). We have argued that the socio-spatial chronology of the long processes of discontent in Tunisia and Egypt were propelled from the most marginalised regions, including rural areas and poor neighbourhoods. The demands were first and foremost social: access to food and natural resources including land and water, employment, housing, health infrastructure and services (Bush and Ayeb 2012; Ayeb 2011a; El Nour 2015b). Second, the food issue highlights how the peasantry in both countries was particularly active in the resistance and contestation that characterised the long revolutionary processes (Bush and Ayeb, 2014; Ayeb, 2017). Finally, despite the clear differences in term of landscapes and agricultural structures, exclusive irrigation in Egypt and mostly rainfed in Tunisia, the process of marginalisation and impoverishment of peasants in both countries was similar. It had been fuelled by years of agricultural and hydro-political neo-liberal policies that largely favoured big investors and which produced similar political consequences.

This chapter examines peasant, agricultural and food questions in Egypt. We reflect on the long mobilisation and role of the peasant in the revolutionary processes, which, in Egypt had begun well before 2010–11 and which continue in the contemporary period. As several authors have noted (El-Mahdi 2011, Bush and Ayeb 2014, Gana 2012, Abdelrahman 2012, Zemni, De Smet and Bogaert 2012), though often dismissed by mainstream media and social networks, peasant resistance in Egypt and Tunisia has never stopped. There was also a long 'historical lineage' to the 2011 uprising (Abdelrahman 2015, 29). The historical and socio-spatial dimensions of the revolutionary processes are key to help understand the significant political involvement and resistance of peasants before and after 2011 (Ayeb 2017).

The Egyptian Paradox: Developed Agriculture, Poor Peasants

Two contradictory dimensions characterise Egyptian agriculture. On the one hand, the current agricultural landscape shows a highly intensive, mechanised and modern agriculture with high levels of profitability and productivity. The specific geographic configuration of the landscape, the relative scarcity of arable land and the complexity of the hydraulic system helped create the concentration of the farmer population into the country's uneven village structures characterised by both very large and small communities. This left the majority of cultivable lands 'available' for farming use. On such lands, it is possible to obtain two harvests per year (and up to three in certain delta regions). Yields have reached levels comparable to those recorded in 'developed' countries: for example, many peasants can easily obtain a hundred quintals of wheat per hectare.[1]

The contribution of Egyptian agriculture to GDP was 21.2 per cent in 1984–85, at the beginning of the period of liberalisation of the economy. By 2013 its contribution had declined to 14.5 per cent. However, this sharp decline occurred despite a remarkable increase of agricultural GDP from US$ 7,506 million in 1984–85 to about US$ 40,158 million in 2012–13, a fivefold increase over 28 years (Aboulnaga et al. 2017, 1).

On the other hand, the development of agriculture since the beginning of the 1950s, and particularly since the 1980s, was strongly influenced by neoliberal reforms. These aimed to develop a mechanised and hyper-intensive agricultural sector oriented towards export that provoked a widespread impoverishment of small-scale family farmers or peasantry. Hence, a rich and developed agriculture is run by a peasantry that is one of the poorest in the world. This is one of the great paradoxes of contemporary Egypt. And it is not accidental.

The paradox is a product of a precise political will, one that has been driven by an economic, financial and political 'elite' who hold almost all levers of power and mobilise for their own benefit (with the exception of military and security institutions that remain an exclusive monopoly of the army). The poverty of Egyptian peasants is the result of the implementation of neo-liberal agricultural policies. These policies privileged investors to generate profits and promote private capital accumulation (Dixon, 2018). This is especially because of the dispossession of the Egyptian peasantry's primary resources: the water of the Nile and the agricultural land.

To a large extent, the same mechanisms also explain the permanence of the country's food dependency. Investors mainly grow non-food (or not-for-food) products for export (around 80 per cent of their production), while peasants produce food mainly for local or national markets (around 80 per cent of their production).

According to the 2010 census,[2] about 50.5 per cent of the total land area of wheat production, 56.0 per cent of the land area of rice production, 55.0 per cent of the land area of maize production, 53.8 per cent of the sorghum land area, 54.2 per cent of the clover land area and 46.7 per cent of the cotton land are cultivated by smallholders (less than 3 feddans) (Aboulnaga et al. 2017, 31). The small-scale family farmers cultivate less than 3 feddans and collectively 'cover' only 35 per cent of the total agricultural area. They produce 47 per cent of national cereal production, 61.3 per cent of big ruminants and 59.3 per cent of small ruminants (Marzin et al. 2017, 44).

Yet the peasant producer is not in a position to deliver their own family or community food security. Farmers are forced to buy a large part of their food provisions from the market, much of which is imported and expensive and sold by investors and middlemen.

The Egyptian peasantry's poverty, which has worsened since the new millennium, is mostly the result of contradictory policies, experiences, reforms and counter-reforms carried out over several decades. The poverty is indisputably more structural than cyclical, although some particular events may have accelerated or slowed its processes and dynamics. The agrarian history of the last two centuries explains some of the fundamental aspects of contemporary Egyptian agriculture and peasantry. However, recent policy, dominated by agrarian reforms and counter-reforms, plays a decisive role in determining the configuration of the social and farming landscape of the Egyptian countryside.

Agriculture in Egypt covers an aggregate/global area of about 3.5 million hectares.[3] It is fully dependent on irrigation and employs almost 3.7 million farmers and peasants, about 29 per cent of the country's labour force or more if we consider members of peasant families involved in agricultural labour (Ayeb 2010). There is an average of 2 feddans per farm and less than 1 feddan for 80 per cent of farmers. These figures, do not take into account farmers settled in the new reclaimed lands in the desert and cover only peasants in the Nile valley and the delta), Egyptian small-scale family farmers collectively experience a widespread impoverishment. The percentage of the poor in the agricultural population is between 50 and 75 per cent rising to 80 per cent if we consider all peasants who perform one or more off-farm activities to supplement their income and cover basic family needs (Ayeb 2010; World Bank 2002, 26, 27; Nagi 2001a, 54, 62, 63; Bush 2002, 16). These farmers and their families were the first to bear the brunt of the 2007–8 food crisis and the repercussions and consequences of its aftermath.

Like many other countries in the Global South,[4] during the first six months of 2008, Egypt experienced a serious food crisis unlike any seen in previous decades. The crisis mostly manifested in a shortage of bread and some other staple foodstuffs, as well as in a sharp rise of prices for certain products including rice and vegetable oils. While food prices had risen 73 per cent since 2006, the increase in price of some products was even higher – 144 per cent for edible oils and 129 per cent for cereals, including wheat and rice. Prices for dairy products, meanwhile, doubled during the same period. According to official sources, this food crisis resulted in the death of at least 15 people during protests or riots in bakery queues, as well as dozens of serious injuries (McGreal 2008; Ayeb 2008).

Food Crises and Uprisings

Several protests and demonstrations in Cairo and other parts of the country were organised around slogans directly related to the bread crisis and state of agricultural policy. Two general strikes obtained limited success because of the widespread mobilisation of security forces that occupied all spaces where demonstrations were planned. At Mahallah El-Kobra, the largest city of the delta and capital of the cotton and textile industry, several strikes, occupations of factories and demonstrations were organised, causing violent clashes with the police. Several people were killed by gunfire, a number were wounded and there were numerous arrests (Abdelrahman 2012; Beinin 2008; 2011; 2012; Beinin and Duboc, 2013).

These various events, triggered by the bread crisis, were probably the most violent and threatening for the Mubarak regime that had been in power since 1981. They recalled the strikes of 1977, which culminated in the cancelation of bread price increments a few days after they were announced. The level of violence then forced President Sadat to retreat as he feared the destabilisation of his regime and his personal safety (Heikal 1988).

The political consequences provoked by the food crisis, and the effects of agricultural world market policies on national market prices, is a product of the structural food dependence imposed on the Global South. As we noted in Chapter 4, food dependence was fostered by agricultural policies promoting the export of produce shaped by the demands of northern-dominated international markets, complemented by reliance on imported food for local consumption. Investing in export-led strategies was preferred to the promotion of food production for internal consumption. Imports were limited to the minimum of what the country could not produce. The result was that as Egypt gradually became an agricultural exporter, its food production was no longer enough to feed its own population. It is in this food agricultural-production contradiction, and how this is underpinned by unequal access to land and other resources, that the key elements and dimensions of Egypt's farming crisis reside.

For the first time in 1974, agricultural imports, including food, (in terms of value) surpassed exports. In 1980, Egypt imported 48 per cent of its food needs. From 1985–86 to 1990–91, Egypt imported on average more than 10 million tons (MTs) of food per annum, or about 200 kilograms per capita. Between 2000 and 2016 the average total production of cereals reached 21.91 million tons per year with a self-sufficiency rate (SSR) around 63 per cent. In 2010, the total production of cereals was 20.10 MTs with a SSR of 68 per cent. Since then, the total production of cereals per year and the SSR was successively 22.42 MTs and 70 per cent in 2005; 19.46 MTs and 55 per cent in 2010; 23.14 MTs and 56 per cent in 2015 and, finally, 23.338 MTs and 62 per cent in 2016.

During the period 2000 and 2016, the average annual production of wheat was 7.96 MTs and the SSR was on average about 50 per cent (see Map 6.1). The total wheat import during the same period was 135.32 MTs with an annual average of 7.960 MTs. The figures for wheat were 6.56 MTs for production and 57.28 per cent for SSR in 2000; 8.14 and 58.87 per cent in 2005; 7.17 and 40.39 per cent in 2010; 9.60 and 47.46 per cent in 2015; and 9.34 MTs and 51.69 per cent SSR in 2016.

Between 1961 and 2016, Egypt produced 240.813 MTs and imported 271.484 MTs of wheat, with an annual average of production about 4.378 MTs and annual average of import about 4.936 and an SSR of 47 per cent. These figures that cover a period of 55 years show that Egyptian food dependency is more structural than circumstantial.

As noted in Chapter 4, between 2000 and 2013, the food deficit in relation to Egypt's overall trade deficit remained high and permanent, with the exception of 2009, when overall Egyptian food imports fell. But contrary to what one might think, the decline in imports is not linked to an increase in domestic production, but to the worsening of the internal economic crisis, the global

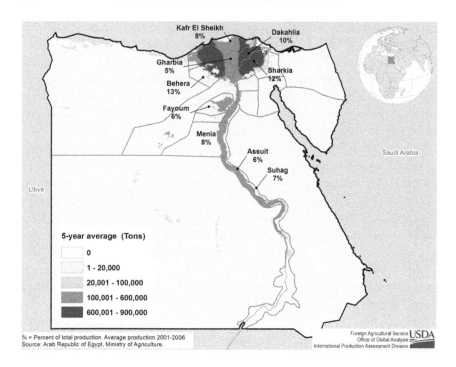

Map 6.1 Egypt: Spatial Distribution of Wheat Production.

Source: Arab Republic of Egypt, Ministry of Agriculture and USDA.

food crisis and the steep rise in prices of agricultural and food products in the world market that severely limited Egypt's import capacity.

With the rapid development of an intensive export-oriented agriculture that accelerated the impoverishment of the peasantry, the permanence and worsening of food dependency was entirely predictable. Food dependency and peasant marginalisation are political choices determined by the GoE and driven by the IFIs and export-oriented agricultural policies. The explanation for the policies that promoted export-oriented agriculture, at the expense of small-scale farmers, lies in more than 60 years of reforms and counter-reforms and in particular of the changes to patterns of land holding and tenure.

Agriculture and Peasants: Agrarian Reform and Counter-Reform

In the early 1950s, 0.4 per cent of agricultural landowners owned 33 per cent of the total agricultural area of the country: 2,000 large farmers owned about 1.1 million feddans, with an average land area of 558.5 feddans per farm. At

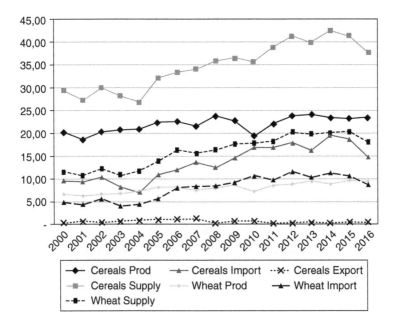

Figure 6.1 Cereals and Wheat: Production, Import, Export and Supply. Egypt 2000–16 (in million tons.)

Source: FAOSTAT.

the same time, 94.3 per cent of the landowners collectively occupied only 36.5 per cent of the land. Seventy two per cent of the farmers had less than one feddan with an average size holding of 0.4 feddan. They occupied collectively only 13 per cent of total farmland (see Table 6.1). The dominant land tenure for small holders was one of renting in or leasing (indirect land tenure) and accounted for 61 per cent of the total land area under cultivation (Aboulnaga et al. 2017, 58).

The 1950s, Nasser's Agrarian Reforms: Hopes and Frustrations

Gamal Abdel Nasser initiated the first major land reform in Egypt just two months after the 1952 seizure of power. The first reform bill was promulgated on 7 September 1952. The goal was threefold: (1) to 'weaken' the power of the large landowners who largely dominated the country's political and economic scene by depriving them of a large part of their land (the main sources of their income and power); (2) to transfer part of the agricultural capital to industry which was almost non-existent at the time (and that the government planned to develop rapidly) and (3) to establish a political and

Table 6.1 Structure of Agricultural Holdings in 1952 (Egypt)

Holding category	No. of holders		Land area		Average farm Area (Feddan)
	Number (1,000)	%	Feddan (1,000)	%	
<feddan	2018	72.05	778	13.01	0.39
1–5 feddans	624	22.28	1404	23.47	2.25
5–10 feddans	79	2.82	526	8.79	6.66
10–50 feddans	69	2.46	1291	21.58	18.71
50–100 feddans	6	0.21	429	7.17	71.50
100–200 feddans	3	0.11	437	7.31	145.67
>200 feddans	2	0.07	1117	18.67	558.50
Total	**2801**	**100**	**5982**	**100**	

Source: Aboulnaga et al. (2017, 58).

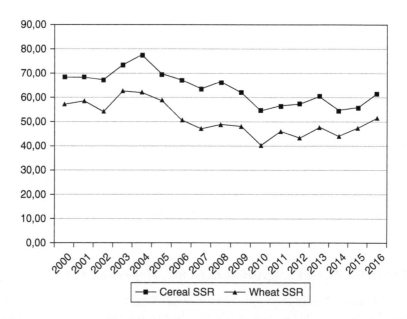

Figure 6.2 Egypt: Cereals and Wheat Self-Sufficiency Rate in Percentage.
Source: FAOSTAT.

electoral base and a source of rural legitimacy by redistributing part of the 'confiscated' land to smallholder and landless farmers. As a consequence of the reform, food security and social capital of thousands of poor families, who received parcels of land of various sizes and land titles, improved (Ayeb 2010).

Demographic pressure, unequal access to agricultural land and the central role of the land market during the 1940s resulted in 'an untenable inflation of land rent that in the late 1940s reached 75% of net operating profit' (Ireton 2013, 441–42). Various forms of resistance contested exorbitant rent increases that were born mainly by medium and smallholder farmers who rented from big landowners. Land price inflation triggered additional developments. It ruined many smallholder-farming families. About 1.2 million families of 'landless peasants' with no access to agricultural land and no opportunity to access non-agricultural activities (up to 45 per cent of the rural population) were forced into the bottom of the rural social hierarchy (Ireton 2013, 441–42). King notes that on the eve of 1953, '44% of all rural dwellers were landless peasants' (2006, 239). At that time, while 95 per cent of landowners controlled only 35 per cent of farmland, about 0.1 per cent owned 20 per cent of farmland and 0.4 per cent owned one-third (2006, 239). As Ireton notes, the price escalation

> of the land rent prompted many large landowners to abandon the use of their land and to rent all or part of it [...] in the form of small plots. A lot of landless farmers in desperate search of land were hence forced to take precarious, short-term and unregistered leases, despite the risks involved (Ireton 2013, 442).

Less than two months after seizing power, the 'free officers' who were aware of the seriousness of rural impoverishment, and of the importance of the social question in the Egyptian countryside, adopted the first agrarian reform. While that reform may not have been revolutionary, it did dramatically contribute to the reduction of inequalities in accessing land and rural poverty.

Land Redistribution: A Mixed Assessment

The agrarian reform had two complementary components. The first concerned the limitation of private land ownership. The second redefined the relationship between owners and tenants of agricultural land, with two key decisions: the conversion of land leases into permanent contracts and the blocking of rents.

The implementation of the agrarian reform was carried out in stages with a progressive limitation of the legal ceiling for the ownership of agricultural land. The Agrarian Reform Law No. 178 of 7 September 1952 first set the limit of land ownership at 200 feddan per person (84 ha) and 100 additional feddans per child. However, even if this limitation affected some families owning several hundred or even thousands of feddans, it did not change the structure of 'capitalist' agriculture. In 1958, a new limitation of 300 feddans (126 ha) per family was decided. In 1961, the land owning limit was reduced to 100 feddans or 42 hectares per family and to 21 hectares in 1969, but the latter reduction was never actually implemented (Ayeb 2010).

Starting in 1953, the state redistributed the land in parcels of 1.26 to 2.1 hectares for each beneficiary (landlords and tenants) according to the quality of the land and the size of the family (Abdel-Fadhil 1978, 18). Through a relatively precise system of redistribution, priority was given to former smallholders, tenants or sharecroppers, to the poorest farmers in the village, to those with the most dependents, and finally to 'foreigners' in the village.

The total amount of agricultural land redistributed under various agrarian reform laws between 1952 and 1970 covered an area of 343,366 hectares (13.5 per cent of available agricultural land) and benefited 341,982 families (approximately 1.7 million people, or 9 per cent of the rural population in 1970) (Abdel-Fadhil 1978, 21). On average the redistribution resulted in less than half a hectare of land per family, a figure too modest to fundamentally change, as claimed by the state, the rural landscape of Egypt.

The agrarian reform laws adopted since 1952 created a vast layer of smallholders and redirected political and social power in Egypt to smallholders and landless peasants, converting many tenants into landlords. Holdings of or under 5 feddans increased from less than 78.5 per cent of the total holdings in 1950 to 84.1 per cent in 1960. The area held by those with 5 feddan increased from 23.1 per cent to 37.8 per cent total agricultural area (Marzin et al. 2017, 44).

The large landowner category (50 feddans or more) fell from about 40 per cent in 1950 to about 21 per cent in 1960. It continued to decline to 16.8 per cent in the 2010 census. Furthermore, the number of landholders with less than 5 feddans has increased from about 877,000 in 1950 to 1.4 million in 1960, and to around 4.1 million in 2010, representing around 92 per cent of all landholders. The percentage of agricultural land held by this group increased from 23.2 per cent in 1950 to 38 per cent in 1960 and to 52.5 per cent in 1980, and declined slightly to about 47 per cent in 2010 (Aboulnaga et al. 2017, 12).

A further determining element of the 1952 agrarian reform, and its subsequent complementary laws, was the redefinition of relations (norms and contractual procedures) between tenants and owners. In the case of share-cropping, the adoption of the equal sharing principle for the cost of operations and harvesting, 'improved by a third or a quarter the share going to the farme (Bakre et al. 1980, 75). The latter also benefited from another transformation brought by the same reform: fixing rent at seven times the value of the property tax, which lowered the cost from between LE 32–37 (Egyptian pounds) to an average of LE21 (Bakre et al. 1980, 75).

Law 17 of 1963 brought further improvements to relations between tenants and owners. The tenant was guaranteed the right to remain permanently on leased land, and agricultural cooperatives became the guarantors of those advantages. In the event of the death of the tenant or leaseholder, the law guaranteed the legacy of the contracts to the heirs, on the sole condition that there was among them a farmer. Except in the case of non-compliance with this condition, the legislation denied the owner the right to unilaterally terminate the contract. Law 52 of 1966 brought this further: even at the end of the lease, the farmer could not be evicted from the land unless some of the clauses of the contract were not respected during the previous lease (Abdel-Fadhil 1990, 18).

Despite these dramatic and far-reaching reforms, the agrarian reform laws have been characterised as 'More reformist than revolutionary and egalitarian, the agrarian reform has not flattened the social pyramid of the owners; it has only blunted the tip' (Bakre et al. 1980, 77). The first law of the agrarian reform (Law 178 of 7 September 1952) did not fundamentally shake the capitalist character of Egyptian agriculture. Instead, the land owning cap of 84 hectares per capita plus an additional 42 hectares per child was maintained. Given the considerable yields of irrigated agriculture compared to rainfed agriculture, owning 84 hectares on good land in the Nile valley and the delta is far from insignificant. The 126 hectares limit (300 feddans) per family introduced in 1958 did not change the extent of the land inequalities between small farmers and large landowners.

In addition to the intrinsic limits of agrarian reform, the relatively disappointing results were further aggravated by the lack of adequate and effective supporting policies. The redistribution of land from large estates to former tenants and agricultural laborers generally took place within the frame of the cooperatives of the agrarian reform (those that implemented the reform). Led by government officials, these constituted a rigid and dirigist working framework for all new micro-owners. However, the cooperative experience in Egypt was quite different from that adopted in Tunisia. In the latter, the 'co-operators' were obliged to transfer their land to the cooperative to which they were only integrated as labourers, Egyptian cooperatives did not collectivise the property of its members. Rather, farmers continued to work their own land under a number of constraints, such as compulsory sale of products to the state through the cooperatives and other designated organisations.

Village cooperatives were also responsible for the redistribution of inputs, repayable on the compulsory delivery of cotton, wheat and rice crops. Still, the early years of the 'socialist' agrarian reform saw some improvements in the standards of living for the smallholder and landless peasants who benefited from the reform. In this regard, El Ghonemy (2002, 24) points out that over a period of 14 years (1951–65), rural poverty in Egypt was reduced by about 50 per cent from 56 to 24 per cent.

The agrarian reform replaced the old 'semi-feudal' relationships with contractual obligations guaranteed by law. Fifty years later in the 1980s, the liberalisation of agriculture completely ended these guarantees and placed the fate of smallholder farmers, already poor and disadvantaged, in the hands of big landowners and investors. This happened mainly through Law 96 of 1992, which acted as the most dramatic economic and social setback to progress for 40 years.

The Counter-Reform

Starting in the mid-1970s, Nasser's heirs, headed by President Anwar Sadat, chose to leave the Soviet 'fold' to align with US policies, to 'denasserise' the country by engaging it in a process of economic liberalisation and privatisation of state-owned enterprises. The agricultural sector was undermined as a consequence of the policy shift. Peasant agriculture was especially damaged after the adoption in 1992 of an agrarian counter-reform, the economic and social consequences of which have been dramatic, as we shall see in this chapter and is referred to elsewhere in this book.

The political abandonment of Nasser's policies during the 1970s was based on an analysis of the economic crisis influenced by the consequences of the 1967 war with Israel. Egypt's military defeat profoundly shook the country's entire economic and political scene. The Egyptian annual GDP growth fell from 4.5 per cent in 1965–66 to 1.4 per cent in 1966–67 and -0.9 per cent in 1967–68 (Kenawy 2009, 591). This was worsened by the death of Nasser in September 1970 and the war of 1973. While there was an increase in GDP growth of around 7 per cent, it was induced by external resources including oil revenue, labour remittances, the Suez Canal and tourism. These rents had no equivalent in terms of a developing internal productive capacity and the rentier economy, which still dominates, made Egypt constantly susceptible to shifts in global market demands. Consequently, the fall in oil prices from the mid-1980s led to a new crisis in the Egyptian economy (Abdelrahman

2004, 100–1; Westley 1999; Amin, G. 1999). The January 1977 'bread riots' were caused by the government's decision, under pressure from the IMF, to cut a large number of essential subsidies and raise prices for basic consumer goods. The riots were particularly violent and had significant impact in Cairo and other urban centres throughout Egypt (Toth 1998, 76). Urban bread riot protests were considered by the elites to be emblematic of the dangerous socio-political conditions caused by stagnation in agricultural production and the related food dependency. According to the political and economic view of those elites, the causes of stagnation lay in poor productivity caused by archaic smallholder farming methods that had reinforced land fragmentation. Agricultural decline was also seen to be the result of bureaucratic state management of agriculture that 'disincentivised production' (Ireton 2013, 473). They advocated for liberal reforms to restructure the agriculture sector and the market to benefit farmers and food producers. While economists and especially IFI policy reformers in Cairo spoke often about the benefits of reform, by improving farm gate prices, for instance, and by providing new incentive structures and reforming markets, the beneficiaries were not the small farmers. The beneficiaries were the minority with access to wealth and power. These included landowners, the institution of the military, ruling NDP bureaucrats and merchants who were able to shape and accumulate capital from the reforms.

From the mid-1980s and the beginning of the 1990s, a long programme of liberalisation of the entire Egyptian economy was introduced by two agreements between the Egyptian state, the IMF and the World Bank. These culminated in a comprehensive plan for economic reform and structural adjustment (ERSAP) formally adopted in 1991. Among the major economic and political changes, it included accelerated liberalisation of the agricultural sector that began in 1987. It aimed in particular to liberalise trade of agricultural production (import-export) and of the production of inputs. Furthermore, it included the privatisation of state-owned agricultural companies, the abolition of compulsory crop rotations, the liberalisation of insurance through the transformation of the Principle Bank for Development and Agricultural Credit (PBDAC) into a commercial bank, the liberalisation of credit ratings and, finally, the redefinition of contractual relations between owners and tenants (Bush 1999; Korayem 1977).

The agricultural reform programme was designed to boost private sector involvement and opportunity. There was an initial preservation of food subsidy policies, theoretically aimed at targeting and enabling the poorest people to access essential food products. These included rice, flour, bread, sugar, vegetable oils and meat. But the consequences of reform were tumultuous for small family farmers and their families; 'the government privatized state-owned enterprises, liberalized the agricultural sector and launched special economic zones to attract private investment. These reforms expanded market opportunities for the private sector in agriculture' (Joya 2017, 206), but small-scale farmers were not intended to be part of these reforms, other than negatively. Probably the biggest impact intended to boost private sector involvement in agriculture was the agrarian counter-reform, also known as Law 96 of 1992. That legislation aimed at the total liberalisation of the previous agricultural land market favouring private investment in the sector and displacing increasingly insecure small farmers.

Law 96 of 1992: The Struggle between Owners and Tenants

The idea for a regressive land reform had been maturing since the mid-1980s. The first proposition directed to modify the legal framework governing relations between landlords and tenants. The reform of the legislation of the early 1950s (Law 178 of 1952) was drafted in 1985 by the Agriculture Committee of the NDP, the erstwhile ruling party. The government announced its intention to submit the new law to parliament in 1986 but it was delayed partly for fear of large-scale revolt. This was because there had been riots in Cairo in February 1986 of conscripts of the Central Security Forces (an Egyptian paramilitary force) (Saad 1999, 395). These conscripts were usually from poor families in rural Upper and Middle Egypt. They were very badly treated, receiving insufficient and poor quality food, and they protested against their conditions. They attacked tourist establishments and nightclubs in the Al-Haram district of Cairo. It was not until 1992 that the decisive phase of the agricultural reform was adopted through Law 96 of 1992. This law, principally concerning tenant-owner relations, repealed several articles of the previous 1952 Agrarian Law.

Chapter 3 highlighted limited national debate regarding Law 96 of 1992 and some of the resistance that emerged to it. There were two contrasting binary positions: those who defended changes in the law and those who did not. This polarised view was often expressed in relation to a perspective on Egypt's agricultural malaise. Reformists advocated the end of security of tenure as a means to promote modernisation of the country in general and agriculture in particular. This position also advocated the role of the private sector in economic development. In contrast, the reform opponents argued for the defence of smallholder farmers, advocating the fight against exclusion and poverty of family farming and farmers including the near landless.

In response to the social and economic consequences of the adoption and implementation of the new agrarian counter-reform law, Egyptian peasants carried out collective and individual peaceful resistance. This lasted until

January 2011 when peasants joined the massive demonstrations that led to the fall of the Mubarak regime on 11 February. There were often violent protests against the implementation of the law especially in the delta governorate of Dakahlia where land pressure is some of the most intense. Farmer advocacy organisations like the Land Centre for Human Rights in Cairo noted high level of conflict that we have documented in Chapter 3. The violent reactions of the police against tenants, especially after 1997 at the end of the five years implementation period, shaped rural politics and repression, which continues.

The involvement of peasants in the debate about tenancy reform was extremely marginal. They were no longer represented by deputies in parliament, and opportunities for them to voice out their concerns were limited. Nevertheless, they could hear and understand how they were publicly depicted by supporters of the reform as the real culprits of the Egyptian agricultural crisis and therefore of the country's economic difficulties as a whole. The stereotypical image transmitted by television was of the lazy peasant tenant abandoning the land to work abroad to acquire consumer goods. This imagery was used extensively during public 'debate' to better justify the liberalisation of the economic sector and the call for investors and big landowners to 'save' the agricultural sector in Egypt. Changes in the legal status of land and farms were hence designed to create a stimulating context, and new opportunities for larger landowners, considered the only legitimate investors in the agricultural sector and who actively promoted market reforms. Policymakers were fostering a standardisation of the farm by reducing the viability and sustainability of small farms and tenants. This was done under the guise of attempts to create conditions for an economy of scale and technical efficiency (Bush 1998, 94).

The parliamentary elections in Egypt reserve seats for professional categories such as peasants. The candidate who represents them is supposed to be a farmer himself. In reality, these people occupy different professional activities and are often the 'owners' of inherited parcels or investors in new reclaimed desert lands. A representative of the NDP in parliament, Shafi Imam Algoundi, elected as a farmer, strongly supported Law 96 of 1992 when it was discussed at the People's Assembly. Five years later, surprised by peasant opposition and segments of civil society, he justified the law by assuring that 'the time of small properties has ended, and the time of large properties will allow an increase in agricultural production'. He wondered, 'What will the one who owns a half-feddan do?' before adding, 'When the owner has 500 feddans, he is obliged to use mechanisation and science to improve his production. These times are not anymore like the old ones when one could see, walking on the roads, the *fellah* lying next to his plot. What is requested today is that all these people work in big properties.'[5]

As Timothy Mitchell noted, 'the eviction of small tenants is not the only part of the longer-term plan of the reformers' (1998, 32). He noted that a conference held in Cairo in March 1995 brought together representatives of USAID, the Ministry of Agriculture, agribusiness consulting firms and some American and Egyptian academics. It was determinant in concluding that 'the future of Egyptian agriculture depended mainly on the wider use of technology to help reduce labor in the fields'. Such labour surplus, as well as maintaining low prices for agricultural products, 'would help to keep the value of the real urban wages low and make the industry more profitable' (1998, 32).

Law 96 stipulated that between 1992 and 1997 the price of rent would increase from 7 to 22 times the land tax value and that renting, sharecropping and the land market (sales, purchases and rentals) would be fully liberalised by October 1997. This new agrarian law was a counter-reform that affected about one million farmers who were engaged in land leasing (tenants, renters or mixed), and was conceived precisely to put an end to the provisions of the 1952 agrarian reform related to tenancy and sharecropping. Thus, on 6 October 1997, all leases became void and all leased lands were automatically returned to the owners, who were then free to recover, sell or re-let them at the price and to the person of their choice. Nothing, with the exception of their financial power in the market, could limit their total freedom regarding the management of those reclaimed lands.

In addition, the new law limited the benefits of the lease to the duration of the contract, determined by mutual agreement at the time of signing. It also limited benefits related to farmers' heirs of first degree (children, spouse, parents). It permanently put an end to lifelong leases and inheritance rights, which allowed children to automatically 'recover' the leases of their deceased parents. In addition, new contracts were legally capped at five years. In fact, contracts are often set for a maximum of just one agricultural year, one season, or even one harvest. In many cases these contracts are no longer registered, rendering the tenant a precarious worker who no longer benefits from any legal security.

Land Concentration and the Exclusion of Small Farmers

Since 1997, more than 800,000 farmers lost their rights to land acquired through permanent leases (Müller-Mahn 1998, 256). This figure is an under-estimate. The statistical data of the agricultural census carried out and published every ten years by the Egyptian Ministry of Agriculture show that the number of tenants affected by the implementation of Law 96 of 1992 amounts to approximately 904,000 (about 25 per cent of farmers) 'controlling' about 1.4 million feddans. Women who were heads of family and whose rent was registered under the name of a deceased or not-fit-to work husband were the first to suffer the direct consequences and lose their land due to the application of Law 96 of 1992. This happened either because they could not pay new rents demanded by the owners or because the owners did not wish to rent to a woman (Bush 2004a, 21). In addition to the change in conditions for rent, the sharp rise in costs for tenants also accounts for why some women (and men) were simply unable to afford to continue to rent. The annual rent of a feddan of agricultural land increased from LE500 (in 1992) to more than LE2,000 (in 1997) and in certain areas of the delta exceeded LE3,000 or LE3,500 (Ayeb 2003).

During field trips to Egypt in May and June 2013 (Bush and Ayeb 2014), we found that cooperative registers no longer contained 'tenant' columns. When these columns would appear, they were usually empty. But that does not mean there were no tenants. On the contrary, the high number of farmers that we met during these visits testified to the contrary. The difference lies in the fact that rentals have become more and more seasonal (a few months per year at most), are only very rarely renewed to the same beneficiaries, and are almost never recorded by a written contract and therefore never recorded anywhere. In other words, what has changed is not so much the number of tenants but the condition of 'unregistered' rentals that hence offer no 'legal security' for the tenants. Tenants are probably instead more numerous than before and visibly poorer than ever.

For the tenants, the most obvious impact of the enforcement of the law was impoverishment resulting from their lost assets base (Saad 2004, 2). A widow mentioned that she had to remove her son from school after receiving a warning from the school for not having paid the fees. Other families could no longer provide their children with daily pocket money. This is particularly relevant for high school and preparatory school because students pay for transportation to school, which may be far from the village (Saad, 2004, 6). In several villages in the Minya governorate, we met rural families who took their children out of school.

In the beginning, I enrolled all my children, boys and girls, in school to give them the chance to find other opportunities than the work of the land and agriculture that no longer attracts young people. But with the decline in income and the rise in land rents I could no longer afford the cost of their schooling. So I started by taking my girls out of school. In any case, they will be married. Last year, I had to take the two older boys out to work with me. That way, they will learn the job and take after me. School has become too expensive and graduates cannot find work anymore (A peasant, father of six children, District of Mallawi, Minya Governorate. 2009).

While removing a girl from school may not be seen as a high drama and might not directly signify a state of great material difficulties, the fact that boys are removed from the school system undeniably reflects a painful choice that only extremely difficult economic situations can 'justify' and explain.

The 2011 uprising prevented the completion and publication of the agricultural census planned for 2010–2012 but we have glimpsed aspects of it in the work we have cited earlier. It remains difficult, without reliable statistical data on the contemporary agrarian structure, to make definitive comments on rural inequalities. Nevertheless, from the data we have accessed, and which is discussed in the next two sections to this chapter, we can say that it is extremely likely, given the patterns that we have observed and recorded, that the two processes initiated in the mid-1990s, namely the concentration and rearranging of access to agricultural land and the impoverishment and dispossession of small farmers, have continued to worsen.

Water: Access and Scarcity?

In addition to limiting access to agricultural land, especially since the 1992 counter-reform, Egyptian peasants, like the majority of the population, suffer from limited access to water for drinking and irrigation. This limitation is all the more complicated because Egyptian agriculture is dependent upon irrigation. So, no water, no production. Moreover, the so-called drinking water, when it is available, is far from a minimum potable and sanitary standard.

In 12 June 2016, the newspaper *Alyoum Essabea* reported demonstrations in several villages of Beheira governorate (West Delta). The protests were against the failure to get supplies of drinking water for more than two months and the permanent lack of irrigation water. The protesters cut off roads and prevented the flow of vehicles to more than seven villages.[6]

Water protest spread throughout Egypt well before January 2011 and they have continued. This is evidenced by another demonstration that took place on 17 September 2013 in Jaafra village, Drao district (Aswan governorate) when villagers cut the road between Cairo and Aswan in protest against lack of water in the village for more than 5 days.[7]

The difficulties of access to water is not related to the overall volumetric availability. Egypt has a relatively large global hydraulic access. This includes 55.5 billion cubic meters of water per year, which constitutes its legal share of the waters of the Nile according to the 1959 agreements signed between

Table 6.2 Access to Clean Water at Home (One or More Taps) in 1996 and 2016 (percentage) (Egypt)

Population		1996 (%)	2016 (%)
Urban	Households	70	97
	Individuals	87	97
Rural	Households	32	91
	Individuals	38	91
Total	Households	56	94
	Individuals	nd	93

Source: www.capmas.gov.eg/Pages/ShowPDF.aspx?page_id=https://census.

Cairo and Khartoum[8] (Ayeb 2010). It also has some 4.5 billion cubic meters of groundwater. Moreover, the fact that water resources are fluvial or underground has a rather important advantage: the regularity of supply through a system of dams and sophisticated canals, including the Aswan Dam, which is the keystone of the hydraulic system with its total storage capacity of about 160 billion cubic meters.

Indeed, contrary to what one might think, despite the relative abundance of water, which translates into a comfortable availability of about 900 cubic metres per person per year, Egypt is experiencing a real hydraulic and social crisis (hydrosocial crisis). This is more complex and incomprehensible as the crisis is totally independent of the annual contribution of the Nile and the relations between the riparian states of the river. More than a scarcity of resources, the situation expresses the fact that this crisis is primarily political and social, constituting water injustice.

Available quantitative data is misleading. This is because it indicates a marked improvement in the rates of access to drinking water in Egypt during the last two decades. Table 6.2 shows this sharp change in access rates between 1996 and 2016 general censuses of population.

The figures of water access in Table 6.2 need a cautionary note of explanation. First, the physical connection to the drinking water network does not automatically mean permanent and secure access to water. There are breaks and failures of supply, destruction and final cut for non-payment of invoices, which means that there are only few urban households with secure and sustainable access to potable water. Second, we know that the water distributed by the network is not drinkable anywhere in the country. Drinking water treatment systems are rarely efficient enough to ensure the biological and chemical qualities that meet the minimum standards of health and hygiene. Third, in several poor neighborhoods or rural villages, the inhabitants install a water distribution system connected to a power source (canal or surface well) uncontrolled and not equipped with any treatment system apart from a few inefficient filters, which are rarely maintained.

However, while access to water appears at least formally to be improving, access to the sewage system for sewage disposal remains extremely limited with related consequences of hygiene and sanitation and poor public health. According to the World Bank (World Bank 2002, 27), in 1999/2000, only 45 per cent of Egyptians were connected to the sewage system. For 2015, according to USAID, the 2000 connection rates were just 20 per cent for the total population, 43 per cent for the urban population and a tiny 3 per cent for the rural population.[9] It is shocking to note that there is still more than 55 per cent of the population in Egypt without connection to a wastewater system. And this in a country that has one of the world's highest population densities with about 2,000 inhabitants per square kilometre (uninhabited desert surfaces are not taken into account in the calculation of the actual density).

In addition, there is a gap in access to drinking water (at home) between the poor and the non-poor (poverty line calculated from household income and expenditure data and generally used by IFPRI and the World Bank): 81.8 per cent of the non-poor have access to drinking water compared to only 60.5 per cent of the poor, a difference of around 20 points. For access to the sewerage system, the gap is larger, with 28 points difference. More generally, the access of poor households to hygienic conditions is very low: only 21.1 per cent of the poor live in houses connected to the sewerage system, and the proportion of poor households connected to a public network of sewerage in Upper Egypt is about half that of the non-poor (World Bank, 2002).

In the absence of a connection to a drinking water network, the rural population use water from irrigation canals and groundwater sources. The double chemical and bacteriological pollution of these sources expose them to many water-related diseases such as diarrhoea, bilharzia, sometimes even outbreaks of malaria and, more commonly, typhoid fever. Other diseases, related to the quality of the water, are also widespread, like kidney difficulties, the prostatitis that can be caused by the presence of a particularly violent bacterium known as escherichia coli. Because they are in charge of the household and all that concerns food, hygiene, cleaning and social reproduction, women are constantly in contact with water and are the most exposed to various waterborne diseases.

Irrigation is another source of infection because it requires farmers to be immersed in the water sometimes up to the knees. In a village where research on exposure of rural populations to schistosomiasis was conducted, researchers found that 55 per cent of full-time peasants were infected (El Katsha and Watts 1997). The use of mobile pumps for irrigation also appears to play a large role in the transmission of the disease. The high speed provided by the machine imposes on the farmer a more sustained pace of work. He has to spend a lot of his time in the canals to install and uninstall pipes, facilitate the flow of water to the plots to irrigate and avoid flooding.

Land Fragmentation and Injustice

We have now explored the main dimensions of the underdevelopment of Egyptian peasant farming and agriculture. We have explained the processes of the underdevelopment in terms of ways in which policy has marginalised small-scale family farming and it has done so with particular intensity since the neo-liberal revolution of the 1970s. Our explanation runs counter to the mainstream tropes regarding land fragmentation as the explanation for agricultural and food dependency and peasant poverty. In addition to this, demographic pressure in Egypt is generally mentioned as a further explanatory element. However, this remains a rather superficial reading. It avoids assessing the real social and economic correlations and overall political and economic processes that led to marginalisation and impoverishment. But this 'technical' or statistical evidence hides the fact that unequal access to agricultural land is a social fact: in 2000, 91.34 per cent of farmers in Egypt shared just 50.6 per cent of the total agricultural area, with farms of less than 5 feddans each, averaging 1.25 feddan per farm. Three per cent of farmers accounted for 33.5 per cent of the total agricultural area, with those farms on average consisting of more than 10 feddans with a size of 26.81 feddans per farm. It is seldom noted that land fragmentation only concerns part of the land held by small farmers, who represent the majority of farmers.

One of the most significant indicators resulting from the change in land tenure was the decline of farm size from 6.13 feddan in 1950 to almost 3.80 feddan in 1960, and then to 2.2 feddan in the last agricultural census of 2010 (Aboulnaga et al. 2017, 10). Thus, the average farm for small-scale family farmer, the category of less than 3 feddans, reduced from 1.14 to 0.91 feddan between 1990 and 2010 (Marzin et al. 2017, 134).

In 2010, those with less than 3 feddans represented 4.7 million farms including the landless, that is, 87.2 per cent of the farms (84.3 per cent of the farmers with land and 2.9 per cent of the landless farmers), and collectively occupied 35.2 per cent of the total agricultural area (Marzin et al. 2017, 134). According to the 2009–10 Egyptian Agricultural Census, small farmers with less than 3 feddans constitute 38.1 per cent of all agricultural producers. 51.1 per cent are of less than five feddans (about 2.1 ha) and approximately 66.74 per cent are farms of less than 10 feddans (about 4.2 ha) (Aboulnaga et al. 2017, 8).

Table 6.3 Percentage of Poor in Different Governorates according to the National Poverty Line (Egyptian Pound (LE) per year, per capita)

	1919–96	2000–1	2004–5	2008–9	2010–11	2012–13
Governorate Poverty line (LE/year)	–	998	1423	2224	3076	3920
Egypt	22.9	20.1	19.6	21.6	25.2	26.3
Urban	22.5	18.4	10.1	11	NA	NA
Rural	23.3	21.4	26.8	28.9	NA	NA

Source: Aboulnaga et al. (2017, 116).

Table 6.3 shows that in 2008–9, on the eve of the popular uprising in January 2011, the rural poverty rate is just under three times urban poverty rate and far exceeds the average poverty level in Egypt. This high poverty rate in Egypt has affected children, many of whom are malnourished. In mid-2014, 31 per cent of children under the age of five were considered to have stunted growth because of malnutrition. Often, families who have little money opt to spend it on cheaper food options rather than nutritious food.

The Egyptian state exempts 'low-income' landless peasants, and peasants with less than 3 feddans (less than 1.26 ha), from land taxes (real estate tax) on their farms. These small-scale holders are generally considered the category of the most vulnerable Egyptian peasants. The available figures show that while the number of these small-scale holdings have been increasing continuously for several decades, the size of their farms is declining. This negatively impacts the growth of the agricultural sector and contributed to the processes of impoverishment of this category of peasants (Aboulnaga et al. 2017, 13).

The income generated from farms of less than three feddans (from different farming activities and utilizing family labour) does not meet the poverty line of US$1.25 per day per capita (the United Nations poverty line[10]) (Aboulnaga et al. 2017, 8).

Farmers of less than one feddan (very small farmers category) accounted for most of the smallholder category. Their proportion increased from 36.1 per cent in 1990 to 48.3 per cent in 2010 while their number increased by almost 33.8 per cent during this period. This has led to a decrease in the average size of their landholding from about 0.48 feddan in 1990 to about 0.43 feddan in 2010 (Aboulnaga et al. 2017, 13).

The landless group included about 565,000 farmers in 1990 (1989–90 census) and in 2010, there were about 965,000 (2009–10 census). This group represented 16.3 per cent of all farmers in 1990 and increased to 17.9 per cent in 2010. The category of small agricultural landholders includes about 2.3 million holders in 1990. Their number increased by 60 per cent to around 3.7 million in 2010 (Aboulnaga et al. 2017, 12).

The percentage of women landowners decreased from 9.8 per cent in 1990 to almost 4.3 per cent in 2010 of the small-scale family farmers. They accounted for about 8.23 per cent of all agricultural landowners in 1990, but this figure dropped significantly in 2010 to only 3.94 per cent of all land-owners. This decline resulted in a decrease in the proportion and total number of women landowners, from about 285,000 to 212,000 between 1990 and 2010 (a decrease 25.5 per cent). Three-quarters of these women were small-scale family farmers. In addition, the percentage of women landowners on medium and large farms fell from 5.26 per cent in 1990 to 3.23 per cent in 2010.

This inequality of access to agricultural land automatically translates into unequal access to water and especially irrigation water. Water availability depends on the size of the farms and, excluding exceptional situations, rights to water are recognised to all without distinction. However, 'masked' pricing, commonly known as 'cost recovery', introduced a new form of inequality that further penalises the smaller farmers. By moving from the traditional and 'communitarian' system of *sakia*, to individual motor pumps, irrigators moved from a system where needs were determined by access to water (volume and access time) to a system where the means (including financial means) imposed and limited water access.

If the Egyptian case proves that poor peasantry can develop prosperous agriculture on very small areas, the sustainability of a farm run by poor farmers is far from obvious. Indeed, a peasant who lives in conditions of social and economic insecurity has difficulty planning for the long term and his whole strategy may instead be focused around the necessity to provide for immediate family needs. In other words, it is not possible to develop a sustainable agricultural sector by keeping farmers in a condition of widespread poverty.

On the one hand, fragmentation of agricultural land and pluriactivity are intimately linked and on the other, are the automatic product of processes of impoverishment of the peasantry induced by increasingly aggressive neoliberal policies since the mid-1970s. In this case pluriactivity is a 'refuge', or what Reardon calls 'refuge pluriactivity', 'where the household turns to other sources of income to reduce the impact of its exposure to shocks in production (Reardon 1998). For his part, Escobal (2001) establishes a direct link between the situation of poverty and pluriactivity arguing that 'the pluriactivity refuge' is linked to farm households in crisis that do not have cash to deal with production shortfalls.

The link between agricultural policies and poverty in Egypt appears clear if we distinguish between the choices of the 1950s and 1960s, dominated by substantially 'socialising' (socialist) and pro-peasant oriented policies, and the more recent years characterised by neo-liberal policies that favour export-oriented agribusiness at the expense of peasant agriculture. As Francois Ireton recalls:

> The examination of rural poverty rates shows that overall, the Nasser period, except in its last years, saw an improvement in the living conditions of rural people: according to the different sources and methods of calculation rural poverty was reported in 1958 between 28% and 35% and between 24% and 27% in 1965, both sources signaling a significant decline. In 1975, according to the same authors, the rural poverty rate rose between 44% and 60% (2013, 471).

Between the two wars with Israel of 1967 and 1973, the Egyptian country-side experienced an acceleration of the process of impoverishment. That was induced by the government mobilising all the economic resources of the country to rebuild the army. Military investment was at the expense of other economic sectors, including agriculture, which has been subject to higher taxes and suspensions of several development and support programmes. The debt crisis of the 1970s worsened all major economic indicators, leading to a with-drawal of the state and the adoption of new policy orientations and policies of economic openness or *Infitah* by President Sadat (Bessaoud and Montaigne, 2009, 71). This was an attempt to put an end to Nasser's 'socialist' policies, perceived as the main cause of blockage of the national economy.

Conclusion

This chapter has shown how neo-liberal agricultural policy has resulted, on the one hand, in the aggravation of Egypt's food dependency and the destruc-tion of its natural resources and environment, and on the other, in the massive marginalisation and impoverishment of the Egyptian peasantry, which number about 4 million (20 million people, including all family members or one-fifth of Egypt's population). We have also shown that Egyptian peasants are considered among the poorest in the world, yet continue to develop and maintain one of the most highly productive forms of agriculture. The paradox is of impoverishment and attempts by small-scale farmers to promote and maintain a diverse and potentially vibrant agricultural system despite GoE policy to undermine it. This contradiction since the mid-1980s has been a feature of Egypt's pattern of rural modernisation, or what we describe more accurately as underdevelopment. It in part explains the rural origins of the revolutionary processes that ended the Mubarak regime in 2011.

After a reminder of the agrarian reforms of the 1950s and 1960s, which largely benefited small farmers, we explored the social, economic, environmental and political consequences of the liberal counter-reforms of the agricultural sector, initiated in the mid-1980s, and formally adopted through the Law 96 of 1992, which profoundly changed relations and modes of production in the Egyptian countryside.

Law 96 of 1992 was the culmination of the liberal reforms initiated by Sadat in the mid-1970s. It fully liberalised the agricultural and land market (sales and rentals) by subjecting it to strict rules of neo-liberal competition, and removed the various (minimal) mechanisms of protection of peasant families, set up during the 1950s and 1960s, which limited agricultural land prices, rents and leases in perpetuity. The same law has encouraged the development of a modern capitalist and export-oriented agriculture. The immediate consequences have been swift and massive. First, there has been the accelerated impoverishment of the small peasantry, whose access to agricultural resources, including land and irrigation water, have been reduced. At the same time, there has been the emergence of a group of wealthy investors close to state power that has enjoyed the protection of the state and security services. Immediately after the implementation of the reform in October 1997, about one million families lost access to land they had in long-term rentals and had been cultivating and maintaining for more than two decades. About one million families were suddenly dispossessed of their unique sources of income and brutally exposed to food insecurity and the various risks of social and economic exclusion.

Faced with these neo-liberal choices, the small- and medium-sized peasants carried out individual and collective actions of struggles and resistance, brutally repressed by the state and by the rich landowners. That has continued in the contemporary period. If the major events of 25 January 2011 were first, the work of urban and youth activists, the following days saw a massive participation of thousands of peasants in Midan Tahrir as well as in other urban places throughout the country. The path between 1992 and 2011 highlights the rural origins of the revolutionary processes. It also reveals and emphasises the importance of the active involvement of the socio-spatial classes of peasantry in developing struggles and resistance.

Notes

1   In Europe, the average yield of wheat per hectare is between 70 and 100 quintals per hectare.
2   For unknown reasons, the 2009–10 agricultural census in Egypt has never been published by the Egyptian Ministry of Agriculture, which usually organises and

conducts it and publishes the results. Therefore, we are obliged to rely on the report published by FAO and CIRAD on small family farming in Egypt, which uses the results of this census. This reference, the only one we could find, was carried out in 2017 by a team of experts around (Aboulnaga et al.). We also use the report published by FAO and CIRAD on small family farming in Middle East and North Africa, (Marzin et al. 2017) which used some figures from the Egyptian agriculture 2010 census.

3   All the figures and statistics on farmers and dating from before 2009–10, in this chapter, do not include Egypt's four urban governorates: Cairo, Giza, Alexandria and Suez.

4   According to FAO's sources, the food crisis has more or less affected 37 countries worldwide and about 800 million people.

5   A claim brought from the opposition newspaper *Al-Ahaly* of 19 July 1997.

6   https://www.youm7.com/story/2016/6/12//2758077.

7   https://www.youtube.com/watch?v=wPcSVj4x2V8.

8   The most important points of this treaty were (1) the sharing of the waters of the Nile with 55.5 billion cubic meters for Egypt and 18.5 for Sudan (2) the acceptance by Sudan of the project to build the High Dam (3) Egypt's commitment to finance the displacement and compensation of Sudanese Nubians whose displacement was inevitable, and finally (4) Egypt's acceptance of the construction of two Sudanese dams: Roseires on the Blue Nile and Khachm al-Guirba on the Atbara. As the annual Nile is 84 billion cubic meters, the remaining 10 billion correspond to the evaporation of Lake Nasser.

9   https://idea.usaid.gov/ – accessed on 19 February 2019.

10   A poor person is defined as someone who consumes about US$ 1.25 a day, but after considering the purchasing power parity (PPP), it amounts to less than LE11.2 per day in 2013, according to CAPMAS.

Chapter 7

FOOD SOVEREIGNTY

Introduction

This book has traced how the trade-based theory of food security is the dominant narrative and policy emphasis regarding food, agriculture and hunger in Egypt and Tunisia. We have documented some of the more insidious impacts of how the storyline of food security has panned out historically with reference to broader regional dynamics that include economic reform, war and environmental crisis. This concluding chapter examines whether an alternative food sovereignty (FS) framework is emerging in Egypt and Tunisia and if it is not, why does the food security paradigm continue to be hegemonic? We also ask even if FS is not a regular feature of food-related discourse in Egypt and Tunisia, have there been any recent dents in the emphasis on food security, and if so, with what kind of relative success for promoting a meaningful and sustainable alternative? We indicate that although farmer unrest and protest, over issues as broad as land boundaries, irrigation access, farming input provision, marketing and distribution of produce, may not use the language of FS, the struggles do in fact centre around many of the claims and agenda articulated by global food social movements and especially those championed by FS broadly defined and La Via Campesina (LVC).

Food Sovereignty

There is no single variant or definition of FS. Like democracy, FS is a process without an end but one that nevertheless as we will see, contains several important key themes that promote peasant and small farmer demands for autonomy and control over food production and consumption. In short, FS offers a comprehensive peasant path to social control and decision-making over food-related issues. Food sovereignty also begs the question of the relationship between the town and countryside, of the importance of maintaining delivery of food to urban areas at prices that are affordable and sustainable. Ultimately, FS offers an agenda for promoting a national sovereign project (Amin S. 2017a). We discussed this idea in Chapter 1 and return to it in this chapter. For the moment we need to understand that there is an agrarian question in the twenty-first century and it is one that contests the genocide of the imperialist triad and which promotes the dominant global food regime. This is a regime that, as we have indicated, systemically undermines the majority of humanity who rely on family peasant production. One of the issues that our analysis has confirmed is that, 'Capitalism, by its nature, cannot resolve the peasant question: the only prospects it can offer are a planet full of slums and billions of "too many" human beings' (Amin S. 2017b, 156). To counter this scenario, Amin advanced the strategy of sovereign national projects that might inch towards an end of the dependence upon the international law of value.

Despite the pitfalls and persistent structural crises of hunger and uneven agricultural performance, recurrent unrest and rural protest is developing a counter-culture that opposes dominant state and IFI policy. The global counter-culture is FS and we see in our two cases, it takes many different forms. If it is to emerge as a new hegemonic force, however, there will need to be a new balance of political forces to challenge government orthodoxy and interference from, among others, the international financial institutions. There is the need for nothing short of an agenda for radical transformation: the re-appropriation of what is private. This will only be possible with a set of political alliances that reduce the dependence of Third World states on the core and goes beyond the reforming zeal of the anti-poverty coalition (Selwyn 2017; 2018). There will be a need for political forces with an agenda for change that links rural struggles for greater autonomy from landlordism and government bureaucrats with working-class resistance to entrenched neo-liberalism. And there will need to be an agenda that links agrarian reform with industrial and service provision reform. The chances of this revolutionary achievement seem potentially stronger in Tunisia than Egypt, but the hurdles in both countries are high. They are hurdles set by imperialist and local landowning interests that receive strong support domestically from authoritarian polities seeking to maintain law and the established order. The regime of President el-Sisi in Egypt is the most authoritarian the country has ever had. The president's legitimacy is conferred and maintained by imperial interests that seek to control Egypt's geo-strategic rent. It is clear that peasant and other struggles will for some time be subject to ruthless repression. This involves routine and systematic imprisonment of cadres promoting even modest political liberalisation, never mind an agenda for delivering social justice (Bush 2018).

Food sovereignty is a framework and set of policy praxis that prioritises the principle and policies to deliver food as a human right rather than as just another commodity exchanged for cash or kind. People's survival depends on growing and distributing food, which can only be provided in a sustainable way if it is made part of national and public sovereignty (Stédile and de Carvalho 2011, 23). Food systems analysis, discussed in Chapter 4, details how dominant class and policymaking influence in the northern capitalist economies, have promoted national sovereignty in relation to food production, without equitable distribution. Food sovereignty, however, in Egypt and Tunisia has been denied because of the dominant food security mantra that relies 'on industrial agriculture, mass food, and international trade to cover the deficit [...] in food requirements' (Amin S. 2011a, xv). The mainstream policies we have documented in this book, have, in fact, highlighted a continuous historical process of de-sovereignisation under the guise of food security.

Food sovereignty as a series of ideas, raising issues for a new policy framework dealing with global and local food availability and access, emerged in most of the literature from the World Food Summit in 1996. In fact, however, we know that FS in Tunisia and Egypt was first a counter-movement from peasantist agronomists and farmers undermined by agricultural modernisation in the 1960s and 1970s (Ajl 2018a). After 1996 it was introduced by LVC, an umbrella organisation of southern and northern rural movements that loosely coalesced in protest against the Uruguay Round of the General Agreement on Tariffs and Trade in 1994. Food sovereignty was also identified as the first declared principle of the 1983 Mexican government's National Food Programme (Edelman 2014,183).

Food sovereignty is a constantly evolving idea and set of farming practices that emerges in the South as a result of agricultural and food crises. These crises have been a persistent feature of capitalist development, of accumulation and the reproduction of capital in the Global North and the Global South, in the capitalist core and periphery. It is difficult to prescribe a universal template for FS (Clapp 2014; Schiavoni 2017) because the pursuit of food as a human right has taken different dimensions. The struggles for it range from town and countryside and rural households to a range of organised and informal protests. They include struggles around land ownership and management of local resources, accessing land and water, and conflicts with corrupt traders and government employees. We might nevertheless identify seven major principles that emerge distinguishing FS from the tropes of food security. These are principles that go far beyond a slogan of food as a human right. Historically the debate about rights has become normalised without effective policy action to deliver them. The principles indicated in Table 7.1 capture the dynamic and range of a qualitatively different set of practices from the status quo of food security.

Taken together, these principles promote an epistemic shift in the way food is understood as a right that must be actively secured and in a transformed system of food production and social reproduction. That, moreover, will need to be sustainable and open-ended (McMichael 2014). To achieve this, it will be necessary for a social movement to promote a politics that promotes and safeguards it. This is why access to locally produced food at affordable prices will shape the way farming and agriculture is politically overdetermined. The dynamic, range and scope of FS was part of the Nyéléni declaration of food

Table 7.1 Seven Principles of Food Sovereignty

Food – basic human right – access to food is a constitutional right	*End Globalisation of Hunger* – enforce code of conduct on MNCs and IFIs
Agrarian Reform – land belongs to those who work it	*Social Peace* – Poverty and marginalisation endanger small farmers
Protect Natural Resources – right to practice sustainable management	*Democratic Control* – Democratise and improve participation in economic, political and social life (especially) for women
Reorganise Food Trade – prioritise production for domestic consumption	

Sources: La Via Campesina (2017); War on Want (2012).

social movements in Mali in February 2007. It has become part of the LVC manifesto and is important to quote at length:

Food sovereignty is the right of peoples to healthy and culturally appropriate food produced through ecologically sound and sustainable methods, and their right to define their own food and agriculture systems. It puts those who produce, distribute and consume food at the heart of food systems and policies rather than the demands of markets and corporations. It defends the interests and inclusion of the next generation. It offers a strategy to resist and dismantle the current corporate trade and food regime, and directions for food, farming, pastoral and fisheries systems determined by local producers. Food sovereignty prioritises local and national economies and markets and empowers peasant and family farmer-driven agriculture, artisanal – fishing, pastoralist-led grazing, and food production, distribution and consumption based on environmental, social and economic sustainability. Food sovereignty promotes transparent trade that guarantees just income to all peoples and the rights of consumers to control their food and nutrition. It ensures that the rights to use and manage our lands, territories, waters, seeds, livestock and biodiversity are in the hands of those of us who produce food. Food sovereignty implies new social relations free of oppression and inequality between men and women, peoples, racial groups, social classes and generations (La Via Campesina 2017, n.p.).

The extensive range of LVC working definition of FS captures many elements of the alternative necessary to redress persistent food crises, of production and consumption. The key component is control and autonomy for farmers to exercise decision making over the land they cultivate and farm, and this includes farm labour, and the landless about which there is more of a silence. The definition of FS also reminds how capitalism expands and does so by enlarging the frontiers at which it operates. Land grabbing is part of a global enclosures' movement but capital does not 'grab' land for itself. It does so as part of the process of creating new social relations of exploitation, of surplus value creation, access to cheap resources and cheap labour to work on the fields and also to hold land as a hedge for investment without farming it at all. In Egypt and Tunisia frontier expansion adversely incorporating farmers into new land and commodity markets has had extraordinary deleterious consequences for the environment and displacement of small scale farmers and farming. At its most stark, frontier expansion fails to reduce chronic hunger and malnutrition of modernity's 'surplus people', of the displaced and dispossessed who are added to the numbers of abjected poor. The frontiers of expanded capitalist agriculture in Egypt and Tunisia are a major illustration of the impact of contemporary phase of the corporate financialised food regime (Dixon 2018). In south east Tunisia, the expansion of the southern frontier at places like Limaoua, in the Governorate of Gabes highlights the intensification of agriculture for crops like peppers and melons, and also apples and citrus. The water demands are intense, the digging of wells reaching extraordinary depths and where financial returns, at least in the short term are high. The intensive use of the soil by a limited number of investors, has done little to ease the pressure on rural Tunisia. The costs to invest in the new land is prohibitive for poor and landless farmers and the investor has to commit to the purchase of a minimum of 10 hectares. Costs include for land registration and purchase of capital intensive technology including irrigation which is prohibitive for small farmers. The cost for digging a well for instance in the new lands in south east Tunisia is 120 dinars per metre. The farm we visited in September 2018 had a well of 160 metres and the farmer had also spent a minimum of 50,000 dinars for machinery and digging. In total the farmer estimated the set up costs for his farm were €60,000 (interviews with new investors, Tunisia, 28 September 2018).

Small farmers could of course invest in farming in new lands if they did not have these costs or if they could share them between a number of farmers or with state subsidy. But this would require the Tunisian state to facilitate collective and shared agricultural investment that was directed towards alleviating the burden on the poorest farmers. Instead, investment has historically been directed to those who already have wealth and are able to add to it accelerating rural inequality that we have described as so extensive. It would also require the state to make a commitment to offset global market pressures on local small-scale family farmers as part of a new revolutionary strategy for rural development.

We have employed the term accumulation by dispossession to describe that displacement which has more generally resulted from what Karl Marx called a 'metabolic rift' (Marx 1867; Bellamy Foster 2000 and 2013; Saito 2017). This term refers to a major contradiction in capitalism, which is the disruption in the relations between people and nature. As technology is increasingly applied to agricultural production, nature is degraded and profits fall. For Marx, labour was only seen to be useful in capitalism if it was creating exchange value. He argued in contrast, that 'real productivity' involved the fulfilment of human need, and advocates for FS argue that 'agro-capitalism' has destroyed the 'ecological conditions of production, by simplifying and over-exploiting ecosystems, eroding soil fertility, contaminating water and spewing greenhouse gases into the atmosphere' (Rosset and Altieri 2017:127; Marx 1970; Bellamy Foster 2013).

Metabolic rift might be a shorthand for understanding the conflict between economic transformation and environmental crises but Chapter 2 noted how careful we need to be not to view society and nature as in a binary relationship. Instead, 'Capitalism is not an economic system; it is not a social system; it is *a way of organizing nature*' (Moore 2015, 2 emphasis in original). And this interconnectedness and systemic relationship between people and their engaged environment, for convenience sometimes referred to as nature, can be interrogated by using the framework offered by FS. The idea of metabolic rift does help us explain the contradictions between the forces of production and the relations of production that generate surplus value. In our two cases we see the immense capacity of the rural sectors in terms of volumes of production, real and potential, and yet we also highlight how the ways in which production is organised is restricted by access to land and other resources that are dominated and shaped by large landowners and which have contributed to environmental degradation.

It is significant that the debate and discussion about FS takes place in the context of financialisation and the dominance of monopoly capital that controls prices of production. Financialisation refers to the structural shift in capitalism skewed towards the dominance of wealth creation emanating from finance, rather than non-financial production. It underpins and structures relations of power and how they are reproduced in late capitalism (Bracking 2016). The debate about FS has emerged as part of the backlash to the commercialisation of agricultural inputs and the chemicalisation of the second food regime after World War II. FS is also a response to the financialisation of family farming as it has become increasingly dependent upon credit to finance seed and other input costs. It is of no surprise that a core element of resistance coordinated by FS advocates promotes the preservation and reproduction of local, as opposed to imported genetically modified, seeds. The debate about FS provides a window to analyse the multifaceted dynamics of the disaster that global capitalism has created in relation to persistent and structural hunger on a global level. The history of global food systems has been shaped by the needs of capitalists to source cheap food for a nineteenth-century manufacturing, and later a more generalised, industrial proletariat. The parallel capitalist imperative that has shaped the global food system has been to supply cheap food at a level of profit for an agrarian bourgeoisie in an emerging and increasingly dominant food sector. One of the conflicts for the managers of global capitalism is that these twin processes embody systemic contradictions within capitalism. On the one hand, there is the need to pacify the working class with cheap food and low inflation, and on the other, to do this while expanding control over global natural resources (Bush and Martiniello 2017).

The contradictions have been amplified in the period of neo-liberalism where the state has been removed from welfare provision and used to police and deliver flexible working conditions and casualisation as global value relations have been reconfigured. This has been done, moreover, by promoting authoritarian populism (Boffo, Saad-Filho, Fine 2018). In the South, the consequence was the lost development decade of the 1980s, debt crisis and the end of redistributive land reform (see Chapters 2 and 4). It also opened the South, and the experience of Egypt and Tunisia highlights this well, to deregulation of land markets, commodification of seeds and other farming inputs, and agro-export promotion at the expense of local consumption that led to land grabbing and a 'global subsistence crisis' (Akram-Lodhi 2012).

Neo-liberal ideologues in the Global North, in the IFIs and in governments tried to resolve crises of capital accumulation and profitability by facilitating a new phase of imperialist land grabs. These accelerated the twin processes of de-peasantisation and de-agrarianisation. The reaction to this has been the development of a counter-culture of FS. The farmer protest and the social movements that emerged to promote this in different forms and with different levels of success have introduced a new agenda of action. Peasant resistance to global food price rises, after 2008, land transactions that have led to dispossession and farmer marginalisation have been described as analogous to the 'canary in the mine'. In other words, farmer protest is a warning of a 'socioecological catastrophe in the making' (McMichael 2014, 936).

Food sovereignty contrasts sharply with food security where the latter is rooted in the essential dimension of international trade, free markets and price equilibrium to generate country access to food. The contrasts between the two approaches are highlighted in Table 7.2. They might be summarised in the contrast between the food security productionist approach and FS concerns with access to food. The binary distinction between the two policy practices has been critiqued for oversimplifying food security as simply associated with the mainstream rather than the more open-ended concept of food security,

Table 7.2 Food Security or Food Sovereignty?

Food Security	Food Sovereignty

• *Dominant narrative*
  – Food security: trade-based, if you can't produce food, import it/mechanise and increase productivity of land and labour
  – Peasant agriculture is doomed because
    – low labour and land efficiencies of non-mechanised agriculture
    – Land fragmentation
    – Urbanisation dispossesses farmers
    – Huge urban congestion only resolved by industrial growth
	• Support don't undermine small family farmers
	• Defend diversity and reject (colonial) trade specialisation
	• Gendered agriculture, improve health provision and sustainability
	• Modern enclosures – outsourcing with land grabs – is unsustainable
	• Economic crisis highlights current food system can't resolve recurrent theme
	  • How to mobilise surplus from peasant agriculture to reconstituted and sustainable industry without eliminating peasants from agriculture?
	• Agro ecology to replace GMO's and corporate chemicalisation of agriculture

which does refer to issues of food, nutrition and stability (Clapp 2014: 208). We have argued that the mainstream remains dominant. The term food security is now so entangled with policy that it is almost impossible to use the term without conceding to the imperatives of the market and asymmetries of power that this entails.

This does not mean that there are no difficulties with the term and use of FS. The ways in which FS can or does address issues of trying to deliver universal access to food is not straightforward. Our biggest concern perhaps is the way the term is used to situate itself in the notion of food as a human right. Rights-based development has been with us for many years and it seems all agencies and actors support and advocate it. However, where rights are seen to be essential and important to provide a context in which they might be legally defended, although that has achieved very little in Egypt, we must not substitute a rights-based approach for one based upon an understanding of social class and the global context in which class power, and imperialist strategies within the food system, operate systemically to prevent FS. Food sovereignty means the processes of agricultural production that delivers the independence of the countryside, and the state, from the subordination of decision-making to the international law of value. We have stressed that peasants, rural producers and their dependents are the fundamental building blocs of society and the independence of this social *class* are what will ultimately facilitate radical, class-based transformation or the dramatic expansion of public good provisions and the squeezing out of private appropriation of labour power and surplus value.

Food sovereignty is seldom debated with this dominant class-based meaning yet political alliances necessary to advance it remain crucial and important. There remains nevertheless immense value in the ways in which advocates for FS help generate and build political and social mobilisation. The term and the political movements linked to it are important. This is not the least because they have shown the temporal character to capitalism by contributing to an historicity of it. Food sovereignty has developed in the context of rural subordination, dependence and pressure from state and capitalist markets and their major actors, MNCs and agribusiness in particular (Bush and Martiniello 2017; Martiniello 2015b). Food sovereignty has generated an opportunity for investigation of the ways in which socio-ecology and political economy interact, creating crises and opportunity for the transformation of the (global) agro-ecological systems.

Moving towards Food Sovereignty

Food sovereignty offers an alternative to the corporate food regime where corporate control is replaced by community and producer initiatives (Akram-Lodhi 2015:564). The issue remains, however, of how can FS deliver the alternative in the context of the dominant corporate food regime and in the context of authoritarian politics that attempts to close space for small farmer resistance to government policy? Additionally, how can FS be delivered where there is evidence that counter-revolutionary forces are at work to undermine activism, to NGOise rural movements for real change and to hijack initiatives for radical social transformation? We can offer optimism of the will, something that is absolutely necessary for mobilisation and discussion and action to deliver what is possible. We also, however, need to express caution and pessimism of the intellect to recognise fully the extent to which big pharma and other interests of international capital are busy sabotaging movements for social justice (Martiniello and Nyamsenda 2018).

We have noted some of the contemporary dimensions of the crisis in what might be the emergence of a fourth food regime. These have been linked to crises of profitability, increased struggle and contestation for access to food, especially during and in the aftermath of the 2008 financial crisis, and in the case of Egypt and Tunisia, in the post-uprising period. There are large global macroeconomic issues that local food protest intersects with relating to issues of international trade, expansion of territorial land grabs by states and companies and how 'flexi crops' shape new patterns of production and distribution on a global scale. There are also the issues linked more explicitly to FS agendas of the relationship between workers in the core and periphery of capitalism, rural and urban relationships between producers and consumers but also around crop choice, pricing and distribution and gendered relations of production and social reproduction (Alonso-Fradejas et al 2015).

The idea of FS is not new to farmers in Egypt or Tunisia. While the use of the term may still be unfamiliar, the struggles waged by farmers have centred on key elements of FS. We have noted how farmers in both countries fought for sustainable and guaranteed access to land, water and irrigation. They have also struggled to access seeds that are not chemically modified, nor out of date. And they have protested against the advance of middlemen traders who grew enormously after the 1990s as the neo-liberal Tunisian and Egyptian state made partial, and not always comprehensive, market reform. The bene-ficiaries of state liberalisation were those social groups, like the military, older landed interests, new entrepreneurs and those linked to the state. That cro-nyism caricatured by the Trabelsi clan enrichment in Tunisia is not a crude crony capitalism. That catch-all phrase does not capture the complex char-acter of the class configuration that exercises power in Tunisia and Egypt. This is especially as the security state in Egypt (Abdelrahman 2017) enforces a mode of accumulation that not only enriches the military but also US and EU capitalist interests in finance, extractives and promotion of regional law and 'disorder'. Since the 1990s, 1987 in the case of Egypt, state policy undermined small farmer livelihoods. Family farmers in Egypt's delta and Upper Egypt, and in central and southern as well as northwest Tunisia, have been increas-ingly disregarded, abjected and pushed away from development opportunities. State policy has supported the interests of larger investors and the purveyors of mechanisation and chemicalised agriculture. The struggle against the rule of capital in agriculture has been the struggle for FS. In both countries, there have been struggles against patterns of agricultural modernisation that have reduced farmer autonomy to adjuncts of industrial- and urban-based devel-opment. Yet what also needs to be remembered is that the state in Egypt and Tunisia has not been operating in a national or even regional vacuum. The regimes in both countries have been subjected to the global (US, EU and Japan) law of value, the uneven incorporation of the respective political econ-omies into globalisation and the financial gains that accrue from the process of imperialism.

There is a history of local and national rebellion against the impact of Egypt and Tunisia's uneven incorporation into the world economy and the deleterious consequences for the poor. We have presented our arguments in this book in the context of understanding the historical trajectory of both countries, of the ups and downs, of optimistic struggles with global and local capitalists and downturns where both political economies and the peasants and farmers within them have been squeezed as part of accelerated austerity. Part of the historical optimism in Egypt had been with the Free Officers seizure of power and the presidency of Abdel Nasser who had so dramatically elevated the (incomplete) transformation of the countryside in his attempt to cap the size of landholdings and the political power of landowners. President Nasser's land reforms of 1952, 1958 and 1961 may not have been extensive, distributing about one-seventh of the country's cultivable land from landowners to smallholders, tenants and landless but it was the only example in the Middle East where seized land was passed on from the state to the *fellahin* (Owen 2000). The benefits for small farmers were remarkably positive in terms of reducing rural poverty, promoting growth and establishing a politicisation of land that continues in Egypt (El Ghonemy 1993; 1999). In so doing there is a measure of hope that FS struggles will be enlarged.

The context of Nasser's land reforms was the generalised expectation in the late 1950s and 1960s for progressive national development, liberation from colonialism and the possibility for food self-sufficiency. These ideals were among those recognised as significant by the newly formed non-aligned movement created after the Bandung conference in April 1955 and the Organisation of African Unity in May 1963. The economist Fawzy Mansour in Egypt explored the possibility for auto-centred development. This was later developed by Samir Amin, who also worked for a short period in the Egyptian Institute for Economic Management from 1957 to 1960. Fawzy Mansour's insistence on the importance of planning and its democratic control extended to the use of local knowledge and technology to boost local control of agriculture (Ajl 2018a, 70). We can now look a little further at the idea of auto centred development, what the necessary conditions would be to deliver it and how significant it is for deepening the debate about FS.

In Tunisia, in the heady optimistic days of a possible new international economic order and Third World nationalism, in the 1960s and 1970s, a 'Tunisian school' emerged. A populist agronomy developed an agenda that captured the contemporary call for FS. Technicians and populist agronomists, Azzam Mahjoub, Abdeljelil Bedoui and Slaheddine el-Amami developed plans for food sufficiency based on local technology and knowledge that was in direct contrast to colonial and then postcolonial agricultural policy (Ajl 2018a; 2018b). These analysts understood the importance of labour-centred farming that was both more sustainable and productive. They envisaged the possibility of promoting a peasant path of development. The political difficulty, however, was to establish hegemonic social forces that would shape agricultural strategy and successfully counter the Washington consensus policy of structural adjustment and neo-liberal economic reform.

The rise of Reagonomics and Thatcherism after 1979 slowed and then pretty much prevented Third World alternatives not only to agricultural policy but also to any divergence from the neo-liberal revolution. And yet the capitalist crisis of the 1970s and lost development decades of the 1980s had something that was in common with the more recent financial crash in 2008. That is, they both generated resistance to austerity and the possibility for alternatives to be debated. It is a key feature of capitalist development that it spurs dissent as a result of the inequality upon which it is founded. As we have noted, however, the construction of a political force to promote sustainable alternatives to the mainstream policy of food security has been repeatedly overturned. There has been much evidence of resistance to neo-liberal reform, to the promotion of export agriculture instead of a strategy to enrich small farmers to improve rural livelihoods and family diets with locally produced food for local consumption. There has been constant reminder to policymakers that farmers resist the consequences of policy that reduces their autonomy. Small farmers' struggles are in fact struggles for greater autonomy from the world capitalist system where the food question is no longer, if ever it had been, simply about the working class, providing cheap abundant food for the proletariat in the Global North. Agrarian questions are reformulated by the growing counter-weight of FS, by the very social reproduction of the food producers themselves (McMichael 2014, 446).

The post-2008 capitalist crisis has promoted the debate about the need for new and fairer settlements between states and workers in the Global North (Coates 2018). However, the 'morbid symptoms' (Gramsci 1971, 276) of cap-italist decay have yet to create a social movement of resistance to the persistent socialisation of the costs of keeping capitalism alive while the high returns to capital continue to accrue to private investors boosting capital accumulation and profit-taking.

An alternative to the mainstream that we have briefly referred to and which promotes a peasant first strategy is delinking (Amin, S. 1990). This alternative development strategy for the Third World is integral to a strategy of FS. The peasant path that delinking and national sovereign projects pro-mote will be a strategy to break from the exploitative global trade regime imposed by the law of value established by the United States, EU and Japan. Comparative advantage has long been the neo-liberal trope and rationale for iniquitous global trade relations and the mantra of food security: produce what you can produce most cheaply and rush those (primary) products onto the global market at prices that cannot compete with the costs of embodied labour of imported Western manufactures. Delinking from global trade networks is a strategy to promote greater dependence upon local agriculture. This requires a rural development strategy that secures the interests of family farmers and incentivises greater agricultural production. This is deliverable with shared farmer rewards allocated democratically and not simply through prices and markets controlled by merchants, land owners and MNCs. This will not necessarily mean that Egypt and Tunisia, or any other underdeveloped country, needs to promote autarky: a complete separation or attempt to be independent from the world economy. It is instead a strategy that tries to create conditions for the development of an economy that focuses upon the production locally of commodities that had prices shaped by local costs and not by the dominant international law of value.

Delinking and separation from existing globalisation is unlikely to take place quickly or easily even where states have political consensus to disengage from dependence upon international actors. At least in the preliminary phases of the alternative development strategy, underdeveloped economies will continue to work alongside exploitative global forces. This continues because of the need to access strategic goods and services but to do so on the terms set by the South. Selective engagement would be short term, however. It would provide the necessary conditions for transition to the alternative path for socialist autocentred development. This will involve the development of national sovereign projects to confront 'apartheid at the global level'. This apartheid was structured around the higher costs of northern commodities and the extraction of unprocessed resources from the periphery. A socialist transition with FS at its heart requires the political conditions to establish autocentered development and then a strategy to promote national (sovereign) development. The latter would help build a project that linked nationally and regionally without continuous dependence upon imported commodities. It is a strategy that is dependent upon a boost to local agricultural production that valued farmers, increased prices paid to rural producers that would help retain farm labour avoiding rural-urban migration and building and consolidating local skilled labour. It is, in sum, a development strategy centred around rural development.

This potential strategy for embedding FS in development and extricating underdeveloped economies from rural impoverishment was championed in the work of Samir Amin. The model for an alternative was founded on his critique of capitalist development in what was the most important critique from the Third World. His *Accumulation on a World Scale* (1974a) highlighted and documented how capitalist development structured the South, or rather the Third World into the production of export goods, which paid for the import of luxury goods for a small local elite. Cheap Third World labour produced food and mineral exports to the centre through a mechanism of unequal exchange: the return to labour in the periphery was less than returns to labour in the centre. This exploitative asymmetrical relationship made it impossible for the South to develop or 'catch up' with the West. There was little prospect in the South of a self-centred system of capitalist development that had proved so important to Europe. Instead of the system that shaped Western development, where the production of capital goods for consumer goods production generated mass markets, the periphery only had (limited) export income that was not used for capital goods and industrial growth but to pay for limited luxury good consumption by an aspiring national bourgeoisie. There cannot be any successful emulation of Western development models in Egypt and Tunisia or elsewhere in the Third World. Instead, a new system of self-reliance, of 'becoming aware' (Lawrence 2018) is necessary for Egypt and Tunisia to establish a successful alternative to the policies and outcomes of imperialism. The new alternative requires a process of partial delinking from the world economy, for a political agenda of sovereign states to work in solidarity and to also develop incrementally a strategy for socialism that would necessarily involve the empowerment of the peasantry.

Conclusion

We have had historical examples from Egypt and Tunisia regarding the need for the development of autonomous development as a response to colonial dependency and uneven incorporation into the world economy (Ajl 2018a). Yet the contemporary period only offers glimpses of attempts to develop meaningful alternatives to food security. The development of strong FS agendas is piecemeal and marginal and seldom with the use of the term FS or with reaching out to broader linked social movements that internation-ally at least advance FS. In Tunisia there is a group called Million Rural Women, linked to La Via Campesina since the summer of 2017, yet its outreach remains limited. There are pockets of autonomy especially in rela-tion to the national seed bank in Tunis and a variety of local seed banks especially in and around the Gabes oasis. These banks preserve and extend the life of local seed varieties and they do so despite pressure from agro chemical companies and the Tunisian Ministry of Agriculture to open the local market to genetically modified organisms. In doing this, farmers are advancing a strong case for their autonomy from international capital. As one organic seed bank collector and distributor, at local markets in Chenini, Gabes noted:

Everything that you have on the table is from seed' and we need to let the youth know how important it is to safeguard heirloom varieties.

Even where local seed may not be as productive it is repeatedly noted by local small scale Tunisian farmers that heirloom varieties are more robust in local conditions. And linked to organic methods of irrigation, using a mix of farm water and manure, farmers are advancing techniques of agro ecology and benefitting from them (Field visits February 2013 and September 2018).

Egyptian farmers continue to protest the seizure of their land from private landlords. It seems landowners have had a green light from el-Sisi's military dictatorship to do this. While there was optimism after the 2011 uprising that farmers would enjoy new freedoms and opportunities from the GoE, it was not forthcoming. On the contrary, farmers have been harassed, they have had crops damaged and there has been considerable police intimidation if farmers have had the temerity to challenge landowner aggression. Small farmers have been tied up in lengthy and costly legal proceedings where big landowners have reclaimed land that they had lost during Nasser's agrarian reforms in the 1950s. And in addition, small farmers have had to try and navigate survival at a time of increased rents, and when costs of farming including seed and fertiliser prices have increased (Human Rights Watch 2019). There is now widespread suppression of alternative development voices in Egypt and it seems the countryside has an extensive surveillance from informants and security agents. In that context the possibility for mobilising a FS agenda is slim, but evidence does suggest a continuation of rural struggles against landlordism and for greater farmer autonomy from neo-liberal markets.

Under the circumstances of repression, FS is less likely to be seen in terms of transforming agrarian systems based on inequality and power of landowners and officials linked to the state. Pathways to FS in these circumstances are likely to address policy and institutional exclusions and to voice out moments of acute marginalisation. There is now a declared decade (2019–28) of family farming announced by the UN (2017) and it will provide a moment or two to demonstrate the case for small farmers. It is nevertheless unlikely that the initiative will create conditions for much poverty alleviation or, address land hunger. For FS to be delivered that is transformatory, it will have to be part of a wide range of policy reforms that promote agrarian reform, restrict land and commodity markets, promote favourable pricing incentives and boost the ability for farmers to retain large proportions of their surpluses. These reforms will ultimately need to be part of broader international food trade regime reforms. They will require the Egyptian and Tunisian state to seize private assets for the public sector and shape rather than be subordinate to the whims and pressures of international finance. That package (Akram-Lodhi 2015) is a long way off. Recent World Bank material continues to use the language of 1960s modernisation theory. In its policy review of Egyptian agriculture, for instance, the World Bank (2017) talks about the potential for the country's agricultural sector to be 'unlocked', but there is little room in that hegemonic discourse for the voices of family farmers and landless workers to be heard.

REFERENCES

Abbas, Raouf, and Assem El-Dessouky. 2012. *The Large Landowing Class and the Peasantry in Egypt, 1837–1952*. Cairo: The American University in Cairo Press.

Abdel-Fadhil, Hussein Mahmoud. 1978. *Al-Tahawwulât al-Iqtisâdiyya wa-l-Ijtimâ'iyya fi-l-rîf al-Misrî (Social and Economic Changes in Rural Egypt 1952–1970)*. Cairo: Al-Hay'a al-Masriyya al-'Amma li-l-Kitâb.

———. 1990. 'Nouvelle Perspective sur l'Avenir de l'Agriculture et sur la Question Agraire en Égypte'. *Tiers-Monde* 31, no. 121 (Janvier-Mars): 15–28.

Abdel Khalek, Gouda. 2002. 'Stabilization and Adjustment in Egypt: Sequencing and Sustainability'. In *Counter-Revolution in Egypt's Countryside: Land and Farmers in the Era of Economic Reform*, edited by Ray Bush, 32–54. New York: Zed Books.

Abdelrahman, Maha. 2004. *Civil Society Exposed: The Politics of NGOs in Egypt*. Cairo: American University of Cairo Press.

———. 2011. 'The Transnational and the Local: Egyptian Activists and Transnational Protest Networks'. *British Journal of Middle Eastern Studies* 38, no. 3: 407–24.

———. 2012. 'A Hierarchy of Struggles? The "Economic" and the "Political" in Egypt's Revolution'. *Review of African Political Economy* 39, no. 134: 614–28. http://dx.doi.org/10.1080/03056244.2012.738419.

———. 2015. *Egypt's Long Revolution: Protest Movements and Uprisings*. London: Routledge.

———. 2017. 'Policing Neoliberalism in Egypt: The Continuing Rise of the "Securocratic" State'. *Third World Quarterly* 38, no. 1: 185–202.

Aboulnaga, A., I. Siddick, W. Megahed, E. Salah, S. Ahmed, R. Nageeb, D. Yassin and M. Abdelzaher. 2017. *Small-Scale Family Farming in the Near East and North Africa Region. Focus Country: Egypt*. Cairo: FAO-CIRAD.

Achcar, Gilbert. 2013. *The People Want: A Radical Exploration of the Arab Uprising*. London: Saqi Books.

ADA (Agence de Développement Agricole – ADA-Maroc). 2018. *Les fondements de la Stratégie Plan Maroc Vert*. Accessed 5 August 2018. http://www.ada.gov.ma/page/les-fondements-de-la-strategie-plan-maroc-vert.

African Development Bank Group. 2012. *Tunisia: Economic and Social Challenges Beyond the Revolution*. Tunis. African Development Bank.

Agricultural Wire. 2017. 'Egypt Seizes 9,000 Tonnes of Sugar in Raids Amid Shortage'. Accessed 24 August. http://agriculturewire.com/egypt-seizes-9000-tonnes-of-sugar-in-raids-amid-shortage/.

Agwah, Ada. 1978. 'Import Substitution, Export Expansion and Consumption Liberalization: The Case of Egypt'. *Development and Change* 9, no. 2: 299–329.

Ahmed, Yasmine Mohamed, and Reem Saad. 2011. 'Interview with Shahenda Maklad'. *Review of African Political Economy* 38, no. 127: 159–67.

Al Ahram Weekly. 2016. 'Man Arrested in Cairo for Carrying Too Much Sugar Released On Bail'. 16 October. Accessed 24 August 2017. http://english.ahram.org.eg/NewsContent/1/64/245914/Egypt/Politics-/Man-arrested-in-Cairo-for-carrying-too-much-sugar.aspx.

Ajl, Max. 2018a. 'Post-Dependency Perspectives on Agriculture in Tunisia'. *Review of African Political Economy* 45, no. 156: 300–308.

———. 2018b. 'Auto-Centered Development and Indigenous Technics: Slaheddine el-Amami and Tunisian Delinking'. *Journal of Peasant Studies* (May): https://doi.org/10.1080/03066150.2018.1468320.

Ajl, Max, and Habib Ayeb. 2018. 'Food Sovereignty and the Environment: An Interview with Habib Ayeb'. Accessed 1 June 2019. http://roape.net/2018/04/12/food-sovereignty-and-the-environment-an-interview-with-habib-ayeb/ and https://osae-marsad.org/2018/04/21/paysanneries-food-council-and-environment/.

Akari, Tahar, and Mustapha Jouili. 2010. 'La transmission des effets de la crise alimentaire sur les dépenses de compensation : Cas de la Tunisie'. Presented at the Joint 3rd African Association of Agricultural Economists (AAAE) and 48th Agricultural Economists Association of South Africa (AEASA) Conference, Cape Town, South Africa.

Akesbi, Najib. 2011. 'Le Plan Maroc Vert: Une analyse critique'. In *Questions d'économie marocaine*, 9–48. Casablanca: Association Marocaine des Sciences Economiques.

———. 2014. 'Which Agricultural Policy for Which Food Security in Morocco?'. In *Seasonal Workers in Mediterranean Agriculture: The Social Costs of Eating Fresh*, edited by Jörg Gertel and Sarah Ruth Sippel, 167–74. New York: Routledge.

Akesbi, Najib, D. Benatya and N. El Aoufi. 2008. *L'agriculture marocaine à l'épreuve de la libéralisation*. Rabat: Economie critique.

Akram-Lodhi, H. 2012. 'Contextualising Land Grabbing: Contemporary Land Deals, the Global Subsistence Crisis and the World Food System'. *Canadian Journal of Development Studies* 33, no. 2: 119–42.

———. 2015. 'Accelerating towards Food Sovereignty'. *Third World Quarterly* 36, no. 3: 563–83.

Akram-Lodhi, H., and C. Kay. 2010a. 'Surveying the Agrarian Question (Part 1): Unearthing the Foundations, Exploring Diversity'. *Journal of Peasant Studies* 37, no. 1: 177–202.

———. 2010b. 'Surveying the Agrarian Question (Part 2): Current Debates and Beyond'. *Journal of Peasant Studies* 37, no. 2: 255–84.

Albrecht, H. 2012. 'Authoritarian Transformation or Transition from Authoritarianism? Insights on Regime Change in Egypt'. in *Arab Spring in Egypt. Revolution and Beyond*, edited by Bahgat Korany and Rahab El-Mahdi, 251–70. Cairo: American University in Cairo Press.

Alexander, Anne, and Myriam Aouragh. 2014. 'Egypt's Unfinished Revolution: The Role of the Media Revisited'. *International Journal of Communication* 8: 890–915.

Allal, Amin. 2010. 'Réformes néolibérales, clientélismes et protestations en situation autoritaire. Les mouvements contestataires dans le bassin minier de Gafsa en Tunisie (2008)'. *Politique Africaine* 117, no. 1: 107–25.

Allal, Amin, and Vincent Geisser, 2011. 'Tunisie: Révolution de jasmin' ou Intifada?'. *Mouvements* 66, no. 2 : 62–68.

Allan, Tony. 2001. *The Middle East Water Question: Hydropolitics and the Global Economy*. London: I. B. Tauris.

Ali, Tariq. 2013. 'Between Past and Future'. *New Left Review* 80 (March–April). Accessed 4 March 2019. https://newleftreview.org/II/80/tariq-ali-between-past-and-future.

Alonso-Fradejas, Alberto, Saturnino M. Borras Jr., Todd Holmes, Eric Holt-Giménez and Martha Jane Robbins. 2015. 'Food Sovereignty: Convergence and Contradictions, Conditions and Challenges'. *Third World Quarterly* 36, no. 3: 431–48.

Al-Noubi. E. 2017. 'The New Minister of Agriculture in His First Statements: Egypt Shall Not Progress Agriculturally without Scientific Research'. Accessed 20 February 2017. http://www.youm7.com/story/2017/2/14/وزيـر-الزراعة-الجـديـد-فـى-أول-تـصريحـاتـه-/3102418.مـصر-لـن-تـتـقوفـارزاعـياً

Althusser, Louis. 2005 (1965). *For Marx.* Verso: London.

Amin, Galal. 1999. 'Major Determinants of Economic Development in Egypt'. In *Twenty Years of Development in Egypt (1977–1997): Cairo Papers in Social Sciences*, vol. 21, no. 3, 42–49. Cairo : American University of Cairo Press.

———. 2014. *Whatever Happened to the Egyptian Revolution?* Cairo: American University of Cairo Press.

Amin, Samir. 1974a. *Accumulation on a World Scale: A Critique of the Theory of Underdevelopment.* Vols 1 and 2 combined. Sussex: Harvester Press.

———. 1974b. 'Accumulation and Development'. *Review of African Political Economy* 1, August-November (Reprinted June 1978): 9–26.

———. 1990. *Towards a Polycentric World.* London: Zed Books.

———. 2011b. *Eurocentrism, Modernity, Religion and Democracy: A Critique of Eurocentrism and Culturalism.* 2nd edition. New York: Monthly Review Press and Pambazuka Press.

———. 2011a. 'Food Sovereignty: A Struggle for Convergence in Diversity'. In *Food Movements Unite!*, edited by Eric Holt-Giménez. Oakland, CA: Food First Books.

———. 2011c. 'Le Printemps arabe?'. *Mouvements* 3, no. 67: 135–56. DOI: 10.3917/ mouv.067.0135.

———. 2013. *The Implosion of Contemporary Capitalism.* New York: Monthly Review Press.

———. 2017a. 'The Sovereign Popular Project: The Alternative to Liberal Globalization', *Journal of Labor and Society* 20, no. 1 (March): 7–22.

———. 2017b. 'The Agrarian Question a Century after October 1917: Capitalist Agriculture and Agricultures in Capitalism'. *Agrarian South: Journal of Political Economy* 6, no. 2 (August): 149–74.

———. 2018. *Modern Imperialism, Monopoly Finance Capital, and Marx's Law of Value.* New York: Monthly Review Press.

André, Romain, Élisa Le Briand, Saint-Araille Anna and Zammouri Saber. 2014. *Mezzouna, après la chute* (Film), 85 min.

Aouragh, Myriam, and Anne Alexander. 2011. 'The Egyptian Experience: Sense and Nonsense of the Internet Revolution'. *International Journal of Communication* 5: 1344–58.

Araghi, F. 2000. 'The great enclosures of our times: Peasants and the agrarian question at the end of the twentieth century'. In *Hungry for Profit. The Agribusiness Threat to Farmers, Food and the Environment* edited by F. Magdoff, J. Bellamy Foster, and F. H. Buttel, 145–60. New York: Monthly Review Press.

———. 2009a. 'Accumulation by Displacement: Land Enclosures, Food Crises and the Ecological Contradiction of Capitalism'. *Review* 32, no. 1: 113–46.

———. 2009b. 'The Invisible Hand and The Visible Foot'. In *Peasants and Globalization: Political Economy, Rural Transformation and the Agrarian Question*, edited by H. Akram-Lodhi and C. Kay, 111–47. London: Routledge.

———. 2010. 'The End of Cheap Ecology and the Crisis of Long Keynesiansim'. *Economic and Political Weekly* 45, no. 4: 39–41.

Ayeb, Habib. 1993. *Le Bassin du Jourdain dans le conflit israélo-arabe.* Beirut: CERMOC.

———. 1998. *L'eau au Proche-Orient: la guerre n'aura pas lieu.* Paris-Le Caire: CEDEJ – Karthala.

———. 2003. *Sur les bords du Nil, l'eau en partage.* Documentary film. http://www.doc2geo.fr/visionner/sur-les-bords-du-nil-l-eau-en-partage.

———. 2008. 'La crise alimentaire en Egypte: compétition sur les ressources, souveraineté alimentaire et rôle de l'Etat'. In *Hérodote.* Revue de géographie et de géopolitique. Bulletin d'Abonnement Institut Français de Géopolitique. N. 131. 4ème semestre, 58–72.

———. 2009. 'Hydropolitique de la Méditerranée'. In *Annuaire de la Méditerranée 2008.* Barcelone: IEME.

———. 2010. *La Crise de la Société Rurale en Egypte: La Fin du Fellah?'* Paris: Karthala.

———. 2011a. 'Social and Political Geography of the Tunisian Revolution: The Alfa Grass Revolution'. *Review of African Political Economy* 38, no. 129: 467–79. http://dx.doi.org/10.1080/03056244.2011.604250.

———. 2011b. *Water in the Arab Countries Global Perceptions and Local Realities* (Spanish). Madrid: Casa Arabe.

———. 2012. 'The Marginalization of the Small Peasantry: Egypt and Tunisia'. In *Marginality and Exclusion in Egypt,* edited by Ray Bush and Habib Ayeb. London, 72–96. Zed Books.

———. 2013. 'Le Rural Dans la Révolution en Tunisie: Les Voix Inaudibles'. *Demmer* (Blog). https://habibayeb.wordpress.com/2013/09/28/le-rural-dans-la-revolution-en-tunisie-les-voix-inaudibles/.

———. 2016. 'Après Ben-Guerdane: Déposessions, Déstructurations et Insécurité alimentaire dans le Sud-est Tunisien'. *Jadaliyya.* http://jadaliyya.com/Details/33192/Après-Ben-Guerdane--dépossessions,-déstructurations-et-insécurité-alimentaire-dans-le-Sud-est-tunisien.

———. 2017. 'Food Issues and Revolution: The Process of Dispossession, Class Solidarity, and Popular Uprising: The Case of Sidi Bouzid in Tunisia'. *Cairo Papers in Social Science* 34, no. 4: 86–110.

Ayeb, Habib, and Archambeau Olivier. 2003. *Sur les Bords du Nil; L'Eau en Partage* Documentary film. http://www.doc2geo.fr/visionner/sur-les-bords-du-nil-l-eau-en-partage.

Ayeb, Habib, and Ray Bush. 2014. 'Small Farmer Uprisings and Rural Neglect in Egypt and Tunisia'. *Middle East Research and Information Project* 272 (Fall): 2–11.

Ayeb, Habib, and Reem Saad. 2009. 'Introduction: Revisiting Agrarian Transformation in the Arab Region'. In *Agrarian Transformation in the Arab World: Persistent and Emerging Challenges,* Cairo Papers in Social Science, vol. 32, no. 2, 1–4. Cairo: American University of Cairo Press.

———. 2013. 'Gender, Poverty, and Agro-Biodiversity Conservation in Rural Egypt and Tunisia'. In *Agrarian Transformation in the Arab World: Persistent and Emerging Challenges,* Cairo Papers in Social Science, vol. 32. no. 2, edited by Habib Ayeb and Reem Saad, 129–55. Cairo : American University of Cairo Press.

Ayeb, Habib, and Ruf Thierry. 2009. *Water, Poverty and Social Crisis* (CD). Paris: IRD.

Bachta, Mohamed S. 2008. 'Tunisie. L'agriculture, l'Agro-Alimentaire, la Pêche et le Développement Rural'. In *Les Agricultures Méditerranéennes: Analyses Par Pays,* edited by M. Allaya, 75–94. Options Méditerranéennes: Série B. Etudes et Recherches no. 61. Montpellier: CIHEAM-IAMM. http://ressources.ciheam.org/om/pdf/b61/00800134.pdf.

———. 2011. 'La céréaliculture en Tunisie: Une politique de régulation à repenser." In *Les notes d'analyse du CIHEAM.* No. 64, 1–18. Paris: CIHEAM.

Badiou, Alain. 2014. 'A Present Defaults – Unless the Crowd Declares Itself'. *Verso Blog*. http://www.versobooks.com/blogs/1569-a-present-defaults-unless-thecrowd-declares-itself-alain-badiou-onukraine-egypt-and-finitude.

Baer, Gabriel. 1962. *A History of Landownership in Modern Egypt, 1800–1950*. London: Oxford University Press.

Bakre, M., J. Bethemont, R. Commere and A. Vant. 1980. *L'Égypte et le Haut barrage d'Assouan: de l'Impact à la Valorisation*. Saint-Étienne: Presses de l'Université de Saint-Étienne.

Bal, Mustafa. 2014. *Anatomy of a Revolution: The 2011 Egyptian Uprising*. New York: Columbia University Press.

Banque Mondiale. 2014. 'Tunisie: Revue des Politiques de Développement; La Révolution Inachevée'. Rapport No. 86179-TN.

Bauman, Zygmunt. 2004. *Wasted Lives/Modernity and its Outcasts*. Polity: Cambridge University Press.

Bayat, Asef. 2013. *Life as Politics. How Ordinary People Change the Middle East*. Stanford. Stanford University Press.

Baylouny, Anne Marie. 2011. 'A Workers' Social Movement on the Margin of the Global Neo-Liberal Order, Egypt 2004–2012'. In *Social Movements, Mobilisation and Contestation in the Middle East and North Africa*, edited by Joel Beinin and Frédéric Vairel

———. 2014. 'Mouvement ouvrier, luttes syndicales et processus révolutionnaire en Égypte, 2006–2013'. In *Soulèvements et recompositions politiques dans le monde arabe*, edited Camau Michel and Frédéric Vairel, 121–42. Montréal: Presses de l'Université de Montréal.

Beckerie, Kristine. 2017. 'US Officials Risk Complicity in War Crimes in Yemen'. Human Rights Watch, 4 May. Accessed 10 August 2017. https://www.hrw.org/news/2017/05/04/us-officials-risk-complicity-war-crimes-yemen.

Belkodja, Tahar. 1998. *Les trois décennies Bourguiba: témoignage*. Paris: Publisud.

Ben Nasr, Maaouia. 2016. La problématique de la sécurité alimentaire en Tunisie. PhD. Université Paris 1, Université Tunis El Manar.

Ben Said, Moncef, Jérôme Coste, Mohamed Elloumi, Vincent Ribier, Jean-Pierre Rolland and Boubaker Thabet. 2011. 'Actualisation Concertee De La Politique Agricole. Orientations pour un Nouvel Agenda Agricole Tunisien'. Tunis. Ministère de l'Agriculture et de l'Environnement et Agence Française de Développement (AFD).

Ben Salah, Ahmed. 2008. *Pour Rétablir la Vérité : Réformes et Développement en Tunisie 1961–1969*. Tunis: Cérès Editions.

Beinin, Joel. 2008. 'L'Égypte des ventres vides'. *Le Monde Diplomatique*. Mai. https://www.monde-diplomatique.fr/2008/05/BEININ/15861.

———. 2011. 'Egypt's Workers Rise Up: Egyptians' Aspirations to Democracy and Social Justice Will Depend on Workers' Willingness to Take to the Streets'. *The Nation*. https://www.thenation.com/article/egypts-workers-rise/.

———. 2012. 'The Rise of Egypt Workers'. *Carnegie Endowment for International Peace*. http://carnegieendowment.org/2012/06/28/rise-of-egypt-s-workers-pub-48689.

———. 2016. *Workers and Thieves: Labor Movements and Popular Uprisings in Tunisia and Egypt*. Stanford, CA: Stanford Briefs, an imprint of Stanford University Press.

Beinin, Joel, and Marie Duboc. 2013. 'A Workers' Social Movement on the Margin of the Global Neoliberal Order, Egypt 2004–2012'. In *Social movements, Mobilisation and Contestation in the Middle East and North Africa*, edited by Joel Beinin and Fréderic Vairel, 2nd edn, 205–27. Stanford, CA: Stanford University Press.

Beinin, Joel, and Zachary Lockman. 1987. *Workers on the Nile: Nationalism, Communism, Islam and the Egyptian Working Class, 1882–1954*. Princeton, NJ: Princeton University Press.

Bellamy Foster, John. 2000. *Marx's Ecology*. New York: Monthly Review Press.

———. 2013. 'Marx and the Rift in the Universal Metabolism of Nature'. *Monthly Review* 65, no. 7. Accessed 26 June 2019. monthlyreview.org/2013/12/01/marx-rift-universal-metabolism-nature/.

Bernstein, Henry. 2010. *Class Dynamics of Agrarian Change*. Halifax: Fernwood.

———. 2014a. 'Food Sovereignty Via "The Peasant Way": A Sceptical View'. *Journal of Peasant Studies* 14, no. 6: 1031–63.

———. 2014b. ' "African Peasants and Revolution" Revisited'. *Review of African Political Economy* 41, no. 143: S95–S107.

Bessaoud, Omar. 2004. "L'agriculture et la paysannerie en Algérie." In *L'Algérie 50 ans après. Etat des savoirs en sciences sociales et humaines, 1954–2004*, 359–84. Oran, Algeria: Centre de Recherche en Anthropologie Sociale et Culturelle.

———. 2007. "La stratégie de développement rurale en Algérie." In *Politiques de développement rural durable en Méditerranée dans le cadre de la politique de voisinage de l'Union Européenne*, edited by J. P. Chassany and J.-P. Pellissier, 79–89. Montpellier: CIHEAM.

Bessaoud, Omar, and Etienne Montaigne. 2009. 'Quelles réponses au mal-développement agricole? Analyse des politiques agricoles et rurales passées et présentes'. In *Perspectives des politiques agricoles en Afrique du Nord*, 51–91. Options Méditerranéennes, Série B. Etudes et Recherches no. 64. Paris: CIHEAM. https://prodinra.inra.fr/record/34661.

Bessis, Sophie, and Souhayr Belhassen. 2012. *Habib Bourguiba: Un Si Long Regne*. Tunis: Elyzad.

Bianchi, R. Robert. 1986. 'The Corporatization of the Egyptian Labour Movement'. *Middle East Journal* 40, no. 3: 429–44.

Boffo, Marco, Alfredo Saad-Filho, and Ben Fine. 2018. 'Neoliberal capitalism: The authoritarian turn'. In *A World Turned Upside Down*, edited by Leo Panitch and Greg Albo, Socialist Register, 2019, 247–70. London: Merlin Press.

Bonefeld, Werner. 2002. 'History and Social Constitution: Primitive Accumulation Is Not Primitive'. Accessed 27 February 2019. http://www.commoner.org.uk/debbonefeld01.pdf.

Borras, Saturnino M. Jr, and Jennifer C. Franco. 2012. 'Global Land Grabbing And Trajectories of Agrarian Change: A Preliminary Analysis'. *Journal of Agrarian Change* 12, no. 1 (January): 34–59.

Boughanmi, H., 1995. 'Les principaux volets des politiques agricoles en Tunisie : évolution, analyse et performances agricoles'. In *Les agricultures maghrébines à l' aube de l' an 2000*, edited by M. Allaya, 127–38. Options Méditerranéennes : Série B. Etudes et Recherches. Paris: CIHEAM.

Bourdieu, P. 1984. *Homo academicus*. Paris: Minuit.

Bracking, Sarah. 2016. *The Financialisation of Power: How Financiers Rule Africa*. Oxford: Routledge.

Bracking, Sarah, and Graham Harrison. 2003. 'Africa, Imperialism & New Forms of Accumulation'. *Review of African Political Economy* 30, no. 95: 5–10.

Braudel, Fernand. 1960. 'History and the Social Sciences: The Long Duration'. *American Behavioral Scientist* February, 3: 3–13.

Breisinger, Clemens, Olivier Ecker, Perrihan Al-Riffai and Bingxin Yu. 2012. *Beyond the Arab Awakening: Policies and Investments for Poverty Reduction and Food Security*. Washington, DC: International Food Policy Research Institute.

Breisinger, Clemens, Teunis van Rheenen, Claudia Ringler, Alejandro Nin-Pratt, Nicholas Minot, Catherine Aragon, Bingxin Yu, Olivier Ecker and Tingju Zhu. 2010. 'Food

Security and Economic Development in the Middle East and North Africa: Current State and Future Perspectives'. International Food Policy Research Institute, Discussion Paper 00985, May.

Bryceson, D. 1999. 'African rural labour, income diversification and livelihood approaches: a long-term development perspective.' *Review of African Political Economy* 80: 171–89.

B'Tselem. 2011. 'Dispossession and Exploitation: Israel's Policy in the Jordan Valley and Northern Dead Sea'. *B'Tselem*. Accessed 21 October 2016. http://www. btselem.org/publications/summaries/dispossession-and-exploitation-israels-policy-jordan-valley-northern-dead-sea.

Bush, Ray. 1998. 'Facing Structural Adjustment: Strategies of Peasants, the State, and the International Financial Institutions'. In *Directions of Change in Rural Egypt*, edited by Nicholas Hopkins and K. Westergaard Peter, 89–108. Cairo: American University of Cairo Press.

———. 1999. *Economic Crisis and the Politics of Reform in Egypt*. Boulder, CO: Westview Press.

———. 2002. 'Land Reform and Counter-Revolution'. In *Counter-Revolution in Egypt's Countryside*, edited by Ray Bush, 3–31. London: Zed Books.

———. 2004a. 'Civil Society and the Uncivil State; Land Tenure Reform in Egypt and the Crisis of Rural Livelihoods'. Civil Society and Social Movements Programme. Paper Number 9. Geneva. United Nations Research Institute for Social Development (UNRSID).

———. 2004b. 'Poverty and Neo-liberal Bias in the Middle East and North Africa'. *Development and Change* 35, no. 4: 673–95.

———. 2007. *Poverty and Neoliberalism*. London: Pluto.

———. 2009 'The Land and the People'. In *Egypt: The Moment of Change*, edited by Rabab El-Mahdi and Philip Marfleet, 51–67. London: Zed Books.

———. 2010. 'Food Riots: Poverty, Power, Protest'. *Journal of Agrarian Change* 10, no. 1: 119–29.

———. 2014. 'Food Security in Egypt'. In *Food Security in the Middle East*, edited by Z. Babar & S. Mirgani. London: Hurst.

———. 2016. 'Agrarian Transformation in the Near East and North Africa: Influences from the work of Lionel Cliffe'. *Review of African Political Economy* 43, no. S1 (September): 69–85.

———. 2018. 'The "Arab Spring" in North Africa: Egypt and Tunisia'. In *Crisis and Conflict in Agriculture*, edited by Rami Zurayk, Eckart Woertz and Rachel Bahn, 91–104. Oxford: CABI.

Bush, Ray, and Habib Ayeb, eds. 2012. *Marginality and Exclusion In Egypt*. London: Zed Books.

———. 2014. *Fellahin*. Documentary film. http://www.athimar.org/Article-57.

Bush, Ray, Lionel Cliffe and Valery Jansen.1986. 'The Crisis in the Reproduction of Migrant Labour in Southern Africa'. In *World Recession and the Food Crisis in Africa*, edited by Peter Lawrence, 283–99. London: James Currey.

Bush, Ray, and Giuliano Martiniello. 2017. 'Food Riots and Protest: Agrarian Modernizations and Structural Crises'. *World Development* 91 (March): 193–207.

Camau, Michel. 1984. 'L'État tunisien: de la tutelle au désengagement'. *Maghreb – Machrek* 103: 8–38.

———. 1999. 'La transitologie à l'Epreuve du Moyen-Orient et de l'Afrique du Nord'. In *Annuaire de l'Afrique du Nord*, tome XXXVIII. Paris: CNRS Editions.

Campling, Liam, Satoshi Miyamura, Jonathan Pattenden and Benjamin Selwyn. 2016. 'Class Dynamics of Development: a methodological note'. *Third World Quarterly* 37, no. 10: 1745–67.

Carnegie Endowment for International Peace. 2015. 'Food Insecurity in War-Torn Syria: From Decades of Self Sufficiency to Food Dependence. Regional Insight'. 4 June. Accessed 29 August 2018. https://carnegieendowment.org/2015/06/04/food-insecurity-in-war-torn-syria-from-decades-of-self-sufficiency-to-food-dependence-pub-60320.

Central Agency for Public Mobilisation and Statistics (CAPMAS). 1996. http://www.capmas.gov.eg/Pages/IndicatorsPage.aspx?Ind_id=1123.

Centre d'Etude et de Formation Interprofessionnelle Solidaires (CEFI). 2012. 'Il faut s'attendre à une deuxième révolution'. Entretien avec Adnen Hajji, décembre 2011 (Interview accordée à Afriques21). Solidaires International, no. 8: 105–9.

Chater, Kalifa. 1984. Dépendance et mutations précoloniales: larégence de Tunis de 1815 à 1857. Tunis: Université de Tunis.

Chayanov, A. V. 1966. The Theory of Peasant Economy, edited by D. Thorner, B. Kerblay and R. E. F. Smith. Manchester: Manchester University Press.

Chenoweth, J., Panos Hadjinicolaou, Adriana Bruggeman, Jos Lelieveld, Zev Levin, Manfred A. Lange, Elena Xoplaki and Michalis Hadjikakou. 2011. 'Impact of Climate Change on the Water Resources of the Eastern Mediterranean and Middle East Region: Modeled 21st Century Changes and Implications'. Water Resource Research 47, no. 6.

Cherif, Youssef. 2017. 'The Kamour Movement and Civic Protests in Tunisia'. Accessed 10 August 2017. http://carnegieendowment.org/2017/08/08/kamour-movement-and-civic-protests-in-tunisia-pub-72774?mkt_tok=eyJpIjoiTnpnMllqUTFOMkkxTjJFNCIsInQiOiIwQUo0oOK1h2OEpJcDRYblg1MjB6dncwcW9zRXo1a2lDUzRhb2hPMXVndFwvRTg2S0d5Qld0dFFA3SGxGYjdNWVFDbXNNReXBTZ2diWnR2TGw4clZDVmxxRRnNnM09GVUFWWWk3ZFpLXC9nbDV5c0h4STg3MnZtMUVcL3BUUXlOdHhHN0l2OCJ9.

Chouikha, Larbi. 2010. 'Évoquer la mémoire politique dans un contexte autoritaire: "l'extrême gauche" tunisienne entre mémoire du passé et identité présente'. L'Année du Maghreb VI: 427–40.

Ciaian, Pavel, Fatmir Guri, Miroslava Rajcaniova, Dusan Drabik and Sergio Gomez Y. Paloma. 2018. 'Land Fragmentation and Production Diversification: A Case Study from Rural Albania'. Land Use Policy 76 (July): 589–99.

Clapp, Jennifer. 2014 'Food Security and Food Sovereignty: Getting Past the Binary'. Dialogues in Human Geography 4, no. 2: 206–11.

Cline, W. R. 2007. Global Warming and Agriculture: Impacts Estimates by Country. Washington, DC: Centre for Global Development and the Peterson Institute for International Economics.

CNFA. 2017. 'Feed the Future Egypt Food Security and Agribusiness Support'. Accessed 1 June 2019. https://www.cnfa.org/program/food-security-and-agribusiness-support/.

Coates. David. 2018. Flawed Capitalism. The Anglo-American Condition and Its Resolution. London: Agenda.

Cockburn, Patrick. 2018. 'The Yemen Death Toll Is Five TImes Higher than We Think – We Can't Shrug Off Our Responsibilities Any Longer'. The Independent. 26 October. Accessed 14 February 2019. https://www.independent.co.uk/voices/yemen-war-death-toll-saudi-arabia-allies-how-many-killed-responsibility-a8603326.html.

Cohen. Robin. 1987. The New Helots. Migrants in the International Division of Labour. Aldershot: Avebury.

Cole, Juan. 2012. 'Creepy Israeli Planning for Palestinian Food Insecurity in Gaza Revealed'. *Informed Comment*, 18 October. Accessed 24 October 2016. http://www.juancole.com/2012/10/creepy-israeli-planning-for-palestinian-food-insecurity-in-gaza-revealed.html.

Cooke, Kieran. 2016. 'Saudi Investment Abroad. Land Grab or Benign Strategy?' Accessed 23 August 2017. http://www.middleeasteye.net/columns/saudi-agricultural-investment-abroad-land-grab-or-benign-investment-strategy-218650423.

Cross, Hannah, and Lionel Cliffe. 2017. 'A Comparative Political Economy of Regional Migration and Labour Mobility in West and Southern Africa'. *Review of African Political Economy* 44, no. 153 (September): 381–98.

Cuno, Kenneth M. 1992. *The Pasha's Peasants: Land, Society and Economy in Lower Egypt, 1740–1858*. Cambridge: Cambridge University Press.

———. 1993. 'The Origins of Private Ownership of Land in Egypt: A Reappraisal'. In *The Modern Middle East*, edited by Albert Hourani, Philip S. Khoury and Mary C. Wilson, 196–228. London: I.B. Tauris.

Daguzan, Jean-François. 2011. 'De la crise économique à la révolution politique?', *Maghreb – Machrek* 4, no. 206: 7–15. DOI: 10.3917/machr.206.0007. Accessed 1 June 2019. https://www.cairn.info/revue-maghreb-machrek-2010-4-page-7.htm.

———. 2011. 'L'Hiver après le printemps? La transformation arabe à l'aune des processus politico-militaires'. *Maghreb – Machrek* 4, no. 210: 19–34. DOI: 10.3917/machr.210.0019. https://www.cairn.info/revue-maghreb-machrek-2011-4-page-19.htm.

Dakhlia, Jocelyne, 2016. 'Peut-on penser dans la transition?'. *Dissonances-Nachaz Blog*. Accessed 31 July 2017. http://nachaz.org/blog/peut-on-penser-dans-la-transition-jocelyne-dakhlia/.

Daoud, A. 2011. 'La révolution tunisienne de janvier 2011: une lecture par les déséquilibres du territoire'. *EchoGéo* 2–13. Accessed 18 September 2018. http://echogeo.revues.org/12612.

Dardeer, A. E. 2017. 'The Egyptian Countryside Company: 7200 Application Forms Were Distributed to Small Peasants and Youth'. 19 February. Accessed 20 April 2017. http://www.almasdar.com/63481.

Datt, Gaurav, Dean Jolliffe and Manohar Sharma. 1998. 'A Profile of Poverty in Egypt: 1997'. FCND discussion paper 49, 102. Washington, DC: IFPRI – International Food Policy Research Institute (IFPRI).

Davis, Diana K. 2016. *The Arid Lands: History, Power, Knowledge*. Cambridge, MA: MIT Press.

Davis, Mike. 2006. *Planet of Slums*. London: Verso.

Daves, E. T., V. H. Warsch. 1976. 'Results Of Agricultural Planning In Tunisia 1961–1971'. In Stone E. R., *Change In Tunisia; Studies In The Social Sciences*, edited by E. R. Stone, 39–51. New York: State University of New York Press.

Dawisha, Adeed, and William Zartman. 1988. *Beyond Coercion: The Durability of the Arab State*. Oxford: Routledge Library Editions.

De Angelis, M. 1999. 'Marx's Theory of Primitive Accumulation: A Suggested Reinterpretation'. Accessed 1 September 2018. http://homepages.uel.ac.uk/M.DeAngelis/PIMACCA.htm.

Dearden, Lizzie. 2014. 'Israel-Gaza conflict: 50 Day Way By Numbers'. *The Independent*. 27 August. Accessed 14 August 2017. http://www.independent.co.uk/news/world/middle-east/israel-gaza-conflict-50-day-war-by-numbers-9693310.html.

Deulgaonkar, Parag. 2017. 'GCC Food Import Bill to Hit $53.1 Billion in 2020, Alpen Capital'. 23 February. Accessed 6 August 2017. http://www.arabianbusiness.com/gcc-food-import-bill-hit-53-1bn-in-2020-alpen-capital-664599.html.

Diamante, Sophia. 2017. '"Go Hungry": Egypt General Tells Millions to Stop Complaining'. *Middle East Eye*. 13 March. Accessed 18 August 2017. http://www.middleeasteye.net/news/general-tells-egyptians-starve-sake-egypt-490453969.

Dixon, W. Marion. 2018. 'Egypt's Indelible Link: Corporate Food, Frontiers, and Popular Revolt'. In 'Critical Agrarian Studies'. *Review Of African Political Economy*. Accessed 5 January 2019. http://roape.net/2018/07/10/egypts-indelible-link-corporate-food-frontiers-and-popular-revolt/.

Droogers, P., W. W. Immerzeel, W. Terink, J. Hoogeveen, M. F. P. Bierkens, L. P. H. van Beek and B. Debele. 2012. 'Water Resources Trends in Middle East and North Africa Towards 2050'. *Hydrology and Earth System Science* 16 (September): 3101–14.

Duffield, Mark. 2007. *Development, Security and Unending War: Governing the World of Peoples*. Cambridge: Polity.

Dumont, René. 1971. 'Notes sur les Implications Sociales de la "Révolution Verte" dans quelques Pays d'Afrique'. United Nations Research Institute for Development. Report 71.5. Geneva.

El-Chazli, Y., and Rayner H. 2015 'Une dynamique émergente: Le Processus Révolutionnaire à Alexandrie'. In *Soulèvements et recompositions politiques*, edited by Michel Camau and Frédéric Vairel. Montréal: Presses universitaires de Montréal, 92–120.

The Economist. 2016. 'Egypt Devalues Its Currency, at Last', 3 November. Accessed 23 August 2017. https://www.economist.com/news/middle-east-and-africa/21709612-government-has-finally-allowed-overvalued-pound-depreciate-egypt.

Edelman, Mark. 2014. 'Food Sovereignty: Forgotten Genealogies and Future Regulatory Challenges.' *Journal of Peasant Studies* 41, no. 6: 959–78.

Egyptian Streets. 2016. 'Egypt's Sisi: Economic reforms difficult but Essential' 15 October. Accessed 1 September 2017. https://egyptianstreets.com/2016/10/15/egypts-sisi-economic-reforms-difficult-but-essential/.

El Ghonemy, Riad. 1993.'Food Security and Rural Development in North Africa'. *Middle Eastern Studies* 29, no. 3 (July): 445–66.

———. 1999. 'Recent Changes in Agrarian Reform and Rural Development Strategies in the Near East'. *Land Reform* 1–2: 9–20.

———. 2002. 'Agrarian Reform Policy Issues Never Die'. Keynote speech at the Conference on Agrarian Reform and Rural development: Taking Stock, Organized by the Social research Center of the American University in Cairo, Egypt, 4–7 March 2002.

El Kadhi, Zouhair, Mohamed Adel Hentati and Sadok El Amri. 2014. 'Les enjeux de la sécurité alimentaire en Tunisie'. Docoument de travail No 4. Tunis. Tunisian Institute for Strategic Studies.

Ellis, Frank. 1993. *Peasant Economies. Farm Households and Agrarian Development*. Cambridge. Cambridge University Press.

Elloumi, Mohamed. 2006a. 'Agriculture et monde rural tunisiens dans le contexte de la mondialisation'. Communication colloque *Méthodes et Théories des Sciences Sociales*, 1–29. Tunis.

———. 2006b. 'L'agriculture Tunisienne Dans Un Contexte De Libéralisation'. *Revue Région Et Développement*, no. 23: 129–60.

———. 2013. 'Les terres domaniales en Tunisie. Histoire d'une appropriation par les pouvoirs publics'. *Études Rurales* 2, no. 192: 43–60.

Elloumi, Mohamed, and Boubaker Dhehibi. 2012. 'Agricultural Policy And Poverty In Tunisian Rural Areas: An Empirical Analysis Using Agricultural Prices And Investment'. *New Medit* 11, no. 4: 2–6.

El Katsha Samiha, and Susan Watts. 1997. 'Schistosomiasis in Two Nile delta Villages: An Anthropological Perspective', *Tropical Medicine and International Health* 2, no. 9 (September): 846–54.

El-Mahdi, Rabab. 2011. 'Orientalising the Egyptian Uprising'. *Jadaliyya.* Accessed 2 February 2013. http://www.jadaliyya.com/pages/index/1214/orientalising-the-egyptian-uprising.

———. 2012. 'Against Marginalization: Workers, Youth and Class in the 25 January Revolution'. In *Marginality and Exclusion in Egypt,* edited by Ray Bush and Habib Ayeb, 133–47. London: Zed Books.

El Nour, Saker. 2015a. 'The Peasants and Revolution in Egypt. From the National Movement of 1919 to the National Revolution of 2011'. *Third World Revue,* no. 222: 49–65.

———. 2015b. 'Small Farmers and the Revolution in Egypt: The Forgotten Actors'. *Contemporary Arab Affairs* 8, no. 2: 198–211. http://dx.doi.org/10.1080/17550912.2015.1016764.

Escobal, Javier. 2001. 'The Determinants of Nonfarm Income Diversification in Rural Peru.' *World Development* 29, no. 3: 497–508.

Evans, N. J., and B. W. Llbery. 1993. 'The Pluriactivity, Part-Time Farming, and Farm Diversification Debate'. *Environment and Planning* 25, no. 7: 945–59.

Evans, Brad, and Julian Reid. 2014. *Resilient Life: The Art of Living Dangerously.* Cambridge: Polity.

Export.gov. 2017. 'Tunisia – Agricultural Sector'. 22 June. Accessed 9 September 2017. https://www.export.gov/article?id=Tunisia-Agricultural-Sector.

Fahmy, Khaled. 1997. *All the Pasha's Men: Mehmed Ali, His Army and the Making of Modern Egypt.* Cambridge: Cambridge University Press.

Fautras, Mathilde. 2014. 'Mohamed Bouazizi, l'ouvrier agricole: Relire la 'révolution' depuis les campagnes tunisiennes'. *Jadaliyya.* Accessed 4 June 2015. http://www.jadaliyya.com/pages/index/18630/mohamed-bouazizi-louvrier-agricole_-relire-la-%C2%AB- r%C3%A9.

———. 2015. 'Land Injustices, Contestations And Community Protest in the Rural Areas Of Sidi Bouzid (Tunisia): The Roots Of The "Revolution"?' *Spatial Justice.* http://www.jssj.org/article/injustices-foncieres-contestations-et-mobilisations-collectives-dans-les-espaces-ruraux-de-sidi-bouzid-tunisie-aux-racines-de-la-revolution/.

———. 2017. 'La terre entre racines, épargnes et spéculations. Appropriations foncières et recompositions de l'espace rural à Regueb (Tunisie)'. PhD. Paris 10 University. https://halshs.archives-ouvertes.fr/tel-01625597v1.

Fawaz, Mahmood M., and Sarhan A. Soliman. 2016. 'The Potential Scenarios of the Impacts of Climate Change on Egyptian Resources and Agricultural Plant Production'. *Open Journal of Applied Sciences* 6, no. 4: 270–86. DOI: http://dx.doi.org/10.4236/ojapps.2016.64027. Published online April 2016 in SciRes. Accessed 7 Auguest 2017. http://www.scirp.org/journal/ojapps.

FEWS Net. 2017. 'Sudan'. Accessed 10 August 2017. http://www.fews.net/east-africa/sudan/food-security-outlook/february-2017.

Fine, Ben, and Alfredo Saad-Filho. 2004. *Marx's Capital.* 4th edition. London: Pluto Press.

Food and Agricultural Organisation of the United Nations (FAO). 1996. *Declaration on World Food Security.* World Food Summit. Rome: FAO.

———. 2009. *The Humanitarian Situation in Gaza and FAO's Response, 23 January.* Rome: Emergency Operations and Rehabilitation Division, Food and Agriculture Organization of the United Nations.

————. 2012. West Bank and Gaza Strip – Executive Brief 21 November. Rome: Food and Agriculture Organisation of the United Nations.

————. 2013a. 'Jordan Basin'. Accessed 2 August 2017. http://www.fao.org/nr/water/aquastat/basins/jordan/index.stm.

————. 2013b. 'Food Security And Nutritional Status in Egypt Worsening Amidst Economic Challenges'. 21 May. Accessed 16 August 2017. https://www.wfp.org/news/news-release/food-security-and-nutritional-status-egypt-worsening-amidst-economic-challenges.

————. 2014a. *Deep Roots*. Rome: FAO.

————. 2014b. International Year of Family Farming. Accessed 3 March 2019. www.fao.org/family-farming-2014/en.

————. 2017. Global Information and Early Warning System. 12 May. Accessed 9 September 2017. http://www.fao.org/giews/countrybrief/country.jsp?code=TUN.

Friedmann, Harriet. 1982. 'The Political Economy of Food: The Rise and Fall of the Postwar International Food Order'. *American Journal of Sociology* 88, S1 (January): 248–86.

————. 1987. 'International Regimes of Food and Agriculture Since 1870'. In *Peasants and Peasant Societies*, edited by T. Shanin, 247–58. Oxford: Basil Blackwell.

————. 1992. Distance and Durability: Shaky Foundations of the World Food Economy'. *Third World Quarterly* 13, no. 2: 371–83.

————. 1993. 'The Political Economy of Food: A Global Crisis'. *New Left Review* 1, no. 197: 29–57.

————. 1994. 'Distance and Durability: Shaky Foundations of the World Food Economy'. In *The Global Restructuring of Agro-Food Systems*, edited by P. McMichael. Ithaca: Cornell University Press.

————. 2005. 'From Colonialism to Green Capitalism: Social Movements and the Emergence of Food Regimes'. In *New Directions In The Sociology Of International Development. Research In Rural Sociology And Development*, vol. 11, edited by Buttel Frederick and Philip McMichael, 227–64. Amsterdam: Elsevier.

————. 2016. 'Bernstein-McMichael-Friedmann Dialogue on Food Regimes. Commentary: Food Regime Analysis and Agrarian Questions: Widening the Conversation'. *Journal of Peasant Studies* 43, no.3: 671–92.

Friedmann, Harriet, and Philip McMichael. 1989. 'Agriculture and the State System: The Rise and Fall of National Agricultures, 1870 to the Present'. *Sociologia Ruralis: European Society for Rural Sociology* 29, no. 2: 93–117. https://onlinelibrary.wiley.com/doi/abs/10.1111/j.1467-9523.1989.tb00360.x.

Gachet, Jean Paul. 1987. 'L'agriculture : Discours Et Stratégies'. In *La Tunisie Au Présent: Une Modernité Au-Dessus De Tout Soupçon?*, edited by Michel Camau, 82–188. Paris: CNRS.

Gana, Alia. 2011. 'Les Inégalités Socio-Territoriales Aux Origines De La Révolution Tunisienne: Défis Du Développement, Enjeux Pour La Recherche'. *La lettre de l'IRMC*, no. 6. http://irmc.hypotheses.org/226.

————. 2012a. 'Agriculteurs et paysans: nouveaux acteurs de la société civile et de la transition démocratique en Tunisie?' Tunis. L'Observatoire Tunisien de la Transition Démocratique (OTTD).

————. 2012b. Les Inégalités Socio-Territoriales Aux Origines De La Révolution Tunisienne: Défis Du Développement, Enjeux Pour La Recherche. Hypothèses, 4 pages.

————. 2012c. 'The Rural And Agricultural Roots of the Tunisian Revolution: When Food Security Matters'. *International Journal Of Sociology Of Agriculture And Food* 19, no. 2: 201–13.

Gani, Walid. 2013. 'Competition And Poverty Reduction: Tunisia'. In *Global Forum Competition And Poverty Reduction*, 249–54. Paris: OCDE/OECD. Accessed 15 February 2019. https://www.oecd.org/daf/competition/competition-and-poverty-reduction2013.pdf.

Gelabert, Esther. 2013. 'Le Printemps arabe en perspective'. *Cahiers de l'action* 2, no. 39: 11–17. DOI: 10.3917/cact.039.0011.

Ghazi, Boulila, and Sami Khedhiri. 2001. 'L'impact Agricole de la libéralisation des échanges entre la Tunisie, L'UE et le monde'. *Économie Rurale* 261: 93–103. https://www.persee.fr/doc/ecoru_0013-0559_2001_num_261_1_5224.

Ghérib, Baccar. 2011. 'Les classes moyennes tunisiennes entre mythe et réalité; Éléments pour une mise en perspective historique'. *L'Année du Maghreb* [Online], vol. VII, 419–35. Accessed 8 August 2018. http://anneemaghreb.revues.org/1296.

———. 2012. 'Economic politique de la revolution tunisienne. Les groupes sociaux face au capitalisme de copinage'. review *Tiers Monde* 4, 212, 19–36.

Glavanis, Kathy, and Pandeli Glavanis, eds. 1989. *The Rural Middle East: Peasant Lives and Modes of Production*. London: Birzeit University and Zed Books.

Gramsci, Antonio. 1971. *Selections from the Prison Notebooks of Antonio Gramsci*, edited by Quintin Hoare and Geoffrey Nowell Smith. London: Lawrence and Wishart.

Green, Duncan. 2012. *From Poverty to Power*. Rugby: Practical Action.

Guilhot, Nicolas, and Philippe C. Schmitter. 2000. 'De La Transition À La Consolidation: Une Lecture Rétrospective Des Democratization Studies'. *Revue française de science politique* 50, no. 4–5: 615–32. DOI: https://doi.org/10.3406/rfsp.2000.395500.

Guillaume, Henri. 2009. 'Mutations Agro-Pastorales, Ruralité Et Développement Dans Le Sud-Est Tunisien'. In *Développement Rural, Environnement Et Enjeux Territoriaux Regards Croisés Oriental Marocain Et Sud-Est Tunisien*, edited by Pierre Bonte, Mohamed Elloumi, Henri Guillaume and Mahi Mohamed, 19–43. Tunis: Cérès Editions.

Hadi, Chérif M. 1984. 'Expansion Européenne et Difficultés Tunisiennes de 1815 à 1830'. In *Dépendance et mutations précoloniales: la régence de Tunis de 1815 à 1857*, edited by Chater Kalifa, 714–45. Tunis: Université de Tunis.

Hagopian, Amy, Abraham D. Flaxman, Tim K. Takaro, Sahar A. Esa Al Shatari, Julie Rajaratnam, Stan Becker, Alison Levin-Rector, Lindsay Galway, Berq J. Hadi Al-Yasseri, William M. Weiss, Christopher J. Murray and Gilbert Burnham. 2013. 'Mortality in Iraq Associated with the 2003–2011 War and Occupation: Findings from a National Cluster Sample Survey by the University Collaborative Iraq Mortality Study'. *PLOS Medicine*. 15 October. Accessed 9 August 2017. http://journals.plos.org/plosmedicine/article?id=10.1371/journal.pmed.1001533#abstract1.

Halawa, Omar. 2015. 'Ethiopia's Renaissance Dam: Five Sticking Key issues into 2016'. *Al Ahram Weekly*. 29 December. Accessed 2 August 2017. http://english.ahram.org.eg/NewsContent/1/64/177677/Egypt/Politics-/Ethiopias-Renaissance-Dam-Five-sticking-key-issues.aspxn.

Hammouda, Hakim Ben. 1995. *Tunisie; Ajustement et difficulté de l'insertion internationale*. Paris: L'Harmattan.

Hanieh, Adam. 2013. *Lineages of Revolt: Issues of Contemporary Capitalism in the Middle East*. Chicago, IL: Haymarket Books.

Harre, Dominique. 2013. 'Métamorphoses des Campagnes et des modes de vie ruraux'. In *L'Egypte au Présent: Inventaire d'Une Société Avant Révolution*, edited by Vincent Battesti and François Ireton, 225–39. Paris: Sindbad Actes Sud.

Harvey, David. 1973. *Social Justice and the City*. London: Edward Arnold.

178   FOOD INSECURITY AND REVOLUTION

————. 1992. 'Social justice, Postmodernism and the City'. *International Journal of Urban and Regional Research* 16, no 4: 588–601.

————. 2003. *The New Imperialism*. Oxford: Oxford University Press.

————. 2005. *A Brief History of Neoliberalism*. Oxford: Oxford University Press.

————. 2006. *Spaces of Global Capitalism*. London: Verso.

Hass, Amira. 2016. 'Israel Incapable of Telling Truth About Water it Steals from Palestinians'. *Haaretz*. 22 June. Accessed 15 February 2019. https://www.haaretz.com/opinion/.premium-israel-unable-to-tell-truth-about-stealing-water-from-palestinians-1.5399404.

Hassaïnya, Jemaïel. 1991. 'Irrigation et développement agricole. L'expérience tunisienne'. Options méditerranéennes. Études et Recherches no. 3. Série B. Paris : CIHEAM.

Heikal, Hassanein M. 1988. *Kharif al-Ghadab (The Autumn of Fury)*. Cairo: Al-Ahram.

Hibou, Béatrice. 2006. *La force de l'obéissance: Économie politique de la répression en Tunisie*. Paris: La Découverte.

————. 2011. 'Tunisie. Économie politique et morale d'un mouvement social'. In *Politique africaine* 1, no. 121: 5–22.

Hobsbawm, Eric. 1994. *The Age of Extremes. The Short Twentieth Century 1914–1991*. London: Abacus.

Hopkins, Nicholas S. 1983. *Testour ou la Transformation des Campagnes Meghrebines*. Tunis: Cérès Productions.

————. 1990. 'Agricultural Labor And Technological Change In Tunisia'. In *Labor And Rainfed Agriculture in West Asia And North Africa*, edited by D. Tully, 253–71. Dordrecht: Springer.

Hoogvelt, Ankie M. M. 1982. *The Third World in Global Development*. Accessed 23 August 2018. https://link.springer.com/book/10.1007%2F978-1-349-16777-7.

————. 1997. *Globalisation and the Postcolonial World*. Washington, DC: Johns Hopkins University Press.

Hubert, Thierry. 1963. 'La Cession À La Tunisie Des Terres Des Agriculteurs Français – Protocoles Franco-Tunisiens Des 13 Octobre 1960 Et 2 Mars 1963'. *Annuaire Français De Droit International* 9: 933–52.

Huffington Post. 2018. 'Plus de 6000 mouvements sociaux au premier semestre 2018 selon le FTDES'. Accessed 7 September 2018. https://m.huffpostmaghreb.com/amp/entry/plus-de-6000-mouvements-sociaux-au-premier-semestre-2018-selon-le-ftdes_mg_5b913724e4b0cf7b003d5762/?__twitter_impression=true.

Hui, Wang, Wen Tiejun and Lau Kin, Chi. 2012. 'The Movement in Egypt: A Dialogue with Samir Amin'. *Boundary 2* 39, no. 1: 167–206. DOI: https://doi.org/10.1215/01903659-1506292.

Human Rights Watch. 2019. 'World Report 2019: Egypt'. Accessed 3 March 2019. https://www.hrw.org/world-report/2019/country-chapters/egypt.

Huntington, Samuel P. 1971. 'The Change to Change: Modernisation, Development and Politics'. *Comparative Politics* 3, no. 3 (April): 283–322.

Hussain, Marwa. 2013. 'Egyptian Activists Launch First Protest against Genetically Modified Food'. *Al Ahram*. 26 May. Accessed 20 June 2016. http://english.ahram.org.eg/NewsContent/3/12/72305/Business/Economy/Egyptian-activists-launch-first-protest-against-ge.aspx.

Institut National des Statistiques (INS). 2012. *Mesure de la pauvreté des inégalités et de la polarisation en Tunisie 2000–2010*. Tunis: INS.

International Rivers. 2017. '5 Myths Surround the Great Ethiopian renaissance Dam'. 30 January. Accessed 2 August 2017. https://www.internationalrivers.org/blogs/732/5-myths-surround-the-grand-ethiopian-renaissance-dam-gerd.

Iraq Body Count. 2017. https://www.iraqbodycount.org.

Ireton, François. 2011. 'Économie politique de l'agriculture: de l'encadrement étatique à la déréglementation'. In *L'Egypte au Présent: Inventaire d'Une Société Avant Révolution*, edited by Vincent Battesti and François Ireton, 437–92. Paris. Sindbad Actes Sud.

———. 2013. 'Economie politique de l'agriculture: de l'encadrement étatique à la déréglementation, par François Ireton.' in *Égypte Au Présent*, Collection: ' Hommes et Sociétés', edited by F. Ireton and V. Battesti, 437–92. Paris: Actes Sud.

Joffé, George. 2016. 'The Impending Water Crisis in the MENA Region'. *The International Spectator* 51, no. 3: 55–66.

Jouili, Mustapha. 2008. 'Ajustement Structurel, Mondialisation Et Agriculture Familiale En Tunisie'. Montpellier: L'universite De Montpellier 1.

———. 2009. 'Tunisian Agriculture: Are Small Farms Doomed to Disappear?'. 111 EAAE-IAAE Seminar 'Small Farms: decline or persistence', University of Kent, Canterbury, 26–27 June. Accessed 20 April 2017. http://ageconsearch.tind.io/record/52816/files/051.pdf.

———. 2011. 'Libéralisation de l'accès aux ressources hydrauliques et processus d'exclusion au niveau du gouvernorat de Sidi Bouzid (Tunisie Centrale)'. In *Méditerranée Appropriation des ressources naturelles et patrimoniales: Compétitions et droits d'accès en Méditerranée.* Colloque: ESG, 28-29-30 Novembre.

Joya, Angela. 2017. 'The Persistence of Neoliberalism since the Arab Uprisings: The Cases of Egypt and Tunisia'. In *The Political Economy of Emerging Markets: Varieties of BRICS in the Age of Global Crises and Austerity*, Routledge Frontiers of Political Economy, edited by Richard Westra, 201–20. Oxford: Routledge.

Kadri, Ali. 2014. *Arab Development Denied: Dynamics of Accumulation by Wars of Encroachment.* London: Anthem.

———. 2018. *The Cordon Sanitaire. A Single Law Governing Development in East Asia and the Arab World.* Singapore: Palgrave Macmillan.

Kapitalis. 2017. 'Plan de développement de l'agriculture et de la pêche 2016–2020'. 9 February. Accessed 5 April 2017. http://kapitalis.com/tunisie/2017/02/09/plan-de-developpement-de-lagriculture-et-de-la-peche-2016-2020/.

Karam, Fares. 2014. 'Saudi Arabia Food Imports Worth $24 Billion Annually'. 27 August. Accessed 6 August 2017. https://www.middleeastmonitor.com/20140827-saudi-arabia-food-imports-worth-24-billion-annually/.

Karem, Yehia. 2015. 'Luttes de classe dans un village égyptien: La Réforme Agraire Au Coeur Des Affrontements'. *ORIENT XXI*. Accessed 10 June 2017. http://orientxxi.info/magazine/luttes-de-classe-dans-un-village-egyptien,0889.

Kautsky, Karl. 1988. *The Agrarian Question.* Two volumes. London: Zwan.

Kefaya. N. D. 'Kefaya (Enough) to Cleanse Egypt! "Judicial and documentary file"'. Accessed 8 September 2017 www.big.assets.huffingtonpost.com/Kefayafasad.doc

Kenawy, E. Molouk. 2009. 'The Economic Development in Egypt During the 1952–2007 Period'. *Australian Journal of Basic and Applied Sciences* 3, no. 2: 588–603.

Khader, Bichara. 2012. 'Le printemps arabe: un premier bilan'. *Alternatives Sud* 19, no. 2: 7–39.

Khaldi, Raoudha, and Abderraouf Naïli. 1995. 'Analyse Des Politiques De La Sécurité Alimentaire En Tunisie'. In *La Sécurité Alimentaire En Méditerranée*, edited by M. Padilla and G. Le Bih An, 91–109. Options Méditerranéennes A. Séminaires Méditerranéens. Montpellier: CIHEAM.

Khalfoune, Tahar. 2005. 'Le Habous, le domaine public et le trust'. *Revue internationale de droit comparé* 57, no. 2: 441–70. doi:https://doi.org/10.3406/ridc.2005.19355.

King, J. Stephen. 2006. *Democratic Failure and the New Authoritarianism in the Middle East and North Africa*. Washington, DC: Georgetown University Press.

Korany, Bahgat, and Rabab El-Mahdi. 2012. 'Introduction'. In *Arab Spring in Egypt. Revolution and Beyond*, edited by Korany and El-Mahdi, 1–6. Cairo: American University in Cairo Press.

Korayem, Karima. 1977. 'Egypt's Economic Reform and Structural Adjustment (ERSAP)'. Working paper. Cairo: The Egyptian Center for Economic Studies (ECES).

Krichen, Aziz. 1987. 'La Fracture De L'intelligentsia Problèmes De La Langue Et De La Culture Nationales'. in *Soulèvements et recompositions politiques dans le monde arabe*, edited by Michel Camau and Frédéric Vairel, 246–84. Montréal: Presses de l'Université de Montréal.

La Via Campesina. 2017. Declaration of Nyéléni, 27 February 2007. Accessed 21 June 2018. https://viacampesina.org/en/declaration-of-nyi/.

————. 2018. 'The Peasant Movement in Palestine: A Crucial Step Toward Defending the Rights of Farmers and Social Justice'. 1 February. Accessed 18 June 2018. https:// viacampesina.org/en/peasant-movement-palestine-crucial-step-toward-defending-rights-farmers-social-justice/.

Lamloum, Olfa, and Ben Zina Mohamed Ali. 2015. *Les jeunes de Douar Hicher et d'Ettadhamen: Une enquête sociologique (Youth of Douar Hicher and Ettadhamen: A Sociological Survey)*. Tunis: International Alert and Arabesques.

Land Centre for Human Rights (LCHR). 2002. 'Farmer Struggles against Law 96 of 1992, Land Center for Human Rights'. In *Counter Revolution in Egypt's Countryside*, edited by Ray Bush, 126–38. London: Zed Books.

Land Matrix. 2017. https://landmatrix.org.

Latruffe, Laurent, and Laure Piet. 2013. 'Does Land Fragmentation Affect Farm Performance? A Case Study from Brittany'. Factor Markets Working Paper no. 40. April.

Laukkonen, Julia, Paola Kim Blanco, Jennifer Lenhart, Marco Keinert, Branko Cavric and Cecilia Kinuthia-Njenga. 2009. 'Combining Climate Change Adaptation and Mitigation Measures at the Local Level'. *Habitat International* 33, no. 3 (July): 287–92.

Lawrence, Peter. 2018. 'Samir Amin on Centre, Periphery and the World Economy: An Appreciation of His Original Insights'. Accessed 6 March 2019. http://roape.net/ 2018/08/21/a-rebel-in-the-marxist-citadel-tributes-to-samir-amin/.

Le Coz, Jean. 1975. 'Mutations Rurales Au Maghreb : Du Dualisme Agraire À L'aménagement De L'espace', In *Introduction À L'afrique Du Nord Contemporaine, Connaissance Du Monde Arabe*. Institut De Recherches Et D'études Sur Le Monde Arabe Et Musulman – IREMAM, 63–80. Aix-Marseille: Éditions Du Cnrs.

Lelieveld, Jos, Steffen Beirle, Christoph Hörmann, Georgiy Stenchikov and Thomas Wagner. 2015. 'Abrupt Recent Trend Changes in Atmospheric Nitrogen Dioxide Over the Middle East'. *Science Advances* 1, no. 7 (August): 1–5.

Lenin, V. I. 1977. *The Development of Capitalism in Russia*. Moscow: Progress.

Liauzu, Claude. 1976. 'Un Aspect de la crise en Tunisie: la naissance des bidonvilles'. *Review Francoise d'Hist. d'Outre-Mer LXIII*, nos 232–33: 607–21.

Library of Congress. 2015. 'Restrictions on Genetically Modified Organisms: Egypt'. Accessed 15 September 2017. https://www.loc.gov/law/help/restrictions-on-gmos/ egypt.php.

Lippman, Thomas W. 2010. 'Saudi Arabia's Quest for Food Security'. *Middle East Policy Council* XVII, no. 1 (Spring). https://www.mepc.org/saudi-arabias-quest-food-security.

Lowder, Sarah K., Jakob Skoet and Saumya Singh. 2014. 'What Do We Really Know about the Number and Distribution of Farms and Family Farms in the World?' Background paper for The State of Food and Agriculture 2014, ESA Working paper no. 14–02, August 8. http://www.fao.org/economic/esa/publications/details/en/c/220356/.

Loughrey, Jason, Trevor Donnellabn, Thia Hennessy and Kevin Hanrahan. 2013. 'The Role of Pluriactivity in Farm Exit and Labour Supply Decisions'. Factor Markets Working Papers. No. 67, August.

Luxemburg, Rosa. (1913) 1968. *The Accumulation of Capital* (Routledge Classics) Oxford.

Lynn Karl, Terry. 1997. *Paradox of Plenty*. Berkeley: University of California Press.

Mada Masr. 2015. 'Sisi inaugurates 1st Phase of 1.5 Million Feddan Reclamation Project'. 31 December. Accessed 29 April 2017. http://www.madamasr.com/en/2015/12/31/news/u/sisi-inaugurates-1st-phase-of-1-5-million-feddan-reclamation-project/.

Mahdi, Mohamed. 2014. 'Devenir du foncier agricole au Maroc: Un cas d'accaparrement des terres'. *New Medit* 13, no. 4 (December): 2–10.

Makhlouf, Ezzedine. 1966. *Structures agraires et modernisation de l'agriculture dans les plaines du Kef. Les unités coopératives de production*. PhD, Université de Strasbourg.

Malm, Andreas, and Shora Esmailian. 2013. 'Ways In and Out of Vulnerability to Climate Change: Abandoning the Mubarak Project in the Northern Nile Delta, Egypt'. *Antipode* 45, no. 2: 474–92.

Marcus, Rachel, Paola Pereznieto, Erin Cullen and Nicola Jones. 2013. 'Children and Social Protection in the Middle East and North Africa: A Mapping Exercise'. ODI Working Paper 335, October. London: Overseas Development Institute.

Martiniello, Giuliano. 2015a. 'Social Struggles in Uganda's Acholiland: Understanding Responses and Resistance to Amuru Sugar Works'. *Journal of Peasant Studies* 42, nos 3–4: 653–69.

———. 2015b. 'Food Sovereignty as a Praxis? Rethinking the Food Question in Uganda'. *Third World Quarterly* 36, no. 3: 508–25.

———. 2016. '"Don't Stop the Mill": South African Capital and Agrarian Change in Tanzania'. *Third World Thematics: a TWQ Journal* 1, no. 5: 633–52.

———. 2017. 'Agrarian Politics and Land Struggles in Northern Uganda'. *Community Development Journal* 52, no. 3(July): 405–20.

Martiniello, Giuliano and S. Nyamasenda. 2018. Agrarian Movements in the Neoliberal Era: The Case of MWIVATA in Tanzania'. *Agrarian South: A Journal of Political Economy* 7, no. 2: 145–72.

Marx, Karl. 1970 [1867]. *Capital (vol. 1)*. New York: Penquin Books.

Marx, Michael, Bernard Fouquet, Bel-Hassen Abdelkafi, Maamri Akremi, Andrea Stoppa, William Sutton, Loic Whitmore and Zacharie Méchali. 2013. *Tunisie: Financement du secteur agricole*, Programme de Cooperation FAO/Banque Mondiale. Rome: Centre D'investissement De La Fao. http://www.fao.org/docrep/018/i3210f/i3210f.pdf.

Marzin, Jacques., Pascal Bonnet, Omar Bessaoud and Christine Ton-Nu. 2017. *Étude sur L'Agriculture Familiale à Petite Échelle Au Proche-Orient Et Afrique Du Nord. Synthèse*. Cairo: FAO-CIRAD.

Mason, Michael, and Ziad Mimie. 2014. 'Transboundary Climate Security: Climate Vulnerability and Rural Livelihoods in the Jordan River Basin, Final Project Report'. Mimeo. London: London School of Economics, and Birzeit, Palestine: Birzeit University.

Mazeau, Guillaume, and Giedre Sabaseviciute. 2014. 'Archéologies révolutionnaires. Regards croisés sur la Tunisie et l'Égypte (2011–2013)'. In *L'Année du Maghreb*. En ligne. Accès: 06 juillet 2018. http://journals.openedition.org/anneemaghreb/2005.

McGreal, Chris. 2008. 'Egypt: Bread Shortages, Hunger and Unrest'. *The Guardian*. 27 May. Accessed 3 March 2010. https://www.theguardian.com/environment/2008/may/27/food.egypt.

McMichael, Philip. 2003. 'Food Security and Social Reproduction: Issues and Contradictions'. In *Power, Production and Social Reproduction*, edited by I. Bakker and S. Gill, 169–89. London: Palgrave Macmillan.

————. 2009. 'A Food Regime Genealogy', *Journal of Peasant Studies* 36, no. 1: 139–70.

————. 2013. *Food Regimes and Agrarian Questions*. Halifax: Fernwood.

————. 2014. 'Historicising Food Sovereignty'. *Journal of Peasant Studies* 41, no. 6: 933–57.

————. 2016. 'Bernstein-McMichael-Friedmann Dialogue on Food Regimes. Commentary: Food Regime for Thought'. *Journal of Peasant Studies* 43, no. 3: 648–70.

Meddeb, Hamza. 2011. 'L'ambivalence de la course à 'el khobza'. *Politique africaine* 121, no 1: 35–51.

————. 2012. *Courir ou mourir dans la Tunisie de Ben Ali*. Thèse. Paris: IEP.

Meillassoux, Claude. 1981. *Maidens, Meal and Money: Capitalism and the Domestic Community*. Cambridge: Cambridge University Press.

Mestiri, Mhamed. 2016. 'Disparités Régionales, Etat des lieux d'une discrimination'. Accessed 15 April 2017. http://nawaat.org/portail/2016/02/09/disparites-regionales-etat- des-lieux-dune-discrimination/.

Michael, D., A. Panya, S. I. Hasnain, R. Serklor and S. Panuganti. 2012. *Water Challenges and Cooperative Response in the Middle East and North Africa*. Washington, DC: Saban Center Brookings Institution.

Middle East. 2013. 'Saudi Arabia: Overseas Investments to Boost Food Security'. Accessed 24 October 2016. http://www.oxfordbusinessgroup.com/news/saudi-arabia-overseas- investments-boost-food- security.

Mikhail, Alan. 2014. 'Labour and Environment in Egypt since 1500'. *International Labor and Working-Class History* 85 (Spring): 10–32.

Minio-Paluello, Mika. 2014. 'The Violence of Climate Change in Egypt'. *Jadaliyya*. 15 July. Accessed 24 October 2016. http://www.jadaliyya.com/pages/index/18548/the-violence-of-climate-change-in-egypt.

Ministère de l'Agriculture et des Ressources Hydrauliques (MARH). 2006. 'Enquête sur les Structures des Exploitations Agricoles 2004–2005'. Tunis. Accessed 7 July 2018. http://www.onagri.nat.tn/uploads/divers/enquetes-structures/index.htm.

Ministère de l'Environnement et du Développement Durable (MEDD) – Direction Générale de l'Environnement et de la Qualité de la Vie – PNUD. 2006. 'Programme d'action régionale de lutte contre la désertification du Gouvernorat de Kasserine' (Rapport). Accessed 10 March 2019. http://www.environnement.nat.tn/envir/sid/dmdocuments/mise_oeuvre/parlcd/parlcd_kasserine.pdf.

Mitchell, Timothy. 1991. *Colonising Egypt*. Berkeley, LA: University of California Press.

————. 1998. 'The Market's Place'. In *Directions of Change in Rural Egypt*, edited by Nicholas Hopkins and K. Westergaard, 19–40. Cairo: American University of Cairo Press.

————. 2002. *Rule of Experts: Egypt, Techno-Politics, Modernity*. Berkeley, LA: University of California Press.

Mitwally, S. 2017. 'Agriculture and Irrigation (Ministers): Weekly Joint Meetings to Resolve the Issues of the Two Ministries'. 20 February. Accessed 25 February 2017. http://today.almasryalyoum.com/article2.apx?ArticleID=535788&IssueID=4243.

Monthly Review. 2013. https://monthlyreview.org/2013/12/01/marx-rift-universal-metabolism-nature/.

Moore, Jason. 2010. 'Cheap Food and Bad Money. Food Frontiers and Financialisation in the Rise and Demise of Neoliberalism'. *Review* 33, nos 2–3: 225–61.

————. 2015. *Capitalism in the Web of Life: Ecology and the Accumulation of Capital*. London: Verso.

Moretti, Franco, and Dominque Pestre. 2015. 'Bankspeak'. *New Left Review* 92 (March–April). Accessed 30 August 2018. https://newleftreview.org/II/92/franco-moretti-dominique-pestre-bankspeak.

Moyo, Sam, Paris Yeros and Praveen Jha. 2012. 'The Agrarian Question: Past, Present and Future'. *The Agrarian South: A Journal of Political Economy* 1, no. 1: 1–10.

Mukhtar, H. 2016. 'The Egyptian Countryside: We Shall Not Leave the Small Peasants and We Shall Teach Them How to Plant the Desert'. 18 October. www.youm7.com.

Müller-Mahn, Detlef. 1998. 'Spaces of Poverty: The Geography of Social Change in Rural Egypt'. In *Directions of Change in Rural Egypt*, edited by Nicholas Hopkins and K. Westergaard, 256–76. Cairo: American Univeristy of Cairo Press.

Mundy, Martha. 2017. 'The War on Yemen and Its Agricultural Sector'. Paper #50, Conference on The Future of Food and Challenges for Agriculture in the 21st Century. 24–26 April. Accessed 10 August 2017. http://elikadura21.eus/wp-content/uploads/2017/04/50-Mundy.pdf.

Mundy, Martha, Amin al-Hakimi, and Frédéric Pelat. 2014. 'Neither Security nor Sovereignty: Agriculture and Food Production in Yemen'. In *Food Security in the Middle East*, edited by Zahra Babar and Suzi Mirgani, 138–58. London: Hurst.

Mundy, Martha, and Frédéric Pelat. 2014. 'The Political Economy of Agriculture and Agricultural Policy in Yemen'. Draft working paper for GRM Workshop: The Future of Yemen, 29 July.

Murphy, Emma. 1999. *Economic and Political Change in Tunisia. From Bourgiba to Ben Ali.* Houndmills: Palgrave Macmillan.

Nagi, Saad Zaghloul. 2001a. *Poverty in Egypt: Human Needs and Institutional Capacities.* New York. Lexington Books.

———. 2001b. 'Poverty in Egypt: Concepts, Realities, and Research Agenda'. *Research Briefs. Poverty in Egypt.* Accessed 20 March 2002. http://www1.aucegypt.edu/src/pdr/Research_Briefs/Poverty_In_Egypt.pdf.

Nakhood, Smita, Alice Caravani, Sam Barnard and Liane Schalatek. 2013. *Climate Finance Regional Briefing: Middle East and North Africa.* Washington, DC: Heinrich Böll Stifung.

Nerfin, Marc. 1974. *Entretiens avec Ahmed Ben Salah sur la dynamique socialiste en Tunisie dans les années soixante.* Paris: Maspéro.

Nichols, Michelle. 2017. 'UN Experts Warn Saudi-Led Coalition Allies over War Crimes in Yemen'. Accessed 10 August 2017. http://www.reuters.com/article/us-yemen-security-un-idUSKBN15D0SB.

OECD. 2016. *Youth in the MENA Region. How to Bring Them In.* Accessed 11 August 2017. http://www.oecd.org/mena/governance/youth-in-the-mena-region.pdf.

OMCT. 2006. 'Egypt Farmers; Agrarian Policy, Human Rights and Violence in Egypt; Information and Recommendations for the European Union in the Context of the Association Agreement between the European Union and Egypt'. Paper for EU, 1 June 1.

ONEQ. 2013. Observatoire National de l'Emploi et des Qualifications / National Observatory of Employment and Qualifications.

Owen, Roger. 1986. 'Large Landowners, Agricultural Progress and the State in Egypt, 1800–1970: An Overview'. In *Food States and Peasants: Analyses of the Agrarian Question in the Middle East*, edited by Alan Richards, 69–96. Boulder, CO: Westview Press.

———. 2000. *State, Power and Politics in the Making of the Modern Middle East.* London: Routledge.

Pambazuka News. 2017. 'Charter of the North African Network for Food Sovereignty'. 13 July. Accessed 21 June 2018. https://www.pambazuka.org/food-health/charter-north-african-network-food-sovereignty.

184   FOOD INSECURITY AND REVOLUTION

PARC. 2012. *Agricultural Development Association Annual Report 2012*. Jerusalem: Palestinian Agricultural Relief Committees.

Patel, Raj, and Jason W. Moore. 2017. *A History of the World in Seven Cheap Things*. Oakland: University of California Press.

Patel, Raj, and Philip McMichael. 2009. 'A Political Economy of the Food Riot'. *Review* 32, no. 1: 9–35.

Perelman, Michael. 2000. *The Invention of Capitalism: Classical Political Economy and the Secret History of Primitive Accumulation*. Durham: Duke University Press.

Poncet, Jean. 1962. *La colonisation et l'agriculture européenne en Tunisie depuis 1881*. Paris: Mouton.

———. 1970. 'L'économie Tunisienne Depuis L'indépendance.' In *Annuaire De L'afrique Du Nord*, 93–114. Paris: CNRS-CRESM.

———. 1976. 'Les Structures Actuelles De L'agriculture Tunisienne'. In *Annuaire De L'afrique Du Nord*, 45–56. Paris: CNRS.

Poortman, C. J., T. O. Ahlers, I. Anderson, L. F. Constantino and D. W. Lister. 2006. 'Tunisie: Examen De La Politique Agricole'. Rapport No. 35239-TN. *Banque Mondiale*. Washington, DC: World Bank.

Radi, Faiza. 2016. 'Shahinda Maklad (1938–2016): "Egypt's People Will Never Be Shattered"'. *Al Ahram Weekly*. Accessed 19 August 2018. http://weekly.ahram.org.eg/News/16591.aspx.

Radwan, Samir, Vali Jamal and Ajit Ghose. 1991. *Tunisia: Rural Labour and Structural Transformation*. London: Routledge.

Ramadan, B. 2016. 'The Head of the Egyptian Countryside Company: Facilitations to Youth and Small Peasants in the One Million Acres Project'. 25 November. Accessed 20 April 2017 http://www.almasryalyoum.com/news/details/1047079.

Reardon, Thomas. 1998. 'Rural Nonfarm Income in Developing Countries. The State of Food and Agriculture'. Rome: FAO.

Reardon, Thomas, Berdegué Julio, and Escobar German. 2001. 'Rural Nonfarm Employment and Incomes in Latin America: Overview and Policy Implications'. *World Development* 29, no. 3: 395–409.

Reuters. 2011. FACTBOX – 'Tunisians Ex-First Family and Its Vast Riches'. 19 January. Accessed 30 August 2018. https://www.reuters.com/article/tunisia-protests-assets/factbox-tunisias-ex-first-family-and-its-vast-riches-idUSLDE70I17820110119.

———. 2016. 'Israel Seizes Land in Occupied West Bank'. Accessed 14 August 2017. http://www.newsweek.com/israel-land-west-bank-seized-palestinians-dead-sea-jericho-437221.

———. 2017. 'Syrian War Monitor Says 465,000 Killed in 6 Years of Fighting'. 13 March. Accessed 10 August 2017. http://www.reuters.com/article/us-mideast-crisis- syria-casualties-idUSKBN16K1Q1.

Reynaud, Alain. 1982. *Société, espace et justice. Inégalités régionales et justice sociospatiale*, coll. Espace et liberté. Paris: Presses Universitaries de France.

RFI. 2011. 'Retour sur la révolution Facebook en Tunisie'. 26 January, http://www.rfi.fr/afrique/20110125-tour-net-notre-envoye-special-tunis Accessed 13 August 2019.

Riadh, Béchir, and Sghaier Monji. 2013. 'Taux de pauvreté et ses mesures en Tunisie' *New Medit* 12, no. 2 (giugno) : 2–10.

Ross, Michael. 1999. 'Resource Curse'. In *World History*.

Rosset, Peter. M., and Miguel A. Altieri. 2017. *Agroecology: Science and Politics*. Rugby, UK: Practical Action.

Rother, Bjoern, David Lombardo, Roisto Herrala, Priscilla Toffano, Erik Roos, Allan G Auclair and Karina Manasseh. 2016. 'The Economic Impact of Conflicts and the

Refugee Crisis in the Middle East and North Africa'. Staff discussion notes no. 16/ 8, 16 September. Accessed 9 August 2017. http://www.imf.org/en/Publications/ Staff-Discussion-Notes/Issues/2016/12/31/The-Economic-Impact-of-Conflicts-and-the-Refugee-Crisis-in-the-Middle-East-and-North-Africa-44228.

Ruf, Werner, K. 1975. 'Le Socialisme Tunisien : Conséquences D'une Expérience Avortée'. In *Introduction À L'afrique Du Nord Contemporaine, Connaissance Du Monde Arabe*, 399–411. Aix-en-Provence: IREMAM.

Saad, Reem. 1999. 'State, Landlord, Parliament and Peasant: the story of the 1992 tenancy law in Egypt'. In *Agriculture in Egypt from Pharaonic to Modern Times*. Proceedings of the British Academy, vol. 96, edited by Alan Bowman and Eugene Rogan, 387–404. Oxford: Oxford University Press.

———. 2002. 'Egyptian Politics and the Tenancy Law'. In *Counter Revolution in Egypt's Countryside: Land and Farmers in the Era of Economic Reform*, edited by Ray Bush. London. Zed Books.

———. 2004. 'Social and Political Costs of Coping with Poverty in Rural Egypt'. Fifth Mediterranean Social and Political Research Meeting. Florence & Montecatini. Organised by the Mediterranean Programme of the Robert Schuman Centre for Advanced Studies at the European University Institute.

Saito, Kohei. 2017. *Capital, Nature, And the Unfinished Critique of Political Economy. Karl Marx's Ecosocialism*. New York: Monthly Review Press.

Santos, Nuno, and Iride Ceccacci. 2015. *Egypt, Jordan, Morocco and Tunisia: Key Trends in the Agrifood Sector*. Rome: Éditions FAO. http://www.fao.org/3/a-i4897e.pdf.

Schiavoni, Christina M. 2017. 'The Contested Terrain of Food Sovereignty Construction: Toward a Historical, Relational and Interactive Approach'. *Journal of Peasant Studies* 44,no. 1: 1–32.

Schilling, D. 2013. 'Egypt's $90 Billion South Valley Project'. *Industry Tap*. 10 January. Accessed 20 Apri 2017. http://www.industrytap.com/egypts-90-billion-south-valley-project/539.

Schneider, M. 2008. ' "We are hungry!" A Summary Report of Food Riots, Government Responses, and States of Democracy in 2008'. December. Ithaca, NY: Development Sociology, Cornell University.

Seddon, David. 1986. 'Riot and Rebellion: Political Responses to Economic Crisis in North Africa (Tunisia, Morocco and Sudan)'. School of Development Studies, University of East Anglia, Issue 196 of Discusssion Paper.

Selwyn, Benjamin. 2015. 'Twenty First Century International Political Economy: A Class-Relational Perspective'. *European Journal of International Relations*: 21, no. 3: 513–37.

———. 2017. *The Struggle for Development*. Cambridge: Polity.

———. 2018. 'A Manifesto for Socialist Development in the 21st Century'. *Economic & Political Weekly* 53, no. 36 (September 8): 47–55.

Sethom, Hafedh. 1979. 'Les tentatives de remodelage de l'espace tunisien depuis l'indépendance'. In *Méditerranée*, troisième série, tome 35, 1-2-1979, L'homme et son milieu naturel au Maghreb, 119–25. DOI: https://doi.org/10.3406/medit.1979.1906.

———. 1993. 'Tunisian Agrarian Structures, the Changes they Have Undergone Since Independence and their Role in Agricultural Development' (Arabic). In *La Revue Tunisienne de Géographie*, 23–24. Tunis. Faculté des sciences humaines et sociales de Tunis, 107–36.

Shaheen, Kareem. 2017. 'Yemen Death Toll has reached 10,000, UN says'. 16 January. Accessed 10 August 2017.https://www.theguardian.com/world/2017/jan/16/yemen-war-death-toll-has-reached-10000-un-says.

Shanin, Theodor. 1997. 'The Idea of Progress.' In *The Post-development Reader*, edited by Majid Rahnema and Victoria Bawtree, 65–71. London: Zed Books.

Shetty, Shobha. 2006. *Water, Food Security and Agricultural Policy in the Middle East and North Africa Region*. Washington, DC: World Bank. Accessed 6 March 2019. http://siteresources. worldbank.org/INTMENA/Resources/WP47web.pdf.

Shihade, Magid. 2012. 'On the Difficulty in Predicting and Understanding the Arab Spring: Orientalism, Euro-Centrism, and Modernity'. *International Journal of Peace Studies* 17, no. 2: 57–70.

Solidaires International. 2012. 'Il faut s'attendre à une deuxième révolution'; Entretien avec Hajji Adnen. CEFI: Centre d'Etude et de Formation Interprofessionnelle Solidaires (décembre 2011). In *Solidaires International*, no. 8 (Interview accordée à Afriques21). 105–9.

Sowers, Jeannie. 2013. *Environmental Politics in Egypt: Activists, Experts and the State*. Oxford: Routledge.

———. 2014. 'Water, Energy and Human Insecurity in the Middle East and North Africa'. *Middle East Report* 271 (Summer). Accessed 10 September 2017. merip.org/2014/07/ water-energy-and-human-insecurity-in-the-middle-east/.

Sowers, Jeannie, Avner Vengosh and Erika Weinthal. 2011. 'Climate Change, Water Resources and the Politics of adaption in the Middle East and North Africa'. *Climatic Change* 104, nos 3–4: 599–627.

Stédile, J. P., and H. M. de Carvalho. 2011. 'People Need Food Sovereignty'. In *Food Movements Unite!*, edited by Eric Holt-Giménez, 21–34. Oakland, CA: Food First Books.

Szakal, V. 2016. 'Migration interne, marché de l'emploi et disparités régionales'. 9 March. Accessed 10 September 2017. http://nawaat.org/portail/2016/03/09/migration-interne-marche-de-lemploi-et-disparites-regionales/.

The Guardian. 2016. 'Egypt Devalues Currency by 48% to Meet IMF Demands for $12bn Loan'. 3 November. Accessed 23 Augsut 2017. https://www.theguardian.com/world/ 2016/nov/03/egypt-devalues-currency-meet-imf-demands-loan.

Thorner, Daniel, Basile Kerblay and R. E. F. Smith, eds. *A.V. Chayanov On The Theory of Peasant Economy*. Chicago, IL: The American Economic Association.

Tignor, Robert, L. (1966) 2015. *Modernization and British Colonial Rule in Egypt 1882–1914*. Princeton Legacy Library, NJ: Princeton University Press.

Toth, James. 1998. 'Beating Plowshares into Swords: The Relocation of Rural Egyptian Workers and Their Discontent.' In *Directions of Change in Rural Egypt*, edited by Nicholas Hopkins and N. Westergaard, 66–87. Cairo: American University of Cairo Press.

———. 1999. *Rural Labour Movements in Egypt and Their Impact on the State 1961–1992*. Gainesville: University of Florida Press.

Touhami, H. 2012. 'Seuil De Pauvrete, Population Pauvre'. Conférence donnée le 7/ 3/2012 à la Faculté des Sciences Economiques de Tunis à l'invitation du Club des Econonètres Tunisiens Economiques de Tunis. Accessed 19 June 2017 http://www. leaders.com.tn/uploads/FCK_files/file/SEUIL%20DE%20PAUVRETE-VDF-Leaders.pdf.

Transnational Institute. 2012. *The Global Land Grab: A Primer*. Amsterdam: Transnational Institute.

Tsakalidou, Ilektra. 2013. 'The Great Anatolia Project: Is Water Management a Panacea or Crisis Multiplier for Turkey's Kurds?'. *Wilson Center*. 5 August. Accessed 2 August 2017. https://www.newsecuritybeat.org/2013/08/great-anatolian-project-water-management-panacea-crisis-multiplier-turkeys-kurds/.

Tucker, Judith. 1993. 'Decline of the Family Economy in Mid-Nineteenth-Century Egypt'. In *The Modern Middle East*, edited by Albert Hourani, Philip S. Khoury and Mary C. Wilson, 229–54. London: I.B. Tauris.

Tyler, Imogen. 2015. 'Classificatory Struggles: Class, Culture and Inequality in Neoliberal Times'. *The Sociological Review* 63, no. 2: 493–511.

United Nations. 2011. 'The Global Food Crises'. In *UNDESA Report on the World Social Situation 2011: The Global Social Crisis*, chapter 4, pp. 61–74. Accessed 29 August 2018. Available at http://www.un.org/esa/socdev/rwss/docs/2011/chapter4.pdf.

———. 2015. 'Report of the Independent Commission of Inquiry Established Pursuant to Human Rights Council Resolution S-21/1'. 24 June, A/HRC/29/52. General Assembly. Accessed 14 August 2017. http://www.ohchr.org/EN/HRBodies/HRC/CoIGazaConflict/Pages/ReportCoIGaza.aspx.

———. 2017. UN General Assembly 72nd session. Resolution Adopted by the General Assembly 20 December, Decade of Family Farming 2019–2028. Accessed 5 March 2019. https://digitallibrary.un.org/record/1479766.

United Nations Human Rights Office of the High Commissioner. 2018. 'Yemen: United Nations Experts Point to Possible War Crimes by Parties to the Conflict'. Accessed 29 August 2018. https://www.ohchr.org/EN/NewsEvents/Pages/DisplayNews.aspx?NewsID=23479&LangID=E.

United States Agency for International Development. 1999. *Agriculture: Vision for 2003. MALR/USAID Agricultural Policy Reform Programme*. Cairo: RDI.

Van der Ploeg, Jan Douwe. 2009. *The New Peasantries: Struggles for Autonomy and Sustainability in an Era of Empire and Globalization*. London: Earthscan.

———. 2010. 'The Peasantries of the Twenty-first Century: The Commoditisation Debated Revisited.' *Journal of Peasant Studies* 37, no. 1: 1–30.

———. 2013. *Peasants and the Art of Farming: A Chayanovian Manifesto*. Halifax: Fernwood.

War on Want. 2012. 'Food Sovereignty. Reclaiming the Global Food System'. Accessed 6 March 2019. https://waronwant.org/sites/default/files/Food%20sovereignty%20report.pdf.

Waterbury, John. 2013. *The Political Economy of Climate Change in the Arab Region*. New York: United Nations Development Programme, Regional Bureau for Arab States.

Water-Technology. n.d. 'Toshka Project – Mubarak Pumping Station, Egypt'. Accessed 7 September 2017. http://www.water-technology.net/projects/mubarak/.

Weir, Patrick. 2015. 'Egypt's Land Reclamation Plan Should Heed History Lesson'. 14 October. Accessed 7 September 2017. https://www.thenational.ae/business/egypt-s-land-reclamation-plan-should-heed-history-lesson-1.90770.

Westley, R. John. 1999. 'Change in the Egyptian Economy, 1977–1997'. In *Twenty Years of Development in Egypt (1977–1997)*. Cairo Papers in Social Sciences 21, no. 3 (American University of Cairo Press): 18–41.

Wittman, H., A. Desmarais, and N. Wiebe. 2010. 'The Origins & Potential of Food Sovereignty'. In *Food Sovereignty: Reconnecting Food Nature and Community*, edited by H. Wittman, A. Desmarais and N. Wiebe, 1–14. Oakland, CA: Food First.

Woertz, Eckart. 2013. *Oil for Food. The Global Food Crisis and the Middle East*. Oxford: Oxford University Press.

———. 2017. 'Agriculture and Development in the Wake of the Arab Spring'. In *Combining Economic and Political Development: The Experience of MENA*, edited by G. Luciani, 144–69. Geneva: Graduate Institute.

World Bank. (1996) 2001. *Tunisia's Global Integration and Sustainable Development: Strategic Choices for the 21st century*. Washington, DC: World Bank. Accessed 23 August 2018. http://documents.worldbank.org/curated/en/208681468312589957/pdf/multi0page.pdf.

————. 2002. *Egypt – Poverty Reduction in Egypt – Diagnosis and Strategy: Main Report (English)*. Washington, DC: World Bank. Accessed 22 April 2005. http://documents.worldbank. org/curated/en/611841468770090531/Main-report.

————. 2006. *Tunisia: Agriculture Policy Review*. Report No. 35239-TN. Washington, DC: World Bank. Accessed 28 April 2017. http://documents.worldbank.org/curated/ en/242951468114530031/pdf/352390TN.pdf.

————. 2007. *Making the Most of Scarcity: Accountability for Better Water Management Results in the Middle East and North Africa*. Washington, DC: World Bank.

————. 2008. *Agricultural and Rural Development in MENA*. World Bank Sector Brief MENA. Washington, DC: World Bank.

————. 2010. *Development and Climate Change*. Washington, DC: World Bank.

————. 2012. 'Interim Strategy Note for the Republic of Tunisia for the period FY13-14'. Accessed 24 April 2017. http://documents.worldbank.org/curated/en/ 786001468173647922/Tunisia-Interim-strategy-note-for-the-period-FY13-14.

————. 2014. *Instability and Fragmentation Continues to Constrain Private Sector Growth in Palestinian Territories*. Press Release, 11 September. Jerusalem: World Bank.

————. 2017. 'Unlocking The Potential of the Agricultural Sector in Egypt'. Promoting Sustainable Investment in Egypt's Food Security Conference, 5 December. Washington, DC: World Bank Group.

————. 2018. 'Agriculture, valeur ajoutée (% du PIB)'. *Banque Mondiale*. Accessed 20 July, 2018. https://donnees.banquemondiale.org/indicateur/NV.AGR.TOTL.ZS?end=20 16&locations=TN&start=1965&view=chart.

World Food Programme. 2014. 'Sudan: Overview'. *World Food Programme*. Accessed 24 October 2016. http://www.wfp.org/countries/sudan/overview.

————. 2017a. 'The Market Monitor: Trends and Impacts of Staple Food Prices in Vulnerable Countries'. Accessed 10 September 2017. https://docs.wfp.org/ api/documents/WFP-0000019676/download/?_ga=2.145430707.60557784 3.1503041438-1742030357.1503041438.

————. 2017b. 'South Sudan'. Accessed 9 August 2017. http://www1.wfp.org/countries/ south-sudan.

Zaafouri, Omar. 2010. 'Les Nouvelles Techniques D'irrigation Ont-Elles Modifié Le Comportement De La Paysannerie En Tunisie Centrale?: Etude D'une Communauté Rurale À Sidi Bouzid'. Presented at *The Usages Écologiques, Économiques Et Sociaux De L'eau Agricole En Méditerranée: Quels Enjeux Pour Quels Services ?* Colloque à Université De Provence.

Zammouri S., R. André, E. Le Briand and A. Saint-Araille. 2014. *Mezzouna, après la chute* (Film), 85 min.

Zemni, Sami, and Habib Ayeb. 2015. 'The Social and Economic Roots of the Tunisian Revolution. Towards a Socio-Spatial Class Analysis'. Paper presented at the London School of Economics, 20 November.

————. 2016. 'Les racines sociales et économiques de la révolution tunisienne. Vers une analyse socio-spatiale classe', Papier présenté au colloque *Les mouvements sociaux en Afrique du Nord et au Moyen-Orient*. Paris, Universié Paris 8 à Saint-Denis.

Zemni, Sami, Brecht De Smet and Koenraad Bogaert. 2012. 'Luxemburg on Tahrir Square: Reading the Arab Revolutions with Rosa Luxemburg's *The Mass Strike*'. *Antipode* 45, no. 4: 888–907.

Zouari Abdel-Jawed. 1998. 'European Capitalist Penetration of Tunisia, 1860–1881: A Case Study of the Regency's Debt Crisis and the Establishment of the International Financial Commission'. PhD. Washington, DC. University of Washington.

INDEX

Lightning Source UK Ltd.
Milton Keynes UK
UKHW010636280220
359497UK00004B/716